Namrata Rana is Director … is an alumni of IIM Ahmedabad and The … ute for Sustainability Leadership (CISL). She work… and institutions on the Net Zero transition and green jobs. Sh… the co-author of *Balance: Responsible Business for the Digital Age*.

Utkarsh Majmudar teaches at leading business schools in India and in the past has worked at several large corporations in India. He is a member of the Board of Governors at the Indian Institute of Management, Raipur. He writes extensively on sustainability issues, has authored many case studies and is the co-author of *Balance: Responsible Business for the Digital Age*.

SHIFT

DECISIONS FOR A NET ZERO WORLD

NAMRATA RANA
UTKARSH MAJMUDAR

First published in Westland Business, an imprint of Westland Publications Private Limited, in 2021

1st Floor, A Block, East Wing, Plot No. 40, SP Infocity, Dr MGR Salai, Perungudi, Kandanchavadi, Chennai 600096

Westland, the Westland logo, Westland Business and the Westland Business logo are the trademark of Westland Publications Private Limited, or its affiliates.

ISBN: 9789390679522

10 9 8 7 6 5 4 3 2 1

Typeset by R. Ajith Kumar
Printed at Thomson Press (India) Ltd

CONTENTS

Technical Notes

INTRODUCTION

THE LAST DECADE WAS THE AGE OF CONNECTIONS ENABLED BY SOCIAL media platforms, collaboration via cloud computing and enablement of distributed work via the gig economy.

The next decade will be different.

Global pandemics and the fragility of economic systems have taken the sheen off capitalism. People are asking, why isn't capitalism solving problems and does exponential, unfettered growth really lead to long-term prosperity? The perpetually growing economy, on which our financial system rests, has now come into conflict with a finite biosphere. This is imposing limits for finance and how we live our lives. The challenges of accelerating climate change, biodiversity loss and collapsing ecosystems are no longer a dystopian possibility, they are here now. There is growing concern about how a new economic order that is inclusive and just can be created in the post-pandemic recovery.

The book focuses on the transition that companies need to make towards the net zero and circular economy without leaving anyone behind. The role of the financial markets in making companies sustainable cannot be understated as finance is the glue that holds the global economy together. The book therefore focuses on the importance of environmental, social and governance (ESG) norms and how they can be integrated into corporate strategies.

2021 to 2030 is the decade of sustainability

This is a time of action. A time for the corporate world to showcase what they really stand for. Long-term horizons for public good and on-ground action will create resilient companies in an increasingly volatile world. Since the Sustainable Development Goals must be implemented by 2030, they require immense support not only from governments but also businesses. Chapter 1 examines the big trends and highlights why we need ESG, and how a balance needs to be created. Chapter 2 then follows through with a detailed insight on the need for net zero carbon emissions.

ESG is the new face of finance

We get what we measure; and that is a big part of the problem. The world's economic system does not take into consideration public goods like air quality, good health, excessive waste and need for a habitable climate. These measures are now becoming necessary for us to have a sustainable future. Chapter 3 covers the importance of ESG norms and uncovers how businesses are adapting to them through our annual study over 8 years of India's top 200 companies.

The big shifts in Circularity, Agriculture, Energy and Water

The issues around climate change and sustainability are fundamentally about the loss of connection with our immediate environment. At another level the big issues of circularity, agriculture, energy and water are interconnected. These interconnections give us hope that speed is possible and that given the right inputs can build positive changes. Chapter 4 highlights the importance of circularity and the challenges of scale in attempting this. Chapter 5 discusses how food, water and energy are interlinked and how this transformation must be addressed.

Net zero is also about social inclusion and green jobs

To transform business for the ESG world, we need a new kind of leadership. In our previous book, *Balance*, we highlighted the need for business to act as a trustee to society and built on the premise that business cannot succeed in a society that fails. Chapter 6 will talk about why it is important to take everyone along in our quest to improve lives. Chapter 7 will examine why the low carbon economy needs a skills and jobs transition.

The decade of building trust

In recent years, trust in institutions, media and brands has been eroded. Consumers no longer trust advertising and doubts are being raised about product labels and certifications too. So is the case with media. Media houses are increasingly being questioned and news is often misrepresented and content altered to represent a certain point of view. So, who do people trust? There are no easy answers to this. Chapter 8 uncovers the various efforts to build trust.

Building back better

The urgent necessity to address these important areas of inequality, climate change and transformation at scale will transform society and business. To manage these transitions and emerge on top will require a deeper understanding of trends and strategies that can unlock newer opportunities. This is an opportunity to redesign and recreate a responsive and better planet that can make us healthy, happy and economically sound. This is examined in Chapter 9 and Chapter 10.

The fight for one's survival is the fight for everyone. World economies are interconnected, so are our lives. Hence leadership for the twenty-first century needs to be about trusteeship, public good and equity. However, trusteeship is only possible if you can build a moral core. The pushes and pulls though between the connected nodes of economics, capitalism and resources, technology and society will make for an exciting journey in the next decade. That is really what this book is about, a journey into the shifts that are redefining capitalism and those that will perhaps help create a better, more sustainable and egalitarian world.

1

CHECKPOINT 2025

2020 AND 2021 HAVE BEEN YEARS LIKE NO OTHER. GLOBALISATION and capitalism, the twin pillars of the world as we know it, stand transformed because the pandemic has shown that people-first policies and not just accumulation of wealth are necessary for a healthy and sustainable world. Modern economic theory had assumed that as companies attained economies of scale, globalisation was a given. This was because everything depended on centralised production of materials sourced from different parts of the world, and subsequent distribution to the world markets. The deeply interconnected world, however, has not dealt well with the disruption brought about by the pandemic and the ensuing direct and indirect impacts. The movement of people across the world hastened the spread of the pandemic and the resulting lockdowns led to a stop in the movement of goods across the world. Globalisation worsened the impact of the pandemic and as a result, our perceptions of how things were being run have been transformed. The importance of health, the need to prioritise public good over profit, and the need to redesign supply chains for resilience and not just cost optimisation have emerged as priorities. One of the most important realisations has been the fact that unless we address climate change quickly, more such pandemics could be on the horizon. While the exact nature of the post-pandemic world is still unknown, one thing is certain. We need a fundamental transformation of our economic system if we are to create an equitable and just society. The next few years are likely to be tumultuous as these changes begin to take shape and 2025 is likely to be the year where we start seeing the new design of economic and societal systems emerge.

The need for a better world

There is little doubt that economic growth has helped pull billions of people out of poverty over the last seventy years or so. But now, its shortcomings are coming into stark relief. Researchers are questioning contemporary economics' most fundamental assumptions, including whether growth can, or indeed should, continue forever. 'More planetary crises are coming,' members of The Club of Rome, a group of politicians, economists and scientists, said in a statement in March 2020, calling for a green reboot after the pandemic.[1] They further went on to state, 'Rather than simply reacting to disasters, we can use (the) science to design economies that will mitigate the threats of climate change, biodiversity loss, and pandemics. We must start investing in what matters, by laying the foundation for a green, circular economy that is anchored in nature-based solutions and geared toward the public good.'

The environmental commons

Growth in nature is always balanced and multi-faceted. While certain ecosystems grow, others decline while their components are recycled. This interplay of growth and decay allows organisms and systems to reach their potential and creates balance.

The financial system, by contrast, recognises only money and cash flows. Our financial system ignores all other forms of fundamental wealth—all ecological, social, and cultural assets. So, for instance, a tree has no value till it is cut down and converted into wood. The fact that it provides shade or helps mitigate greenhouse gases eludes the financial system. This kind of thinking has led to several imbalances. The list of things that are in excess or severely degraded and their consequences is a large one. Growth has not been equal; the richest two thousand own more than 4.6 billion others.[2] Companies are flush with funds, but the real incomes of people have declined. Excessive carbon emissions have led to climate change, excessive consumption to waste, excessive water usage to droughts, excessive concretisation in cities has caused flooding and so on. The consequences of imbalance are mostly seen in the long term and if allowed to go unchecked, disruption caused by business activities may lead to huge imbalances in society. So, while capitalism has flourished, the people and the environment have been left behind.

Forests, climate, water, biodiversity and so on are all public goods or things owned by society. In a society that put a high value on material goods, the public goods also known as the 'commons' have been severely degraded. Forests, oceans, soil, water and wildlife are struggling with the onslaught of an imbalanced world. Today, 7.3 billion people consume 1.6 times what the earth's natural resources can supply. This is leading to deforestation, extinction of wildlife and a threat to the planet itself as our current agrarian system is a huge emitter of carbon. Further, a third of the food produced is wasted. When it comes to the oceans, things are equally bad. The oceans are polluted with plastic and many natural habitats in the oceans that were earlier teeming with marine life are now on the brink of collapse. This is serious news because the oceans produce more than half the oxygen we breathe, and they significantly impact the water cycle that produces rain and freshwater. As a result of all this, the climate is changing faster than earlier anticipated. Extreme temperatures and weather events are being seen across the world. These changes are putting freshwater systems increasingly at risk. Freshwater species are declining at an alarming rate of 76 per cent—much faster than terrestrial or marine species—and freshwater habitats are in worse condition than those of forests, grassland or coastal systems.[3]

The digital commons

Capitalism is driven by a system of perpetual growth. But we are on a planet with a finite set of resources and unless these systems are allowed to work appropriately and in synchronicity, we run the risk of devastation. There have been several debates on this as economists have said that the rise of technology will drive a services economy and thereby disconnect economic growth from material resources. This hasn't really come true. Increasing technological advances have led to a reduction in costs and a huge increase in consumption. Further, imbalances exist in manmade public goods too, such as the internet and the data that resides in it. These are known as the digital commons. Digital companies like Facebook and Twitter are places for social interaction, companies like Microsoft and SAP provide software that allows us to do certain tasks and platforms like Paytm (an Indian digital payments platform), Uber and Airbnb provide services based on technology. Digital companies manage resources and infrastructure, impact the flow of data and information and function as 'information gatekeepers'. Since information is the cornerstone of today's society, it gives the provider a moral responsibility to function as a trustee for the public good. But there are many instances where data captured for one purpose has been stolen or used for nefarious purposes. Also, many large platforms are now run by algorithms generating a whole new set of issues.

As measures to manage the pandemic strengthened during 2020–21, so did technological intrusion. Software applications designed to trace and monitor possible infections can now also be used for surveillance by both companies and governments. As technology gets entrenched into our lives, deeper questions have arisen: how much can we trust technology to be fair, inclusive and reliable? How can you trust someone you will never see? Also, what are the responsibilities of individuals and companies with respect to information sharing, as companies often get away by saying that information control is in the hands of the individual. As we are now transitioning to a digital-first economic system where even currencies are likely to be digital, our ability to define 'digital trust' is in the spotlight.

Governing commons means emphasising public good above profit

This means that 'the commons', whether in the form of the environment or data residing online, need a different form of governance, one that cannot be at the mercy of a system driven by profit. The situation is compounded by the fact that our economic measures of success, the Gross Domestic Product (GDP), measures the market value of all goods and services produced, thereby incentivising more and more consumption. The GDP is considered the measure of economic growth and therefore, a measure of the quality of life. Nobel Laureate Simon Kuznets, the original architect of the GDP, has however stated that this was not its purpose. This is because the GDP does not shine a light on the positive or negative effects (externalities) created in the process of production and development.

Economists define growth in financial terms: quarterly profits, return on investments, number of jobs created and wages paid, gross domestic product and so on. In many cases, peoples' salaries are based on these criteria. Hence, while we measure automotive production, we don't measure the emissions they cause when they are used for transportation of people and things. Non-financial criteria, such as good health and well-being, pollution and biodiversity loss, are considered 'externalities' and not included in their assessments—and that is exactly what the problem is today. The things we have forgotten to measure, or consider as externalities are fighting back. While wealth metrics have increased over the years, the damage to other things has been immense.

Therefore, the welfare of a country cannot be inferred from the measurement of national income. And for these reasons, the *Economist* magazine went so far as to call the GDP a 'Grossly Distorted Picture' of human achievement.[4] When we speak about 'development', we need to specify which kind of development we have in mind. If 'development' is used in the current narrow economic sense, it will further perpetuate the imbalances. If, however, the process of development is understood as more than a purely economic process and includes social and ecological aspects, and is associated with qualitative economic growth, then such a multidimensional systemic process can indeed be sustainable. Thus, we need a system that measures overall well-being of a nation. This could possibly be done by adjusting GDP for negative impact on society. This requires creation of new metrics for the damage being caused. This is difficult and complicated, but a beginning in this direction is a must.

While most big businesses are still driven by shareholder value, it is increasingly becoming clear to policymakers that economic growth, social balance and ecological wellbeing cannot be seen under the same lens. The three need to be separated from one another.

The need for balance

The discussion around the new emerging shifts in business and finance are therefore repeatedly highlighting the need for balance between profit and equality and between growth and environmental stability. To understand this a bit more, we need to look at why this problem has been exacerbated in recent times. The culprit hasn't just been the economic system, but technology, which has shifted the balance.

To set up a factory, a hundred years ago, you needed land, a big building and machinery. Additional investments were required to store the goods you made and then to ship them off to buyers. This meant large investments in capital. Capitalism as a system therefore prioritised and incentivised the creation of capital. Investor returns took precedence over everything else and making money was the role of business. Today, almost the entire world operates according to this philosophy, where private capital is used to generate goods and services for profit.

This system has worked well for the last century, but things are different now!

The world is becoming digital. In the digital world, everything moves faster and enables many new connections. Information travels from one end of the world to the other quickly enabling both extraordinary collaboration and consumption. Teams can now work with each other irrespective of location. Unlike the past, products, many times, are available as a seemingly endless flow. We don't buy CDs or DVDs anymore, we consume music on demand, we read books on Kindle and when we need to travel we just rent an Uber. We have moved from an acquisition-led system to a need-led system where we consume when the urge strikes us because several product and service categories are now so readily and perpetually available. Even during the pandemic, while the flow of physical goods had stopped, the digital world found itself in the middle of a massive acceleration. Netflix viewing reached stratospheric levels, Zoom calls zoomed multiple times over and this trend was seen across digital platforms.

With increasing digitisation and rapid technological enhancement, we are already in the post-industrialisation era. A part of the massive digital revolution is impacting almost everything around us. The World Economic Forum calls this phase the 'Fourth Industrial Revolution'.[5]

The income gap has widened

Compared to industrial economies, digital enterprises are markedly more asset-light. To create more services, technology companies don't need more people, land or machinery, because software is endlessly replicable. Hence they can constantly focus on better technology to reduce input cost and labour and maximise returns for themselves. So, while new age companies need capital, it takes much less to generate an equivalent cash flow. Capital is therefore no longer the scarcest ingredient in their economic success formula and accumulating large amounts of capital becomes possible.

Moreover, the benefits of technology are not leading to an equitable growth in incomes. Rapid technological progress may or may not lead to productivity growth for many reasons. The simplest way of explaining this without getting into economic models is that, unless the surplus generated through automation is ploughed back into the economy for human welfare, the surplus simply resides with the owner of the technology. As a person gets richer, there is a limit to how many cars and clothes one can buy. The outcome of this is huge economic inequalities and concentration of power; and, this is precisely what is happening. Which is why, new age automation is not having a uniform effect on employment and the global trends of falling growth, a shrinking middle class, reducing jobs and a huge increase in inequality are just the beginning of further inequality and societal imbalances.

At the end of 2019, Credit Suisse[6] indicated that millionaires around the world—who number 1 per cent of the adult population—accounted for 43.4 per cent of global net worth. In contrast, the 54 per cent of adults with wealth below $10,000 together mustered less than 2 per cent of global wealth. India is no stranger to income inequality and the gap is widening. India's richest own more than four times the wealth held by 70 per cent of the country's population.

Further, income distribution is impacted by gender too. For instance, women do a significant amount of work, but get paid much less and their share of wealth is far smaller. A study by Oxfam[7] indicates that globally men earn 23 per cent more than women and own 50 per cent more wealth.

The pandemic will impact income distribution too. While millions of households struggled to meet basic needs in the pandemic, the wealth of several billionaires increased manifold.[8] The 1,000 richest people on the planet recouped their COVID-19 losses within just nine months, but it could take more than a decade for the world's poorest to recover from the economic impacts of the pandemic.[9] The pandemic has also led to reduction in female labour participation as pressures of home work and office work mounted significantly.

Economics measures technological progress through an indicator called total factor productivity, or TFP.[10] It measures the productivity gains left over after accounting for the growth of the workforce and capital investments. When TFP is rising, it means the same number of people, working with the same amount of inputs, are able to make more than they were before. If TFP goes flat, then so do living standards. In America, since 1970, TFP has grown at only about a third the rate at which it grew from 1920 to 1970. In India, an analysis by Citigroup has similarly raised an alarm on a dropping TFP. India's labour productivity growth averaged a dismal 1.7 per cent in the thirty years between 1950 and 1980. It improved to an average of 3.8 per cent in the next twenty years and shot up to an average 8 per cent between 2005 and 2011, which were also India's best growth years. Since 2011, labour productivity growth has started decelerating and the 4.3 per cent growth posted in 2017 was much lower than what is required to sustain GDP growth in excess of 8 per cent.[11] It basically means that we are poorer and working longer hours.

Technology has worsened the balance of power

Office workers have longed for flexible working jobs where they could earn as much as they do in a full-time job and yet have more free time for other pursuits. The digital world enabled this as companies were able to open large marketplaces which gave independent workers and suppliers access to high end technology and enabled them to offer goods and services. Uber (car rental), Airbnb (Hospitality), Delhivery (delivery service), Zomato (food delivery) are all such platforms. Some of these platforms took on gig workers. The term 'gig economy' was coined to reflect this system where independent contractors took up 'short term' or 'freelance' assignments. For the platforms it worked well—fixed costs could be minimised and workers (at least initially) seemed more motivated. Moreover, there were no additional costs such as leave and travel reimbursements, retirement benefits, office costs and more.

For gig workers, this soon turned into a mixed bag. While some liked this style of working, for many others it became extremely stressful as part-time workers did not have the same benefits that full-time employees did, leaving them without the job security and peace of mind that nine-to-fivers enjoyed. This reached catastrophic levels when the pandemic occurred, as large numbers of gig workers became instantly unemployed, leading several families to fall back into food insecurity and poverty.

Furthermore, large companies are accused of profiting from the imbalance of power between the management and the worker. The gig workers don't have access to a union which can help in collective bargaining. The platform decides the rules and as more people join it, the more powerful the platform becomes since supply is larger than demand. Individuals in this ecosystem start losing their identity and get tied to the platform.

In 2018, the *New York Times* reported that taxi drivers in New York were committing suicide, driven in most cases by financial distress. These stories of despair, mostly because of increasing competition from taxi aggregators like Uber, long hours and grinding debt, prompted the New York City Council to weigh new legislation to help taxi owners reduce their debt and to increase driver wages.[12] In India, suppliers to some of the hospitality and food delivery digital platforms have revolted en masse. Realising the futility of fighting the mega platforms one-to-one, hotels, restaurants and small retailers coalesced around their respective trade organisations to fight for better terms or otherwise simply opted out.[13]

For most people who are part of the service sector, these stories are both surprising and worrying. The traditional economy companies too have caught on to this trend and they are also gradually employing people on a contractual basis for niche projects. These are short-term contracts that hire people only for specific tasks. This reduces operational expenses and manages time effectively. [14]

Short-term thinking

Several business models of the twenty-first century, largely based around technology, are about disruption or creating an imbalance and profiting from it. The venture capital ecosystem pours oodles of cash into perpetually loss-making but exponentially growing unicorns because this endless flow of cash wipes out the competitors, and then prices can be raised and discounts forgotten. Which is pretty much what has happened. In sector after sector in India, the largest companies left standing are today in positions that can be described as duopolies. Consumers have hugely benefited from the start-up wars, with low prices and great service.

The gig economy is an example of short-term thinking that maximises shareholder value. This type of approach pervades almost every aspect of business decision making. The dominant refrain of 'let's think about this quarter and forget the rest' has had a serious impact on the ability of companies to create genuine long-term value. When we define value as quarterly profits, we don't invest. But, if you manage for long-term value, you would automatically account for other stakeholders such as customers, employees, communities, and long emergencies like climate change. The current economic model and nebulous definitions of value incentivise the liquidation of natural capital for profit and exploitation of people for sky-rocketing valuations.

Why the SDGs matter

So, what is the way out? How can we build back our fragile, pandemic-torn economies? Create more equity and a resilient and robust ecosystem?

We already have a framework that addresses almost all the critical things that need to be addressed.

During the 2014 UN Sustainable Development Summit, members from 193 countries of the United Nations collaboratively committed to adopting the Sustainable Development Goals (SDGs). The countries also committed themselves to meet the 2030 agenda for sustainable development. The 17 SDGs and 169 interlinked targets within these addressed a variety of issues—from ending poverty to stemming climate change and provided a pathway to a sustainable and more prosperous world. Many companies the world over are linking their sustainability and social responsibility actions to the goals established in the SDGs. Our study[15] indicates that 60 per cent of the top 100 Indian companies incorporate SDGs into their strategic decision-making around business responsibility.

Eighty-two per cent of the companies focus on SDGs number six, eight, twelve and thirteen that represent decent work, clean water and sanitation, responsible consumption and production, climate action, good health and well-being and quality education.

2020 was planned to be a seminal year by the UN as this was to be the start of a decade of action to deliver the SDGs by 2030. The 'Decade of Action' called for accelerating sustainable solutions to all the world's biggest challenges—ranging from poverty and gender to climate change, inequality and closing the finance gap.

The coronavirus pandemic then hit the world, and at first glance, it seemed that the SDGs would be unachievable. The direct and indirect impacts are so enormous that it will perhaps take years to figure out what actually happened. A new ILO analysis of the labour market impact of COVID-19 suggests a massive drop in labour income. Global labour income is estimated to have declined by 10.7 per cent, or $3.5 trillion, in the first three quarters of 2020, compared with the same period in 2019. This figure excludes income support provided through government measures.[16] According to the IMF's latest World Economic Outlook, the cumulative loss to global GDP over 2020 and 2021 could be about $9 trillion.[17] This will worsen poverty, keep children out of schools, increase child marriages, impact immunisation programmes and worsen health outcomes. The World Bank expects the first increase in extreme poverty since 1990, with between 40–46 million more people surviving on less than $1.9 a day.[18] Estimates now suggest that the COVID-19 outbreak will result in an increase in HIV, TB and malaria-related deaths over the next five years, as up to 80 million children may lose out on routine vaccines.

So COVID-19 should not be an excuse to delay action, but rather the reason to accelerate action on the SDGs. However, the multitude of challenges, such as job losses and shifts due to technology, the need to prioritise health, deceleration in world economies and inadequate measures of GDP, basically mean that governments which were previously the biggest stakeholders in improving human welfare are now feeling increasingly unable to combat the challenges they are facing.[19] This is a huge issue as economic policy has usually been based on the assumptions that technological potential can and will drive productivity improvements and that the growth of GDP per capita is correlated with improvements in human welfare. Traditional economic principles therefore are not proving successful in managing the economic downturn that countries are facing. In such a scenario, people are increasingly looking at companies to solve their problems and to take on social causes. This is why many of the world's top companies are aligning themselves to social and environmental causes.

Policy makers and thought leaders are now talking about building back the world economy in a better way. To do that however, we need to recognise that we are living within interconnected systems. The earth is a system which functions in a particular way. Similarly, the financial markets, social media platforms and global supply chains are all systems. And sometimes several of these systems could be interconnected in ways that are not apparent till much later.

Business responsibility till now was defined in simplistic terms, where 'sustainability' referred to environmental issues and impacts of the core business and 'CSR' had loosely come to mean philanthropic activities that a company undertook over and above the ordinary course of business. These meanings still hold true if you assume that the structure of society and its expectations remain the same, *ceteris paribus*, if the structure of society changes, so does everything else.

Responsibility in the age of pandemics and automation needs new economic models, business constructs and maybe even the structure of a different world.

The rise of ESG

The global economic paradigm is changing as companies are under tremendous pressure from people across the world to account for the social impact of their businesses (see Technical Note 9). Moreover, endless growth with profit as the sole metric is no longer being considered as sustainable. The focus on business responsibility has often been termed by the financial community as ESG, environmental, social and governance issues.

Environmental: Focusses on a company's environmental disclosure, environmental impact, and any efforts to reduce pollution or carbon emissions.

Societal: Refers to the workplace mentality (diversity, management, human rights) as well as any relationships surrounding the community (philanthropy or corporate citizenship).

Governance: Accounts for compensation, shareholder rights, and the relationship between shareholders and management.

The focus on ESG has been picking up momentum in the last few years and companies have increasingly focussed on generating sustainability reports and cause marketing campaigns to promote themselves. Now though, we have reached a tipping point with global investors who are demanding action and want this action to not just be local or limited. They want transformation at scale because nothing else will do in the current state of climate emergency. A compliance-driven approach where you simply submit a sustainability report is passé. Companies will need to look at everything that forms the core of their business to drive value and consider their impact on the environment and society.

2019 saw many global businesses pledging to reduce emissions, transform supply chains, focus on better materials, reduce income inequality and improve public health. In August 2019, members of the Business Roundtable who are CEOs of top American companies, announced, 'Shareholder Value Is No Longer Everything'.[20] Analysts viewed this as a response to an increasing backlash against income inequality, mounting distress against low wages and hard-to-come-by jobs.[21]

In 2020, changes wrought in business were many. The biggest change in the sustainability narrative has been the entry of banks and large financial institutions, which have made important commitments towards financing the transition to a clean, green economy. Of the world's largest fifty banks, twenty-five have made public sustainable finance commitments totalling more than $2.5 trillion.[22] For instance, Goldman Sachs plans to spend $750 billion over the next decade financing and advising companies focussed on climate transition and inclusive growth. Banks have also signed up to the new UN-backed Principles for Responsible Banking[23] and a host of other initiatives such as Science Based Targets[24] or RE 100[25] which commits to source 100 per cent of energy from renewable sources.

ESG issues are now becoming critical in investment decision-making. Investors are incorporating these to reduce risk and seize opportunities by fine-tuning equity exposures, searching for excess returns, remaking bond portfolios and tapping the green bond market. Today, ESG represents about one-quarter of all professionally managed assets around the world. Global ESG assets are on track to exceed $53 trillion by 2025.[26] A big push towards this is being given by governments as more than $3 trillion in fiscal stimuli globally will be dedicated to financing a green recovery (see Technical Note 7).

Once considered a niche market for institutional clients with specialised investment needs, ESG investing has gone mainstream. It now spans multiple asset classes and is used by a diverse group of investors. Companies across the world are now speaking about environmental and social issues in their corporate reports. About seven years back, when this trend was just emerging, the authors started a project to track social and sustainability activities of the top Indian companies. The study called Responsible Business Rankings has been tracking the top 200 Indian companies for seven years. The study indicates that Indian companies are putting in significant efforts to improve their ESG performance. Improvement in performance is not driven by a particular category of company. No matter how we dissect the study sample, we find increased scores. This indicates improvement across the board.

ESG stocks provide better returns than others. Take a look at the returns provided by the top performing companies in the Futurescape Responsible Business Rankings (see Figure 1.1). So while the Nifty gave a 12 per cent return the ESG stocks gave an average return of 16 per cent. Research is consistently showing that companies that rank high on ESG provide higher returns and tend to have a lower cost of capital. In 2020, ESG investments and funds have regularly outperformed all others and ESG investments are now at an all-time high.

So, how does ESG help add value to a company's prospects. There are five ways it can do so:

- **Growing the top line**: It has been seen that consumers are increasingly making their purchase decisions based on sustainability of the product. Thus, a sustainable product is likely to add value to the company.
- **Cost reduction**: Reduction in energy usage or water usage is likely to reduce costs for the company.
- **Avoidance of regulatory roadblocks**: Regulators are positively inclined toward companies with strong ESG practices. Also, increased regulatory pressures are less likely to impact a company focussed on ESG and may even gain subsidies and faster regulatory clearances.
- **Productivity improvements**: Employees prefer to work in companies that have a strong sustainabilty orientation. This is likely to raise employee morale and productivity.
- **Reduced stranded assets**: Companies that proactively move towards newer technologies or have reduced investment in older technologies are less likely to be left with stranded assets.

FIGURE 1.1

RETURNS ON ESG STOCKS

ESG stocks	January 1, 2014	December 27, 2020	Return (annualised)
Infosys Ltd.	273.05	1,236.05	28.62%
Tata Chemicals Ltd.	93.80	476.20	31.10%
Wipro Ltd.	174.61	382.20	13.95%
Hindustan Unilever Ltd.	509.29	2,402.25	29.50%
Godrej Consumer Products Ltd.	256.50	721.00	18.80%
Grasim Industries Ltd.	368.32	897.15	16.00%
Bharat Petroleum Corporation Ltd.	71.47	377.55	31.97%
Nifty50	6,221.15	13,749.25	14.13%

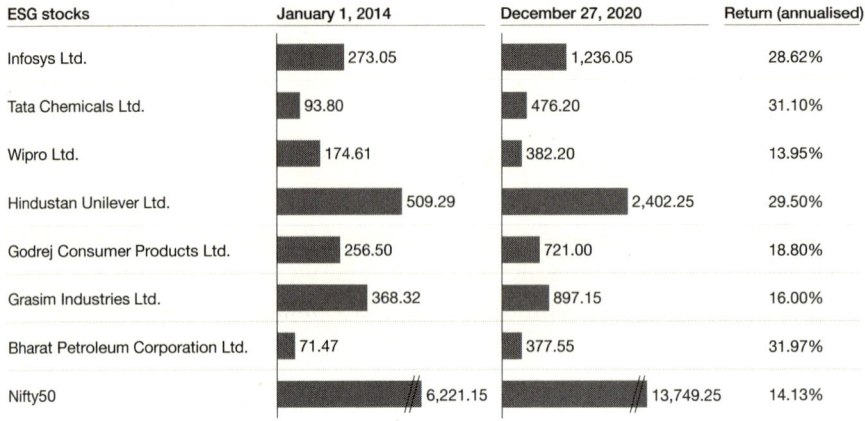

[1]Companies chosen on the basis ofconsistent ESG performance from Break up Futurescape Responsible Responsible Business Rankings. Stock price data and Nifty data from Yahoo Finance, adjusted for stock splits and dividends

Overall, the pandemic has made us rethink the capitalist system and our lackadaisical approach towards the environment. A reimagination of the role of the market and the state is urgently needed. Further, businesses need to step up in different ways and collaborate at a scale that till now has not been heard of. It is therefore very likely that this may herald the beginning of a new economic order. The Indian government is already using SDGs as a roadmap for formulating national policies and regulations. It is incumbent upon corporations to complement these actions.

But we can't wait till 2030 to find out whether we won or lost. We need an interim checkpoint, perhaps 2025 can be that.

2

THE NET ZERO TRANSITION

TO AVOID THE WORST CLIMATE IMPACTS, GLOBAL GREENHOUSE GAS (GHG) emissions will need to drop by half by 2030 and then reach netzero around mid-century.[1] Large investors, governments and businesses are seeing a unique opportunity to drive a shift to a low-carbon future. And the shift to low carbon is not an end in itself; it can drive resilience, prevent crises and lead to growth with better health and wellbeing.

Ignoring the climate crisis could cause the global economy to lose between \$150 and \$792 trillion by 2100, if countries do not meet their current targets to cut down GHG emissions.[2] In contrast, it would cost G20 countries between \$16 and \$103 trillion to limit warming to 1.5 to 2 degrees Celsius. The urgency to limit emissions is spurring countries, cities, companies and people. As of February 2021, netzero targets (either economy- or company-wide, or for a specific sector) cover at least 454 cities, 120 countries, 1,391 companies, 569 universities and 74 large investors across all continents.[3]

The impact of climate change

Our entire progress and growth has been due to our ability to harness energy to do various tasks. Cooling, heating, cooking, travel, manufacturing—everything depends on energy. Moreover, GDP growth has been directly correlated to energy consumption as during the past five decades, while global GDP has quadrupled, energy consumption has increased 2.5 times.[4]

An increase in energy usage is also directly correlated with the use of natural resources as global extraction of minerals has increased 3.4 times.

Climate change is caused because human activity, such as burning of coal and oil, is causing excessive amount of GHGs to enter the earth's atmosphere, causing our climate to heat up dramatically. Several GHGs such as carbon dioxide and methane occur naturally and trap some of the sun's heat close to the earth's surface. This is also known as the greenhouse effect and helps sustain life on earth. Human activity such as burning coal, oil and gas at an unprecedented scale since the Industrial Revolution has increased carbon dioxide levels in the atmosphere by more than 45 per cent. This is the highest they have ever been in at least 800,000 years. The sectors that contribute the most to GHG emissions are energy and transport (73.2 per cent), agriculture (18.4 per cent), industrial processes (5.2 per cent) and waste (3.2 per cent) (see Figure 2.1). Energy use has two main contributors—energy use in industry (24.2 per cent) and transport (16.2 per cent) [5]

While most GHGs stay in the atmosphere, significant portions are quickly removed by plants on land or taken up by oceans. The lockdowns across the world due to the pandemic led to huge reductions in carbon emissions. Global GHG emissions fell by 6.4 per cent in 2020,[6] the largest annual drop since the Second World War. This tells us in no uncertain terms that even if we remove the cars, planes and transport from all the world, we still have a long way to go to remove 90 per cent of the carbon in the atmosphere.

The earth is heating up and extreme weather events are becoming more common. However, till recently, scientists have avoided linking specific climate disasters to human impact. In the past few years, scientists have run simulations with climate models to determine how much human impact has contributed to a specific event such as a heat wave. This kind of research, called attribution research, is enabling scientists to pinpoint the direct impacts of human activity on the climate and ensuing natural disasters. As people struggle to cope with flooding, cyclones, excessive pollution, extreme cold and extreme heat, the vast, global, interconnected supply chains that companies work through are breaking down. Earth is losing the ability to regenerate its resources and natural systems are collapsing with over extraction due to mining, water bodies are polluted due to the presence of industrial effluents and plastic and biodiversity is at huge risk with thousands of species nearing extinction.[7]

FIGURE 2.1
WHERE DO GLOBAL GREENHOUSE GAS EMISSIONS COME FROM?

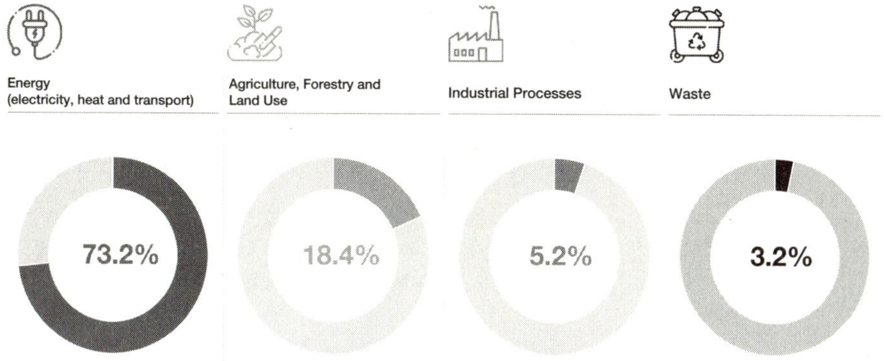

The work of the Intergovernmental Panel on Climate Change (IPCC) shows the dire consequences we face if we fail to limit the global temperature increase to 1.5°C. Even at 1.1°C of global warming, which is by how much the global temperature has increased by so far, the impacts we have seen from a changing climate have been intolerable. At 1.5 degree of warming, 14 per cent of the global population will face severe heat and at 2 degrees, 37 per cent of the global population will face unbearable heat. Further, climate change will impact almost all sectors, albeit in different ways.

The world's leading climate scientists agree that we have only twelve years to limit global warming to a maximum of 1.5°C.[8] The planet is giving us several warning signs. Arctic ice is melting at an unprecedented rate, wildfires have devastated large parts of the US and Australia, unprecedented flooding and crazy storms are happening with increasing frequency. Climate change could wreck the global economy and shrink global GDP by almost 23 per cent by 2100.[9] It is therefore essential that we do our best to hold global temperatures as low as possible.

If we continue our current policies and keep adding carbon to the atmosphere we will cross over into temperatures that will make life on earth impossible. Rising temperatures and changing monsoon rainfall patterns from climate change could cost India 2.8 per cent of GDP and depress the living standards of nearly half the country's population by 2050.[10] India's average annual temperatures are expected to rise by 1°C to 2°C by 2050 even if preventive measures are taken along the lines of those recommended by the Paris Climate Change Agreement of 2015. If no measures are taken, average temperatures in India are predicted to increase by 1.5°C to 3°C (see Figure 2.2).

According to a World Bank Report,[11] in India today, approximately 600 million people live in locations that could either become moderate or severe hotspots by 2050 under a business-as-usual scenario. States in the central, northern and north-western parts of India are the most vulnerable to changes in average temperature and precipitation. By 2050 Chhattisgarh and Madhya Pradesh are predicted to be the top two climate hotspot states and are likely to experience a decline of more than 9 per cent in their living standards, followed by Rajasthan, Uttar Pradesh, and Maharashtra.

Seven out of the top ten most-affected hotspot districts will be in the Vidarbha region of Maharashtra. Almost half of South Asia's population, including India, now lives in vulnerable areas and will suffer from declining living standards that could be attributed to falling agricultural yields, lower labour productivity or related health impacts. Some of these areas are already less developed, suffer from poor connectivity and are water stressed.

Climate change and loss of biodiversity is likely to increase pandemics at an unprecedented scale. The World Health Organisation has warned that this won't be the last or the worst pandemic. Seventy-five per cent of all emerging infectious diseases come from wildlife, and more deadly pathogens exist in nature. Destruction of natural habitats and climate change both drive wildlife closer to people. Catastrophic levels of global warming await unless countries quintuple their carbon-cutting ambitions. A warmer earth means more mosquitoes and ticks bringing disease to new places, more allergies and asthma. The pollution blanket we have put around the earth makes our lungs more susceptible to infection.

To avoid the worst climate impacts, global GHG emissions will need to drop by half by 2030 and reach net zero around mid-century (see Figure 2.3).

Net zero for a green economy

But, what exactly is 'Net Zero'? 'Net Zero' refers to achieving an overall balance between emissions produced and emissions taken out of the atmosphere.

> Net emissions = Total carbon released ***less*** total carbon taken out of the atmosphere

FIGURE 2.2

IMPACT OF CLIMATE CHANGE

Agriculture

- Soil erosion, reduction in crop yields due to severe weather and crop diseases
- At 1.5 degrees 8% of plant species will lose their habitable area and 16% at 2 degrees

Energy

- Higher demand for cooling, difficulties in generation more power due to extreme weather events

Forests

- Increase in forest fires and changes in forest species

Health

- Climate crisis is also a health crisis. Lack of water and food will cause hunger and starvation, Extreme events will make it difficult for people to survive. There will be higher incidence of diseases and pandemics

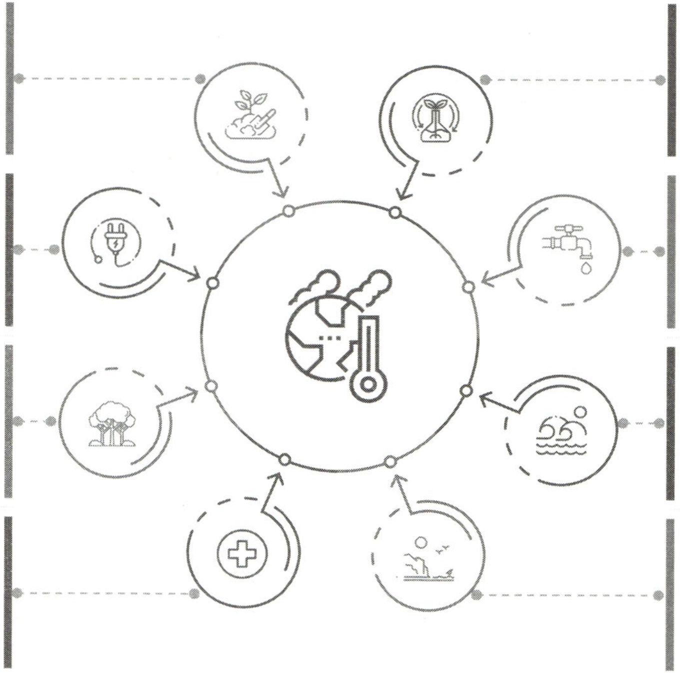

Biodiversity

- Huge loss in biodiversity and extinction, change in timings and duration of crop growing seasons
- At 1.5 degrees 6% of insect species will lose their habit able area and 18% at 2 degrees
- At 2 degrees 99% of coral reefs will decline

Water

- Certain areas may have too much water and others may have too little.

Oceans

- Ocean acidity is already 26% higher than before industrial times and is projected to worsen further. Fisheries will be heavily impacted with loss of marine life and a decline in ocean habitats.

Coastal Areas

- Flooding, erosion, extreme weather events, changes in eco systems

Source: Adapted from UNFCC, https://unfccc.int/sites/default/files/resource/Climate_Action_Support_Trends_2019.pdf

Adapted from WRI (07/10/18) based on data from IPCC (10/2018).[12]

As long as carbon released equals carbon taken out of the atmosphere, we are net zero. Else we are net positive as is the case today. As a society we would like to be net negative but that is a long way off. There are two ways to achieve net zero carbon emissions. First, by attacking the first part of the equation. Here one can reduce or stop releasing GHGs by cutting emissions and shifting to green energy sources such as solar and wind.

Or one can attack the second part of the equation by removing CO_2 from the atmosphere through natural solutions such as reforestation or through technology such as carbon capture technologies. This takes into account that some emissions are produced by 'hard-to-mitigate' sectors, such as steel manufacturing and aviation, where reducing emissions is either too expensive, technologically too complex or simply not possible. Here, carbon capture and storage technologies can come into play, which can capture the carbon released and ensure that it is converted into a compressed liquid state and stored. Nature-based solutions can be used effectively to remove carbon. These include planting trees and forests, better farming techniques, seaweed forests, peatbogs and mangroves. At a macro level, it does not matter in which part of the world the action is being undertaken. Increases in carbon emissions in China can be matched against carbon reduction through increased afforestation in the Amazon. Or increased use of solar and wind energy in Europe. As long as we are net zero or carbon neutral at a global level we should be fine (see Figure 2.3).

Translating the concept of net zero is relatively more difficult when it comes to companies. However, the basic principle remains the same.

> Net emissions = Emissions caused by company ***less*** credits for carbon reduction or carbon reduction activities

If the emissions equal the credits, then the company is said to be net zero. Here carbon credits refer to credits received for reduction in carbon by the company or other companies (see Technical Note 1). The credits are tradeable and enable companies to be net zero. Almost everyone is focussing on ten key things that need to be done (see Figure 2.4). This includes investing in green energy, eliminating waste and halting deforestation among others.

According to the EU roadmap to achieve an 80 per cent reduction in emissions by 2050, investment in clean and energy-efficient technologies

FIGURE 2.3
HOW TO GET TO NET ZERO

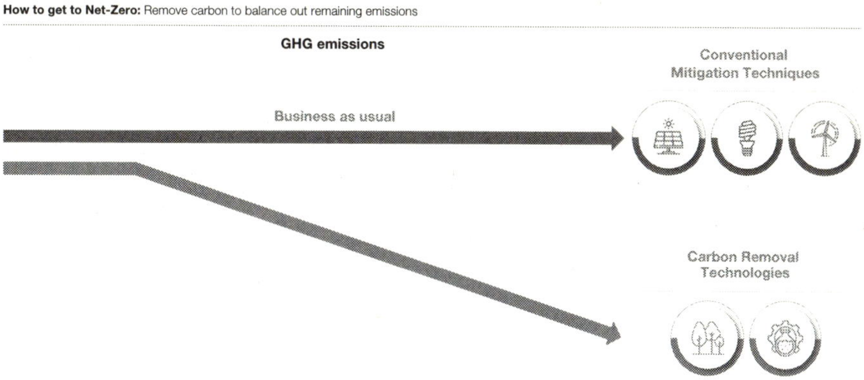

needs to be increased by 1.5 per cent of GDP per year, or €270 billion. This investment will be largely paid back, or even over-compensated, through lower energy bills; fuel savings amount to €175–320 billion on average per year by 2050. The low carbon economy will also improve air quality, reducing air pollution control and health care costs by up to €88 billion a year by 2050.[13]

Today, we have the technologies necessary to reach net zero as solar and wind now provide power for 67 per cent of the world—and it is affordable.[14] But, more than technology, we need a shift in policy and behaviour to achieve this. There are many things that can be done. For instance, the UK has announced a ten-point green plan that will help create 250,000 jobs. The plan looks at promoting electric cars and green transport, a focus on wind, hydrogen and nuclear power, planting more trees and making London the centre of green finance.[15] At the 2020 UN General Assembly, China announced that it would peak its GHG emissions before 2030, and aim to achieve net zero GHG emissions by 2060.

While India, unlike China, the European Union (EU), Japan and South Korea has so far not committed to a 'Net Zero emission' target as its national goal, India is a signatory to the Paris Agreement under the United Nations Framework Convention on Climate Change (UNFCCC). The Paris Agreement aims to take collective climate actions to keep the global average temperature rise well below 2 °C by the end of the century and make best efforts to limit warming to 1.5 °C. As part of its post-2020 commitment, called Nationally Determined Contribution (NDC), under the Paris Agreement, India has three quantitative goals—cutting down the carbon footprint by 33–35 per cent by 2030 from the 2005 level; achieving about 40 per cent cumulative electric power installed capacity from non-fossil fuel-based energy resources by 2030 and creating an additional carbon sink equivalent to 2.5 to 3 billion tonnes of CO_2 through additional forest and tree cover by 2030.[16]. The Economic Survey of India[17] is an annual exercise in determining the state of the Indian economy. The discussion on SDGs and climate change in the 2021 document reflect India's transformative actions that include solar power projects, afforestation, sustainable agriculture and mandatory energy consumption in large energy-consuming industries. India has also become the second largest green bond market after China and has joined the European Commission-led International Platform on Sustainable Finance (IPSF).

Joining hands with the government to take India towards the path of lower GHG emissions, twenty-four top private companies, including Tata, Reliance, Mahindra, ITC, ACC, Adani and Dalmia Cement, signed a declaration on climate change by voluntarily pledging to move towards 'carbon neutrality'. The nine mitigation measures announced by these companies include promotion of renewable energy, enhanced energy efficiency, material efficiency, improved processes, water efficient processes, green mobility, R&D, afforestation and waste management.[18]

Success can't be measured in words, declarations and assumptions. It will be defined by actual results and looking back at the 2020's as the decade of transformative action. There is much more to do to help leaders in politics

FIGURE 2.4
10 IMPORTANT THINGS TO REACH NET ZERO

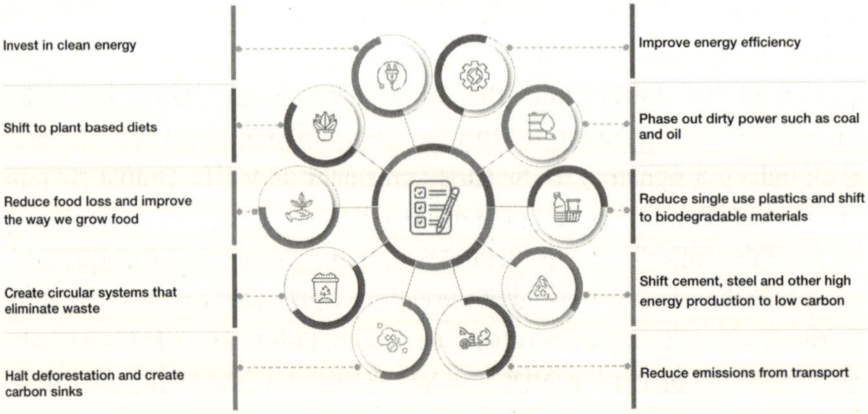
Invest in clean energy
Shift to plant based diets
Reduce food loss and improve the way we grow food
Create circular systems that eliminate waste
Halt deforestation and create carbon sinks
Improve energy efficiency
Phase out dirty power such as coal and oil
Reduce single use plastics and shift to biodegradable materials
Shift cement, steel and other high energy production to low carbon
Reduce emissions from transport

and business understand what it really means, and what it will take to get there. Hence, while we need to take a long view we need shorter milestones that will take us to net zero by 2050. Scientists and experts have consistently said that the sooner we act, the lower will be the cost and the risk. There will be a new generation of people in corporate leadership by 2050 and the current ones may get away by only making declarations for 2050 and doing nothing at all. Hence, 2030 targets and close scrutiny on actions are the only things that will get us to net zero.

The rapid scale up

Scientists have been crying hoarse about climate change for the last two decades. Why are countries and companies suddenly accelerating the sustainability and climate change action now? There are three main reasons for this. First, new technologies exist that can make the shift to low carbon possible and economically feasible. Second, the risks of climate change are already causing damage and the financial system is taking heed, and third, governments are pushing the net zero agenda after realising that this move can generate jobs.

Net Zero technologies exist and new ones are evolving

The transition to net zero carbon dioxide (CO_2) emissions requires significant investment in clean energy technologies. A wide range of fuels and technologies need to be deployed, tailored to individual parts of the energy sector and to country-specific circumstances. Some technologies exist and are in advanced stages of scale up. Wind and solar are scaling up very quickly. People are installing solar panels on rooftops, thereby reducing the need for accessing coal-based power from the grid. Improvements in storage technologies and lowering prices of solar panels will induce more people towards rooftop power generation. People are also gradually moving towards electric vehicles.

At the same time, efforts are underway to enhance energy efficiency. We are living in a world that wastes a huge amount of resources in terms of loss of energy and by discarding goods that have been produced. It is estimated that between 20 to 30 per cent of the energy we generate is wasted due to transmission and distribution losses. The technical losses are due to energy dissipated in the conductors, transformers and other equipment used for transmission and distribution of power. This needs to be prevented. Further, buildings and industries around the world are using older technologies and end up wasting another 30 to 50 per cent of the energy they receive. Hence there is a massive gap that, if addressed, can make energy usage more efficient. The International Energy Agency (IEA) shows a potential of up to 40 per cent reduction of resources if we re-examine the ways we produce and consume electricity.

Installing more efficient technology in buildings, energy efficient lighting, green roofs and smart sensors will create an all-electric, fully connected, flexible and adaptive infrastructure for tomorrow. Our cities and infrastructure will evolve to become waste-free, energy-efficient and circular, connected by collaborative platforms. Increasing digitisation of the energy grid and improvements in the way we design buildings, industries and cities will accelerate this need to create an efficient energy value chain. At the same time, the coming years will see more breakthroughs in battery, materials, biochemistry and digital innovation all of which have the potential to cope with the inherent issues related to a fast transition. In India, Schneider Electric's project with the HCL Foundation is one of the largest groups of rural micro-grids in Asia-Pacific, which supplies electricity to more than 6,000 households, in homes and for street lighting, micro-enterprises, schools covering more than 10,000 students, and several clinics. The micro-grids are connected to the Schneider Electric EcoStruxure for Energy Access platform, a remote, cloud-based, real-time monitoring and control solution, used to manage the load and the income generated by micro-enterprises.[19]

However, this kind of organic growth of renewable energy and increased efficiency is not enough to remove CO_2 from the atmosphere. We need acceleration at scale to meet the CO_2 targets and the sooner the better. Transformative changes are needed to enable this through science, real world tools and scale. We need to find solutions for the 47 per cent high-intensity areas that contribute the remaining hard-to-abate emissions—heavy trucking, iron and steel, cement, shipping, and aviation. For these, hydrogen is being explored as a viable option. The next few years will see an interesting energy paradigm with new tech jostling for space and existing paradigms being upended. A new coalition called the Mission Possible Partnership,[20] with backing from Jeff Bezos's Earth Fund and the Bill Gates founded Breakthrough Energy, is looking to find new energy solutions for the hard to abate emissions. A fund has been setup to support cutting-edge research and invest in new tech, but that's not all. The most important part of this coalition is their readiness to play the long game. The investment horizon is 20 years, unlike that of most funds who have a 5–7 year window.

Carbon removal, that involves sucking emissions from the atmosphere, will be essential to tackle the growing climate crisis. Carbon capture methods exist, but most haven't scaled up or are in their infancy. There are only about twenty such projects operating commercially, in the US, Canada, Norway and China. But, efforts are underway to change that. A $100 million competition hopes to spur the development of carbon capture technologies at scale.[21]

Adopting net zero emissions targets is not that simple. Zero carbon manufacturing and transportation technologies do not exist. Hence companies have to offset the carbon emissions—in effect, by buying the reductions from a third party. After announcing ambitious net zero targets, Microsoft announced the purchase of offsets from fifteen vendors around the world.[22]

However, energy intensity per unit of GDP had already started showing a decline in 2019 as the world gradually shifted to renewable energy.[23] In June 2019, the UK became the world's first major economy to pass laws to end its contribution to global warming by 2050. The target will require the UK to bring all GHG emissions to net zero by 2050, compared with the previous target of at least 80 per cent reduction from 1990 levels.[24] The British government has also launched a £315 million hunt to find new technologies that can shrink the carbon footprint of the most polluting factories to help meet the UK's climate targets.[25] Almost every sector that depends on energy is looking at disruptions caused by the changes in energy.

Net zero business models

Sustainability is more than reducing carbon emissions and sounding purposeful; it is a systemic change in the ways of doing business. Simple statements about how bad things are, or what should change are past their sell-by date. We are in a climate emergency and it is a time to act, not a time to mouth platitudes. But more than a focus on any of this, we need structural changes so that these shifts towards clean energy and sustainability are scaled up. Due to these transitions, business models that drive much of the world economy are now changing. Previous business models have been based on unique capabilities—better design, sourcing strengths, service innovation and more. Over time, these strengths have coalesced to how well an organisation can develop a market positioning ahead of its competitors. For companies this has led to focussing on building brands while outsourcing to anyone who could manufacture cheaper and supply quicker. Mapping of carbon emissions was considered an 'externality', which the business could easily ignore. But now, measuring carbon emissions and actively taking steps to reduce it, is a necessity. Human rights abuses have been reported across the global supply chains of several large companies, as they mainly focussed on cost reduction and didn't particularly care for poor working conditions, child labour and so on. Business responsibility can no longer be outsourced.

For companies that are navigating the changing policy and regulatory systems, the writing is on the wall—change fast or become irrelevant. Climate change and digital transformation are creating new risks, and at the same time, new opportunities are opening up too. A new kind of leadership is needed that builds trust, is driven by values and is open to change. The leader has to be a trustee to all the stakeholders, rising above the stereotypes to decide what she will and will not do. As a trustee to the organisation, there is no exit strategy and the leader has to take a long-term view of the organisation. This is needed for businesses to transform from within and move towards a digital, low carbon world. Enabling cleaner, more efficient operations and supply chains also allows better performance across all operations to help bring down costs and emissions. For investors, scale and ambition are everything. Net zero carbon emissions take precedence over marginal improvements in reducing carbon. Compliance targets are in fact lagging investor demands. Keeping these trends in mind, using smart decision-making and intelligent design will prevent future emissions, even as the business and organisation grows.

As net zero pledges come in thick and fast from policymakers and businesses, these ambitious words need to be turned into concrete actions.

What are the implications of this net zero transition?

1. **Green supply chains:** The choices made by the big brands will impact global supply chains and unleash second and third order effects in products, materials and components/ingredients.
2. **Brand purpose:** With their products being inherently sustainable, brands will use this to drive trust and distinctiveness in consumer communication.
3. **Digital innovation:** Driven by AI, cloud and IoT, this will make products more intelligent and also drive the ability to cater to customer demands.
4. **Strategic partnerships:** These will emerge to navigate the new paradigms of sustainability, digital innovation and sustainable markets. Peer learning and knowledge sharing will play an important role in raising standards for a net zero world.
5. **Energy transition:** As factories will shift to renewable energy, so will offices and stores.
6. **New design:** Necessitated by the cost of managing reverse supply chains and inspired by consumer demands, products will be radically redesigned—natural, local, environmentally friendly themes will be prominent.

So how can a company reduce the amount of carbon it generates? At a broad level, there are three options—create low carbon products, manufacture in a way that cuts down on emissions and low carbon logistics for sourcing raw materials and supplying to end consumers. With investors demanding increased transparency, carbon footprints and reporting is no longer optional. For some brands, carbon is becoming part of the core brand proposition as several companies have announced that they will be carbon labelling their products. For instance, Unilever, one of the world's largest FMCG companies has said that each of the company's 70,000 products would show on their labels how much greenhouse gas was emitted in the process of manufacturing and shipping them to consumers.[26] Now with market leaders creating products, communication and tools to map carbon impacts, there is hope that we might be able to cut carbon at scale. With the carbon conversation now becoming a part of the brand, carbon reporting, compliance and capture are likely to pick up speed.

Corporate decisions around carbon footprinting (see Technical Note 2) aren't just based on the desire to do good, they have genuine business benefits. Industry leaders are of the view that carbon efficiency will become a differentiator for companies as customers become more aware of the impact of their decisions. However, creating industry-wide transformation in large businesses requires intervention in markets, technology, and people. To do this, there are four primary levers for change:

1. **Markets:** Create public awareness and a demand for low-carbon goods
2. **Technology:** Measure, map and enable at scale
3. **People:** Motivate people in the company as well as suppliers to accept the changes
4. **Collaboration:** Cross industry collaborations and benchmarks are needed as supply chains are interlinked

With the use of technology, companies can create brands with purpose which can do a lot more to decarbonise and transform business models. A strong positive business case and shareholder returns can empower big businesses to make big carbon reductions. This also means that empowering people to build carbon efficiency in supply chains will help build cost savings and can minimise or reduce the need for companies to invest in reverse logistics to minimise consumer waste. But the bigger trend in manufacturing is one of localisation. Modular equipment and custom machines like 3D printers are enabling manufacturers to create decentralised manufacturing centres which can hyper-personalise based on local demand and conditions.

Net zero in project finance and investments

Financing the net zero transition is being enabled and pushed by banks and financial institution the world over by moving capital out of high-carbon activities and mandatory climate risk disclosures. As the notion of climate risks becomes mainstream, so does the demand of financial institutions to quantify their potential impact. In Feb 2021, a deluge that resulted from a glacial melt on Nanda Devi washed away at least two hydroelectric power projects—the 13.2 MW Rishiganga hydroelectric power project and the Tapovan project on the Dhauliganga river, a tributary of the Alakananda.

Climate risks are increasingly expected to play an important role in financial decisions. If a company is setting up a new project and hoping to raise funds, banks and financial institutions are likely to do a climate stress test. Climate risks can be qualified as physical risks arising from extreme meteorological and climatological events; transition risks arising from the transition to a low-carbon economy; and liability risks which are triggered by the increased compensation paid to economic actors affected by climate change.

Financial institutions are now actively decarbonising their portfolios by divestment from high-carbon industries, such as oil and mining, working with companies to adopt carbon mitigation plans and offsetting emissions. But, funds can do far more than all this when it comes to making new investments. A coalition of 70 funds representing assets of $16 trillion have designed a net zero framework to remove carbon emissions across their portfolios by 2050.[27] The framework provides a comprehensive set of recommended actions, metrics, and methodologies to enable both asset owners and managers to become net zero investors. The framework identifies five core components of a net zero investment strategy and covers four asset classes—sovereign bonds, listed equities, corporate fixed income and real estate.

While we transition to renewable sources of energy, there is the hidden risk of stranded assets. Many fossil fuel-based power generation companies will need to shut down well before their life. These assets will then become stranded. People will lose jobs as the plants become non-operational and may require reskilling or their numbers will add to the unemployment figures. Further, of the many renewable energy technologies and those still developing, some will take off and others may fall back. Banks will face the issue of non-performing assets as the planned future cash flows from these assets dries up. The land on which the plant is set up will become locked and therefore unavailable for other economic activities. Customers who previously relied on the power will have to look at other sources. Shocks will also be felt across the value chain as upstream suppliers like coal producers will see a decline in demand and transporters will have nothing to carry. Currently, countries like India, China and the United States import the bulk of their energy requirements. Substituting fossil fuel with renewables implies a move from imports to self-sufficiency. This is likely to have an impact on exchange rates, trade balances and the economic power structure of the global economy.

Net zero is a jobs and skills transition

The fight against climate change was built up as a fight against growth and jobs. But the pandemic has highlighted the risks of inaction. What has also happened is that several new technologies across industries have emerged that are cleaner, greener and can generate jobs. Hence, a net zero target is both attainable and acceptable. The net zero transitions in food, infrastructure and energy alone are expected to generate $10.1 trillion of annual business opportunities and 395 million jobs by 2030.[28] Jobs in these areas will include things such as protecting the environment and ecosystem restoration, new agriculture enabled by precision tech and bio based inputs, cleaning up oceans and managing fisheries in new regenerative ways, sustainable management of forests.

There are many such opportunities ahead as the energy transition involves transforming the local economy and creating new skills that care for the new energy sources. For instance, the UK Continental Shelf (UKCS) is the region of waters surrounding the United Kingdom, in which the country has mineral rights. The UKCS includes parts of the North Sea, the North Atlantic, the Irish Sea and the English Channel; the area includes large resources of oil and gas. Ambitious net zero targets for the UKCS depend on investment in integrated, low-carbon technologies. And the direct, indirect and induced effects of this investment could contribute $3.46 trillion to the UK economy between now and 2050. This shift will transition out the 245,000 people employed in oil and gas in 2020 to jobs in renewables, hydrogen and projects in other areas. By 2040, people employed in oil and gas will fall to 95,000 and green energy jobs will rise from the current 20,000 to 210,000.

The global manufacturing sector accounts for some 35 per cent of global electricity use, 20 per cent of CO_2 emissions and 25 per cent of primary resource extraction. It has a major impact on the environment and must be factored into the climate change equation. At the same time, the sector's economic importance cannot be ignored as it currently accounts for 23 per cent of worldwide employment. Mondelēz International employs over 80,000 people in over 80 countries and sells snacks in over 150 countries.[29]

Toyota operates 69 manufacturing companies in 27 countries and regions globally, excluding Japan. It markets vehicles in more than 160 countries and regions worldwide.[30] Today, the world's biggest companies are transforming their energy utilisation to renewable and also adopting sweeping changes to deliver on this promise. Making efforts to switch to solar, hydro, wind, geothermal, and biomass energy is picking up momentum across the world. The sheer scale of the energy transition in these large companies alone is expected to create new jobs and opportunities.

As shown by our research, in Indian companies, renewable energy has gained a lot of mind share in the past few years. Business operations are energy-intensive; thus, companies have started expanding their captive renewable energy capacities or are purchasing renewable energy for their operations. The disclosure of the share of renewable energy in total electricity consumed, however, continues to be limited. Only a few companies shared short-term targets to increase the share of renewable energy in their operations. For instance, Tata Motors aspires to operate on 100 per cent renewable energy in the coming future. It is a signatory to the RE100 initiative and so is Dalmia Bharat. Companies mainly use renewable energy in their core operations. Some also use it for powering streetlights and solar water heating. Maruti Suzuki, which has been using solar power for lighting its manufacturing plants and office areas, now has also started using solar energy in the manufacturing of cars. Solar continues to be the most deployed source of renewable energy across all sectors except consumer staples, where 88 per cent of companies reported that they utilised biofuel as compared to 75 per cent of companies using solar energy.

While the leading Indian companies focus on utilising renewable energy in operations, very few have renewable energy related programmes for their supply chain members. Most companies require their suppliers to comply with environmental norms, but only around 10 per cent of companies reported initiatives or guidelines that were specific to incorporating renewable energy in supplier operations.

Finish lines are only worth the action they drive. Which is why when we look at all these net zero declarations, we need to ensure that the actions match the statements of intent. The biggest potential for the net zero transformation lies in the creation of a green economy.

Net zero ecosystems are being created

In the past few years it has been repeatedly highlighted that companies only disclose the emissions of their company-owned offices and factories. For instance, only 2 per cent of India's top companies report emissions from logistics.[31] Further, considering the size of the distribution networks, if one were to account for the emissions caused during distribution of products to consumers, no large company can ever hope to be sustainable. The global manufacturing market reached $38 trillion in 2018, contributing to a 15 per cent increase in global production output. Within this market, a broad range of goods is produced and processed, ranging from consumer goods, heavy industrials to storage and transportation of raw materials and finished product. But transformative changes are afoot.

Public-Private Partnerships

Companies like Maersk, one of the largest logistics companies in the world, are not just changing the way they make products, they are changing their products themselves and launching industry-wide collaborations. A.P. Moller–Maersk is a transport and logistics business that employs over 85,000 people across operations in over 120 countries. In 2018, the Executive Board of Maersk approved a new company ambition for climate change: to have netzero CO_2 emissions from their operations by 2050. Since 2017, Maersk has invested $1 billion and engaged fifty-plus engineers each year in developing and deploying energy efficiency solutions. A major contribution will come from replacing older vessels with new and more efficient ones, taking advantage of the company's continuous work to optimise hull dimensions, hull shapes, propulsion systems and auxiliary systems. Another significant contribution will come from further optimising the Maersk network in terms of both network operations and voyage execution. Over the next few years, the company will be able to reap the benefits from investments in connecting and digitising vessels as part of the Connected Vessels project. This will focus on upgrading data collection and reporting systems on shipping vessels, real-time, coordinated data for the routes sailed, reducing time spent in ports that will lead to lower fuel consumption, less time wasted and fewer delays. These initiatives are expected to reduce fuel consumption corresponding to a removal of approximately 847,000 tonnes of carbon over five years.

Efficiency gains however, are not the only solution. Deeper impact can only be achieved through decarbonisation and hence, the company is working on a range of collaborative efforts with several partners to drive the transformation of the shipping industry towards use of carbon-neutral fuels. Maersk has launched Eco Delivery, a way of transportation that uses sustainable biofuel to provide immediate carbon reductions. One of the largest fashion and design groups in the world, H&M Group, has chosen Maersk Eco Delivery to reduce the company's carbon footprint in transportation. The initiative uses sustainable biofuel to power selected Maersk-vessels and helps H&M to make progress towards its ambitious sustainability goals.[32]

The company is slowly moving from managing internal CO_2 emissions to managing the entire logistics system. Copenhagen Airports, Maersk, DSV Panalpina, DFDS, SAS and Ørsted have formed the first partnership of its kind to develop an industrial-scale production facility to produce sustainable fuels for road, maritime and air transport in the Copenhagen area. The project will produce green hydrogen based on offshore wind power as soon as 2023. This initiative is pathbreaking in sheer scale and ambition and will have multiple large scale impacts. At one level, it will certainly help reduce the emissions of all project partners, and the next level impact will be that the City of Copenhagen will also be able to achieve its targets for decarbonisation by 2025. Further, the project is expected to create jobs and new value chains to reinforce Denmark's role as a green energy leader.[33] When the facility is fully scaled-up by 2030, the project could deliver more than 250,000 tons of sustainable fuel for buses, trucks, maritime vessels, and aeroplanes annually. The fully scaled facility can reduce annual carbon emissions by 850,000 tons.

Involving citizens in sequestering carbon

The world's first large-scale 'biochar' urban carbon sink is located in Stockholm, Sweden. This is part of Stockholm's aim to become a fossil free city by 2040 and involve citizens while doing so. Residents provide garden waste to the city, which is turned into biochar—a charcoal-like product that can sequester carbon in soil for thousands of years. This biochar is used as a soil conditioner in public and private plant beds, therefore creating a vast carbon sink. The by-product of the biochar production process, pyrolysis gas, is used to help generate energy for the city's district heating system. The pilot plant was able to process 1,200 tonnes of organic material each year, which in turn produced an estimated:

- 300 tonnes biochar
- > 1,000 CO_2 equivalent carbon sink
- > 1,000 MWh generated in renewable heat production

This initiative empowers all citizens to be able to contribute to a carbon sink for Stockholm in the fight against climate change. Storm water management and wider ecosystem services enhancement have been a bonus. Stockholm has already received nearly 100 requests from other cities and organisations that are interested in replicating the programme.

Net zero will be driven by strategy and expertise

So, at one level, we could start thinking that if we were to plant lots of trees we would be able to avert devastating climate change and all will be well. With the Arctic showing temperatures in excess of 30 degrees and several other parts of the world facing record-breaking heat, this kind of quick, magical thinking is easy to accept. But, hold on, it's a trap. Climate change is large, complex and scientific. Headline-grabbing ideas are fabulous to capture the public's imagination, but just like the pandemic has shown us, there is no substitute for expert-driven scientific advice.

There is no doubt that trees would be useful in carbon sequestration, but to plant that many trees, we need land and resources to grow them too. To fix global warming, we need to stop burning fossil fuels and there is simply no getting around that fact. And businesses need to step up. Sustainability is not magic, it is hard work that requires companies to redesign every small aspect of their business to reduce emissions. Nature-based solutions are needed at scale and they need to work together with mitigation efforts. There is no scope for either/or. We need everything together and at scale and it needs to be based on scientific facts.

Net zero is now the gold standard for corporate emission targets. More than 2000 companies have so far committed to net zero carbon emissions by 2030. With no general consensus on what net zero means for industry, businesses are left to interpret the goal themselves with market forces at play. As a result, the goal is being interpreted in very different ways and sometimes incorrectly. We certainly need to plant more trees, but for companies, a unidimensional solution, such as only planting more trees, is not the answer. Instead, a calibrated, scientific approach is needed which looks at internal operations, measures impacts and executes sustainability transformation at scale.

The transformation of companies is a result of the confluence of forces which now expect them to not just mitigate environmental and social impacts but require them to create regenerative business models that have a positive or neutral impact on the environment. Hence the shift towards ESG-driven frameworks is only expected to accelerate.

Overall, to transition to net zero there are four main things that companies will need to do:

1. **Align organisational purpose, strategy and business models**: Within a commercial context businesses can explicitly set out to improve people's lives whilst operating within the natural boundaries set by the planet.
2. **Set evidence-based targets, measure and be transparent:** Businesses can contribute to a sustainable future by setting bold evidence-based targets, measuring the right things and reporting progress.
3. **Embedding sustainability in practices and decisions:** Businesses can embed new ways of thinking in their operational practices and decision making.
4. **Engage, collaborate and advocate change:** Businesses can use their influence to engage communities, and build public and government appetite for sustainable business.

The transition to a sustainable economy by keeping these things in mind will require new collaborations with customers, communities, competitors and peers, to harness and deploy new innovations. In addition, it will need a new kind of financial system to enable these shifts. The financial world will therefore increasingly measure and value the true impact on society of a business. Businesses will need to embrace new measures to understand their full impact and dependencies on the natural world and society.

Measures around non-financial reporting will therefore increasingly become stringent.

For asset owners who seek to invest in a way that is aware of and responsive to climate change, solutions in the marketplace have traditionally focussed on mitigation: reducing the effects of climate change on a portfolio by, for example, reducing exposure to GHGs and increasing exposure to 'green' energy companies. As extreme weather events become more frequent and the economic impacts of climate change are more widely understood and accepted, investors will require companies to disclose how they are adapting their business strategies to accommodate the impacts of climate change.

Net zero will be an economic, business and people transition.

3

ESG TRANSFORMS BUSINESSES

FOR LONG, COMPANIES HAVE TALKED A LOT ABOUT SUSTAINABLE businesses and done little on the ground. When facing pressure groups and adverse publicity, companies have resorted to 'greenwashing'. Which basically means running an advertising campaign that promotes them as 'sustainable' while actually being the opposite. Further, convincing companies to transform has not been easy and most have resorted to setting up sustainability departments rather than instituting company-wide changes.

Fed up with the incrementalism that has pervaded corporate speak on governance issues and climate change, shareholders are holding companies to account for their actions. There are a set of investors who are becoming 'active' by taking stakes in companies and making demands of management teams and boards across the globe. Prominent activist investors such as Blackrock and Vanguard forced Exxon in 2017 to publish a sustainability report.[1] After intense pressure from investors, Royal Dutch Shell was forced to set carbon emission targets and link them to executive pay.[2] In May 2021 a court ordered Royal Dutch Shell to cut its global carbon emissions by 45 per cent by the end of 2030 compared with 2019 levels, in a landmark case brought by Friends of the Earth and over 17,000 co-plaintiffs. The oil giant's sustainability policy was found to be insufficient by the Dutch court in an unprecedented ruling that will have wide implications for the energy industry and other polluting multinationals.[3] Moreover, corporate reports are documenting this as a key issue. Credit Suisse's 2019 Fourth Quarter Corporate Insights speaks of 'Shareholder Activism: An Evolving Challenge'.

Leaders in finance are building awareness and taking action. Larry Fink, the CEO of Blackrock titled his 2021 annual letter to CEOs as 'A Fundamental reshaping of Finance'[4] wherein he spoke of exiting investments that 'present a high sustainability-related risk'. The letter further highlighted corporate purpose and contribution to society as 'the engine of long-term profitability'.

But, regulatory pressure and activism can only go so far. To build genuine change, the financial system needs to incentivise companies to function as per societal norms that allow profit for shareholders, a healthy earth for society and the wellbeing of employees. While companies focus a large part of their efforts on sustainability and social responsibility reports and certifications, the hard truth is that these things don't really matter. This is because if business needs to transform, the financial markets need to play an overwhelming role in the transformation. Annual reports, quarterly earnings calls, and investor briefings need to take not just financials into consideration, they also need to account for all the non-financial information that till now has been ignored by large parts of the financial community—climate impacts, environmental and social footprints, governance and corporate risk.

The idea that a relatively small group of shareholders receives all of the economic benefits of the company yet externalises all of the environmental and social impacts to the public, is slowly becoming harder and harder to swallow. Hence, concepts such as ESG, circular economy and CSR are picking up (see Figure 3.1). But simply doing good is not sufficient, the data driven

FIGURE 3.1
SUSTAINABILITY TERMS

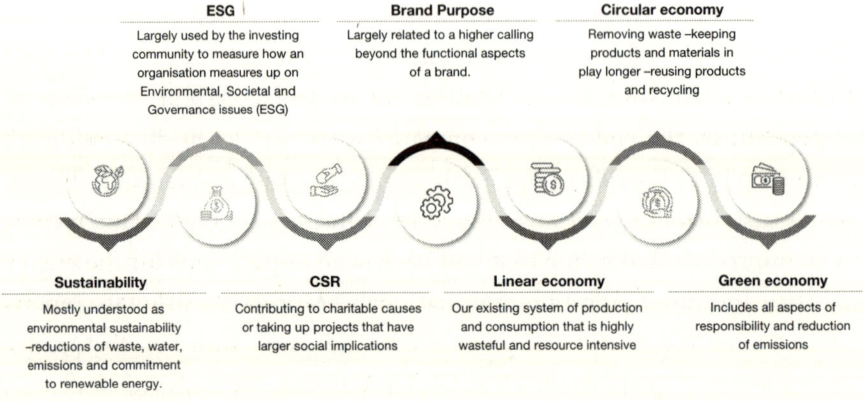
ESG
Largely used by the investing community to measure how an organisation measures up on Environmental, Societal and Governance issues (ESG)
Brand Purpose
Largely related to a higher calling beyond the functional aspects of a brand.
Circular economy
Removing waste –keeping products and materials in play longer –reusing products and recycling
Sustainability
Mostly understood as environmental sustainability –reductions of waste, water, emissions and commitment to renewable energy.
CSR
Contributing to charitable causes or taking up projects that have larger social implications
Linear economy
Our existing system of production and consumption that is highly wasteful and resource intensive
Green economy
Includes all aspects of responsibility and reduction of emissions

financial community values facts and a data driven scientific approach to measuring responsibility.

Our eight-year-long research into India's top 200 companies follows a data driven approach to understanding environmental, social and governance parameters. The scoring is based on a weighted average of these three criteria wherein 35 per cent weight is given to the environment, 30 per cent to social and 35 per cent to governance. The highest score that a company can get is 100. As the parameters suggest, the study covers how pervasive the sustainability practices of companies are, how well the key stakeholders are integrated within a company's responsible business framework and how well structured is the governance for responsible business.

Our research has found that scores across years and parameters have been consistently improving (see Figure 3.2). A significant amount of effort is being put into ESG by top Indian companies. Over the years, we have found that certain companies featured frequently in the list, while others, slow to start, suddenly picked up pace. We took a closer look at how these companies worked and what they did to consistently perform better than their peers. The top performers started early, changed their business models to include sustainability, consistently measured performance and took people along in this journey. Not only did these companies transform, top scoring ESG stocks even gave higher returns.

FIGURE 3.2
ESG PERFORMANCE OVER THE YEARS

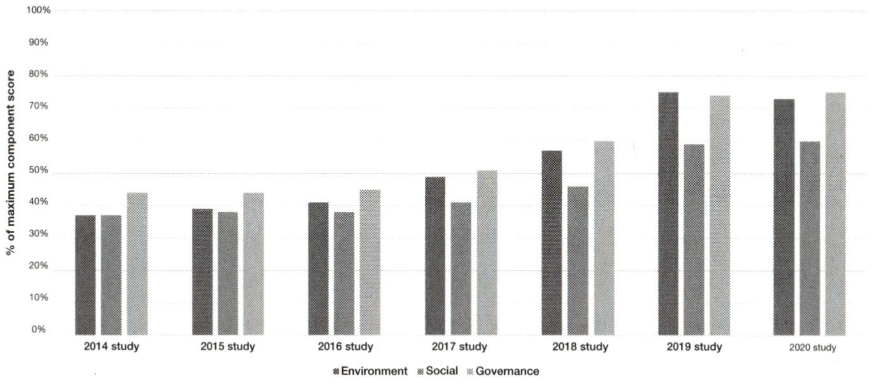

Markets take note of ESG

Our journey with ESG started in 2012. Most of the analysis at that point of time was centered around how much companies were spending on these activities. We quickly realised that these performance measures were specious. So, we started figuring out how to measure performance. We brainstormed long and hard to come up with a set of parameters that covered a company's environmental, social and governance parameters to evaluate a company. The list of parameters has now grown to over ninety (see Figure 3.3). Data was a primary concern. Collecting primary data is time consuming and places significant reliance on companies providing time and access. So, we decided to stick to publicly available information that was audited or assured. We score companies on the basis of publicly available information contained in sustainability and other allied reports. These scores are based on the action statements in the published reports against our proprietary checklist. After a rigorous evaluation and quality check, the results are published in the form of ranks. Over the years we have seen the quality of information improve as well as significant improvement in the sustainability actions of companies.

Over our journey we have accumulated a plethora of data on the ESG performance of companies. This gives us a perfect bird's eye view of the development of ESG performance of Indian companies. Practically no one else has this unique insight. Yet a recurring thought was in our minds. Companies earn profits and the stock markets reward them with stock price increases. That is the shareholder wealth maximisation principle. On the other hand, there is the stakeholder wealth maximisation principle around which the ESG actions of companies are built. Doing well and doing good are not inseparable. The market should recognise both doing well and doing good.

So, we decided to check out our hypothesis. Do markets reward companies that do better on ESG? If they do so, is it because these companies are inherently more risky? Could we create an index that minimises the risk? Does this portfolio earn better returns? Finally, we examined what a portfolio would look like if we were to track the index closely.

We picked the top 100 companies in our study and looked at the top ten performers and evaluated stock market returns in high ranking ESG stocks

FIGURE 3.3

ESG PARAMETERS

Environment

Focuses on a company's environmental disclosure, environmental impact, and, any efforts to reduce pollution or carbon emissions

Climate change	Natural Capital	Pollution	Opportunity
GHG disclosure	Water mapping	Process waste, including waste water discharge	Opportunities in Renewable energy
Air emissions	Water management	Plastic waste	Opportunities in Green buildings/ factories
Responsible finance*	Responsible sourcing	Packaging waste	Opportunities in Sustainable product/ service
		Electronic waste	Opportunities in Employee awareness
		Organic/ food waste	Opportunitis in Green logistics

Social

Refers to creating societal wellbeing either in the worlplaceor in society at large, it includes diverse concepts such as diversity, human rights, philanthropy and corporate citizenship.

Human capital	Customer	Social Opportunities
Employee management	Health & Safety	Opportunities in community welfare
Employee welfare	Environment	Opportunities in Employee management
Health & Safety	Social	Opportunities in Supply chain management
Human Capital development	Financial Literacy	
Supply chain labour standards	Responsible Advertising	
CSR Volunteering		

Governance

Accounts for compensation, shareholder rights, and the relationship between shareholders and management

Corporate governance	Corporate policies	Disclosure
Board committees	Customer data privacy	Responsible business reporting framework
Executives Management	Biodiversity policy	External assurance
Alignment with principles/frame works like SDGs	Responsible business policy	Impact assessment
	Employee policies	Material issues
		Partnerships/ Collaborations

vs stock market returns in the Nifty 50 stocks (Nifty is the flagship index on the National Stock Exchange of India Ltd).

From 2014 to 2020, ESG stocks earned 4 per cent more than Nifty50

If you invested money in just ten ESG companies at the beginning of 2014, how would you have fared at the end of 2020? Surprisingly, very well. If an investor distributed her investments equally between the ten stocks (i.e., investing Rs 10,000 in ESG companies, Rs 1000 each) the investor would have earned an annual return of 16 per cent. As against that, investing the same money in the index (Nifty50) would have returned only 12 per cent, 4 per cent lesser.

ESG stocks consistently beat the market

If the investor could invest only in 2015, they would earn 13 per cent in the ESG portfolio as compared to 9 per cent on Nifty50. Still making 4 per cent more than Nifty50. As you go down the table with reducing periods for which the money is invested, you will find that ESG investors keep beating the market except in the really short period—that's where market peculiarities take over (see Figure 3.4).

What if our investor was not reckless? Suppose, she ended up picking stocks indiscriminately and ended up with stocks that are at the bottom of the pile in our ESG rankings. How would she fare? Not too well, we are afraid. Her equally weighted portfolio (investing equally in each of the ten stocks) of low-score ESG stocks will give her a return of only 5 per cent as compared to 12 per cent on Nifty50. This is just the opposite of the smart investor we saw earlier.

Investing in stocks that perform well on ESG is the way for investors to make more money.

ESG is helping build back better

COVID-19 is an unprecedented global challenge for both health and economic well-being.

As per the UNDP Human Development Index (HDI), India is ranked 131 out of 189 countries in 2020. Moreover, India also reflects huge inter-regional disparities in its human development indices. Concerned by the

FIGURE 3.4

ESG STOCKS CONSISTENTLY BEAT THE MARKET

	Nifty50	Equal-weight -portfolio (Top ESG stocks)
2014-2020	12%	16%
2015-2020	9%	13%
2016-2020	12%	15%
2017-2020	14%	14%
2018-2020	10%	5%
2019-2020	14%	7%
2020	15%	19%

Adjusted for stock splits and dividends
Data source: Yahoo Finance

problems created by the pandemic, there are new conversations almost every day on what needs to be done and everyone has a perspective, based on the window they look out from. For instance, economists cite changes in fiscal and monetary policy, environmentalists talk about green jobs and the UN's SDGs, energy companies talk about the need to promote renewables in all forms and so on.

The pandemic, for now, seems to have connected a multitude of issues. Public health is connected to the economy and both of them worsen with inequality. Climate change impacts everything and can worsen health, economies and inequality. The way we generate and use energy impacts the economy, the climate and public health, and the list goes on. The pandemic has equally highlighted that trust holds society together.

Driven by the urgent need to tackle the climate crisis, policy changes in many countries are afoot. For instance, projects such as planting a trillion trees to absorb excess carbon have been initiated. IPCC[5] estimates that nature-based solutions, including healthy forests, could provide up to one-third of the emissions reductions required by 2030 to meet the Paris Agreement targets. Trees are the world's best machines when it comes to absorbing carbon. Human activity emits about 11 gigatons of carbon and it is estimated that forests, fields, grasslands and oceans absorb about 6 gigatons.[6] So if we plant more trees, the 5 gigatons that go into the atmosphere could get absorbed.[7] Most countries are now looking at increasing their forest cover to reduce emissions. Countries like the UK and India are actively looking at creating such 'carbon sinks' by planting forests in urban areas as well. Initiatives such as these, as well as the energy transition, are also expected to create green jobs.

Companies are realising that stringent regulations around reducing emissions and corporate responsibility are around the corner and rather than wait for these to happen, they need to be proactive about the changes that need to be made. Hence, ESG frameworks are being adopted all across the world.

Take the case of Amazon. In September 2019, Amazon CEO Jeff Bezos announced a massive new commitment to fight climate change called 'The Climate Pledge'. The Climate Pledge, co-founded by Amazon and Global Optimism, is a commitment to reach net zero carbon by 2040. As part of this pledge, Amazon would measure and report emissions on a regular basis, implement decarbonisation strategies, and offset any remaining emissions. In June 2020, Verizon, Infosys, and Reckitt Benckiser signed The Climate Pledge as well and more companies are expected to become part of this collective.[8] The company has adopted a five-pronged approach to measure and reduce its carbon footprint. This includes transportation, electricity, packaging, devices and a financial model to enable the necessary reduction in emissions and shifts to environment-friendly processes and materials. Amazon has also signed up to Science Based Targets. As part of this strategy, 80 per cent of Amazon's energy use is to be renewable by 2024. Amazon has also announced five new renewable energy projects.[9] To date, Amazon has announced thirty-one utility-scale wind and solar renewable energy projects and sixty solar rooftops on fulfilment centres and sort centres around the globe. Together, these projects totalling over 2,900 MW of capacity will deliver more than 7.6 million MWh of renewable energy annually, enough to power 680,000 U.S. homes. Amazon has also started a climate fund to focus on greening and preserving wildlife. Amazon committed funds to conserve, restore, and support sustainable forestry, wildlife and nature-based solutions across the Appalachian Mountains and an urban greening programme in Germany, which uses nature-based solutions to help cities become more climate-change resilient. The programme will collaborate with city officials and local community organisations to create and implement plans for increasing biodiversity and planting trees, revitalising urban wetlands and adapting existing green spaces.

Global industry associations are also gearing up and have set up stringent sustainability targets for their member companies. For example, the Tire Industry Project of the WBCSD serves as a global, voluntary, CEO-led initiative, undertaken by eleven leading tire companies[10] with an aim to anticipate, identify, analyse and address the potential human health and environmental impacts associated with tire development, use and management through end-of-life.

Since, Indian companies are downstream suppliers to several large organisations and part of the interconnected global supply chains they are impacted too. Our research shows that there are seven main strategies that Indian companies are following to improve their ESG performance.

1. Aligning strategy and business models
2. Building transparent and measurable targets
3. Designing for circularity
4. Creating green supply chains
5. Adopting Nature-based solutions
6. Brands with purpose
7. Education for all

1. Aligning strategy and business models

We realised that the top performing companies started early and it took on an average five to seven years from the beginning of their sustainability journey to show improvements across various parameters.

Successful businesses found ways to create value while making investments in climate-friendly technologies. They also aligned their core purpose to sustainable development and worked with a range of stakeholders to understand the full lifecycle of their products and services. Further, they realised that merely following a compliance driven approach was insufficient. Hence they set targets that were ambitious and innovative so that they could lead the sustainability narrative.

The Aditya Birla Group (ABG) operates in a wide range of sectors—metals, textiles, carbon black, telecommunications, and cement. Birla Cellulose is the pulp and fibre business of the ABG group and is a leading producer of viscose staple fibre (VSF) globally. It has operations spread across six countries consisting of eleven sites manufacturing pulp and viscose fibres. The company earlier followed a compliance driven approach to sustainability. However, a report published in 2017 by the Changing Markets Foundation,[11] made them realise that they needed to go far beyond compliance and set sustainability standards that were far in excess of local rules and regulations. The Dirty Fashion report described the environmental damage caused by manufacturing practices used in viscose fibre production [12]and also highlighted links between the polluting factories and global markets by identifying fashion brands and retailers such as H&M, Zara (Inditex), ASOS, M&S and Tesco.

This situation had emerged because there were no comprehensive standards for viscose manufacturing. Prevailing regulatory standards in the countries where the manufacture of viscose took place covered requirements partially, and the prescribed limits were characterised by wide variations. Changing Markets Foundation realised this gap and published what it called a 'Roadmap towards Responsible Viscose Fibre Manufacturing'. In this context, Birla Cellulose acknowledged that the measures taken by them had not been adequate for the expectations of the external stakeholders and decided that it was time to move from focussing on compliance with local regulations to the globally acceptable, more stringent European environmental norms.

To deliver the sustainability vision and ambition of being the most sustainable viscose manufacturer, a business sustainability strategy was drawn up. This required all internal and external stakeholders to be involved in the decision-making. Where required, the company hired people who could help meet its goals. Implementing this was a mammoth task. It required setting benchmarks, gap assessment, and studying the technical feasibility of new technology within the constraints of existing infrastructure at the sites. The company re-allocated its resources, and a roadmap was laid out so that they could complete their plans by 2022. The company committed to a capital investment of $170 million to upgrade and install the best available closed-loop technologies at all fibre sites in a phased manner by the year 2022.

Materiality and Risks: The company identified key materiality issues together with all the stakeholders (internal and external) to create a transparent and robust approach. Birla Cellulose had done an extensive study of the risks associated with the business across and especially in the field related to sustainability and regulatory compliances. Some of the risks identified were raw material risks, environmental risks, regulatory compliance risks, health and safety risks, market risks etc. Birla Cellulose's strategy included responsible sourcing and manufacturing and partnerships for scale and impact.

Responsible Sourcing: Pulp is the main raw material for the manufacturing of fibre. Birla Cellulose strictly implemented its requirements of controlled wood supply across all its pulp suppliers to ensure that the wood used by them was sourced from sustainably managed forests and plantations.

Responsible Manufacturing: In the manufacturing of pulp and fibre, the company ensures that during each stage of the process, input materials such as wood, chemicals, energy and water were sourced responsibly and used judiciously. And, in the end, materials were recovered sustainably for reuse, by the implementation of the best available closed-loop technologies. In closed-loop pulp manufacturing, the idea is to recycle most of the input materials such as wood, chemicals, water, energy, and other raw materials used during production, and prevent the process from negatively impacting the environment.

Partnerships & Collaborations: Birla Cellulose has partnered with leading NGOs, think-tanks and multi-stakeholder organisations doing research and advocacy in this sector (like Sustainable Apparel Coalition, Canopy, ZDHC,

Changing Market Foundation, Textile Exchange) and has aligned its goals and targets. It has collaborated with technology institutes, its suppliers, and the downstream value chain to improve the processes and technologies for a more sustainable value chain.

Today, Birla Cellulose's sustained efforts on sustainability have been recognised globally and it is in the No.1 position in the Canopy Hot Button Report 2020, a testimony of its efforts in sustainable forest management and development of next generation solutions.[13] The company has also made rapid progress in introducing green products in the market. The eco-enhanced Livaeco by Birla Cellulose™, and the circular product Liva Reviva, which is made using industrial cotton waste, have captured the imagination of markets and consumers in a short span of time. Grasim, their pulp and fibre business registered in India has moved up in the Futurescape Responsible Business Rankings from a much lower 96 in 2017 to 9 in 2020.

2. Building Transparent and Measurable Targets

Companies who made changes to their business models realised that sustainability cannot be achieved without the participation of the larger ecosystem—suppliers, employees, customers and society at large. Business leaders in top performing companies in our study understood the importance of balancing environmental and social impacts. They aligned their governance to ensure that they avoided a silo-based approach, set evidence-based targets, measured them consistently and transparently reported them. Enhanced disclosure of non-financial performance and a generally more transparent approach facilitated a more informed dialogue with stakeholders, and greater trust in the role of business in meeting challenges.

Values drive sustainability: The Dalmia Bharat Group owns businesses in the cement, refractories and sugar sectors. It has a core philosophy that says, 'Clean & Green is Profitable and Sustainable'. The group is more than five times water positive and its cement business was the first cement company in the world to commit to moving towards 100 per cent renewable energy. Their sugar business was the first sugar company in India to generate a sustainability report and has committed to significant targets in the coming years. People, planet and performance are the three important business pillars of the Dalmia Bharat Group.

The group is also a signatory to Terra Carta, launched by His Royal Highness, Prince Charles. Terra Carta is a sustainable roadmap to 2030 for businesses to move towards an ambitious and sustainable future. The Terra Carta is based on a series of recommendations developed by a coalition of global business leaders in almost every sector. Together, a charter of ambitious, but practical action aimed at building a truly sustainable future has been developed that addresses the global climate and biodiversity crises. The Terra Carta outlines ten areas for action and comprises nearly 100 actions for businesses to build a truly sustainable future. It will serve as the guiding mandate for the Sustainable Market Initiative which will catalyse, showcase and celebrate progress along the way and over the next ten years.

Robust Measurement Systems: Dalmia Bharat is able to commit to these global frameworks because it has a robust framework for measuring environmental and social parameters and the governance to ensure compliance. In addition to corporate measurements around sustainability metrics, the Dalmia Bharat Foundation, which is the CSR arm of the group, follows an approach that periodically measures the social impact of its projects. For instance, they use social return on investment (SROI) as the appropriate tool to measure the impact of their water-based initiatives. It also helps in evaluating the progress of projects in terms of the returns on each rupee invested and in reviewing the future course of action to enhance effectiveness. Measuring the productivity of their investment has helped Dalmia Bharat understand the impact of its actions as well as guided the managers in pinpointing areas where they could do better. The foundation started in 2011 by working with 130,000 people in ninety villages that were located near its six factories. Over the last ten years, the foundation has reached 1301 villages and helped one million people in twenty locations. The story of the Dalmia Bharat Foundation is not one of numbers alone (see Figure 3.5). It is a story of passion, grit and determination to succeed against all odds. The foundation plans to reach 5,000 villages by 2030 and work with them in its three core areas of climate action, livelihoods and social infrastructure.

FIGURE 3.5
DALMIA BHARAT FOUNDATION 2030 ROADMAP

Climate action	Livelihood	Social Infrastructure
Harvesting and conserving water for productive us -50 million m3 by 2030 Ensuring access to clean cooking and solar lighting -5000 villages by 2030	Transforming households, including unemployed youth added into skilled workforce for enhanced income 200,000 households by 2030 100,000 skilled youth by 2030	Addressing basic health, education and rural infrastructural needs of the communities–5000 villages by 2030

3. Designing for Circularity

Globally, solid waste is sent to landfills or incinerated. Creation and disposal of waste is found to have a detrimental effect on the natural environment. Contemporary concepts, such as circular economy, are thus becoming mainstream, which suggest maximum product utilisation and sustainable waste disposal. The size of this new business opportunity is expected to be around $4.5 trillion globally by 2030. The business models in the circular economy focus on four key things:

- Reducing wastage of material and energy during production
- Extending the life of products by repairing them
- Preventing products from reaching landfills and ensuring that they are reused and recycled
- Ensuring products are designed in such a way that they can be repaired, recycled and reused

Indian companies are realising the tremendous potential hidden in the circular economy and designing business models that support it. JSW Steel is one of India's largest steelmakers. The company believes that there is no such thing as waste and has put elaborate systems in place that help reduce waste, recycle and remanufacture it. It expends significant effort in minimising the consumption of non-renewable resources from the environment, such as coking coal, and constantly upgrading systems to optimise the use of available material.

One of the biggest issues they addressed was the one of steel slag. Steel making leads to a waste called slag. JSW realised that the disposal of slag was a serious problem and figured that slag could be used to make cement. So, they started the cement business. Again, cement is an energy and water intensive business. The learnings of energy efficiency and water management at steel plants could be used in the cement business. It utilised alternative fuels derived from industrial and municipal wastes to minimise the consumption of natural resources like coal, diesel etc. It also reused fly ash from the power plants in cement manufacture. Since not all slag could be used for the manufacture of cement, the coarse aggregate slag could be combined with slag cement to produce paver blocks that could be used to pave walkways and parking lots. The group then set up an infrastructure businessaround utilising cement and steel.

JSW has focussed on research and development and collaboration with technical institutions to bring sustainable practices and products into its ambit. The experiment with paver blocks is an excellent example of collaborative technology development. So is the production of cement using steel slag. The company is also constantly innovating to create newer grades of steel, which have specific properties such as lightness, durability and strength. These value-added products may contain a lesser amount of steel while possessing better qualities suited for various applications. In a circular economy, product reuse needs to be considered at the design stage itself so that post the intended application of a product/resource, it can be repurposed quickly and efficiently for secondary uses.

The circular economy, or a system that eliminates waste from manufacturing and keeps the materials from going into landfills through reuse and recycling, is now being propagated in the organisation so that it can move towards a system that regenerates the environment, rather than harming it. Inspired by a study[14] that shows how just five key areas—cement, aluminum, steel, plastics and food—can eliminate 45 per cent of worldwide emission, JSW Steel is making significant investments in research to find new avenues to reduce and reuse waste. At present, JSW claims to have achieved more than 90 per cent solid waste utilisation and getting closer to its goal of zero waste to landfill with 100 per cent utilisation of all waste by 2030. The company has adopted a traditional 4R-principle, that is Reduce, Reuse, Remanufacture, and Recycle. JSW believes that every piece of steel can eventually be recycled to meet the growing global demand. In 2020, JSW was able to use over 5 million tonnes of recycled input materials for crude steel of over 16 million tonnes. JSW Steel was recognised as a

Sustainability Champion for 2020 by the World Steel Association for the third year in a row.

4. Creating green supply chains

For the longest time, global supply chains have been opaque. For instance, if you want to source organic cotton, you can certainly find a number of sellers. The problem is that there is no reliable way to tell whether the cotton is organic or not. The same has been the case with almost every fibre in the textile industry. Manufacturers ask if the recycled polyester was really recycled and if the cotton was BT cotton or a blended fabric. Similar questions have been asked of the food supply chain as well. How do you know that organic food is organic? How do you know that the coffee you are drinking was sourced from a particular farm? Is the coffee ethically sourced?

Indian companies such as Welspun have been investing in creating transparency in supply chains. Welspun India Ltd. is a global leader in home textiles, supplying to seventeen of the top thirty global retailers like Bed, Bath and Beyond, JC Penny, Macy's. 'ASDA and Debenhams.[15] Its manufacturing facilities located in India are equipped to deliver high quality products, benchmarked to international standards. Welspun employs more than 20,000 people and is the largest exporter of home textile products from India.[16] It produces bedding (bedsheets, pillow covers, and mattresses), bath solutions (towels, bathrobes, and bath rugs), advanced textiles (non-woven materials, wet wipes and filters) and flooring solutions (carpets, carpet tiles and artificial grass). In India it sells under the brand name SPACES, a towels and bed sheets brand with a premium positioning. Welspun has supplied its products to top retailers in over fifty countries.

An early realisation for the company was that it was very difficult to track the cotton that it received from the ginners. Cotton from many farms came mixed and it became difficult to trace whether a particular batch of cotton was sustainable or even what it was claimed to be. Thus, utilising its own farms for producing BCI[17] cotton and organic cotton was the way forward for Welspun. Also, pesticide use in cotton farming was rampant. Through its own farms, Welspun could control the pesticide usage. Farmers were tending to grow GMO cotton crops and Welspun worked to change mindsets to move towards natural cotton. Cotton farming was known to be water intensive farming. Thus Welspun moved away from flooding the field to using techniques like drip irrigation. Failures of cotton crop were a significant risk to cotton farmers. Welspun promoted silkworm farming and multi-crop farming as a risk-reducing diversification for the farmers. Welspun also supported the farmers by getting loans from banks and subsidies from the government. At the raw material stage it procured better cotton and inorganic cotton, provided better farming techniques to the farmers and ensured adequate remuneration to the farmers.

Welspun's farm extension team adopted sustainable farming principles (organic and BCI) aimed at making the production cycle better for the farmers and the environment. With an increasing number of buyers demanding sustainable cotton products Welspun de-risked its business by taking an early action on implementing sustainable practices. Reduced water usage at farms and factories, reduced use of pesticides, reduced chemical usage, energy efficient methods of production, use of sustainable modes of transportation, creating products out of waste material and promoting lesser use of hot washes has added to Welspun's sustainability credentials.

Welspun knew that building trust in the quality of their product was paramount. They started a project that traced the cotton fibre from the farm it was grown at to the product it eventually became. This was a patented process called Wel-Trak. Welspun customers used this global cotton integrity process for fibre verification from the origin and at every stage of production.

As a result of all this effort, Welspun's buyers trust it to deliver high quality products that are sustainably produced.

5. Adopting nature-based solutions

To minimise damage and regenerate the environment, experts are advocating the use of 'nature-based solutions' that consist of forest protection, agroforestry, urban trees, mangrove restoration, and green infrastructure creation. Several organisations have started focussing on these types of activities to mitigate their environmental impact.

In 2016, Apollo Tyres announced the launch of a critical mangrove restoration project in the Kannur district of Kerala[18] in partnership with the Wildlife Trust of India. The Kannur Kandal Project—'kandal' being the

Malayalam word for mangroves—aims to ensure the survival of existing mangroves and increase the acreage of such coastal wetlands across Kannur[19], potentially making it a prototype for other coastal districts in Kerala and the rest of the country. Biodiversity conservation is a global initiative for Apollo Tyres, wherein projects are undertaken in India, Hungary and the Netherlands. In India, mangrove conservation is a key initiative.

Mangrove forests are unique ecosystems, extremely rich in biodiversity, growing along inter-tidal coastal habitats such as shorelines, estuaries and backwaters. They are both refuges and nurseries for a large variety of threatened terrestrial and aquatic species, and an important source of fodder, medicines and firewood for people living in coastal communities. They also act as barriers against cyclones and tsunamis (evidenced in their important role in reducing the impact of the 2004 Indian Ocean tsunami), prevent coastal erosion, and maintain inland water quality by preventing sea water intrusion. However, mangrove forests have faced considerable destruction the world over, with less than half of the original acreage remaining. About half of that loss has occurred in the last fifty years, and a significant amount in just the last two decades, especially due to human population growth and intrusive development.

The acreage of mangroves in Kerala has also reduced drastically over the years, with only 1750 hectares of an estimated historical 70,000 hectares remaining. Conversion into coconut plantations or other agricultural land, aquaculture, unscientific water regulation, population pressures, real estate development, inadequate enforcement of laws, etc. have all contributed towards mangrove destruction. Kannur has 7.55 square kilometres of mangroves, i.e., around 45 per cent of Kerala's total mangrove forest cover. Nearly 90 per cent of these forests—which support at least ten species of mangroves, eighty-seven species of fish, eighty-three species of birds and thirteen species of mammals—are under private ownership and are therefore highly threatened.

The Apollo Tyres funded project is based in Kunhimangalam village, which is one of the largest mangrove villages of Kerala. Land secured with the support of the international NGO World Land Trust has been used to establish a Mangrove Interpretation Centre, located in the natural ecosystem, for mangrove-based research and education, and the promotion of mangrove restoration through community and government participation. A mangrove nursery has been established and community-based initiatives, including Mangrove Action Plans, have been initiated to enhance public awareness, promote active community participation and reduce threats to mangroves. Special efforts are being made to generate scientific interest about mangroves among the youth.

To popularise scientific knowledge on nature and conservation, the project has been organising an environment and nature quiz. This has now become an annual flagship event under this initiative covering college students from the states of Kerala, Tamil Nadu, Maharashtra and Andhra Pradesh.

6. Managing the health of communities and employees

Even before the pandemic, healthcare-based social responsibility projects of corporate India received the second largest spends. All of India's top 100 companies, whether in services or manufacturing, had healthcare-based projects that largely focus on health camps, preventive health and hospitals. Syngene, the subsidiary of biotechnology leader Biocon has set up technology-enabled primary healthcare clinics at public health centres in Karnataka. AstraZeneca, has had a long running program for youth and adolescents. The Young Health Programme of AstraZeneca aims to make a meaningful difference to the health and well-being of the marginalised and disadvantaged young boys and girls by helping them make informed choices to protect their health. It does this by spreading awareness of diseases through Health Information Centres and training adolescents to become Peer Educators, who engage and inform their peers and the community on health issues. Till 2020 the programme had supported 350,000 young people including 3,500 young people trained as peer educators.

The COVID-19 crisis has showcased effectively that public good needs to take priority when it comes to good health. With social distancing being enforced during the pandemic, the web of family, friends and social interactions that aided mental well-being largely vanished. Also the information on TV, newspapers and the internet was tinged with fear and dread about an uncertain future. This has led to collective stress, anxiety and deteriorating mental health all across the world. This was further exacerbated by the fact that physical and mental health services in many countries ceased to function. According to the World Health Organisation, health is a state of complete physical, mental and social well-being and not merely the absence of disease or infirmity. Most of the focus in India has been around disease management and cure. Mental health, on the other hand, was mostly ignored because it has no real physical manifestation. Now however, things are changing. Neerja Birla, Founder and Chairperson, Mpower, a pioneer in mental healthcare says, 'Mental health issues have more than doubled since 2020. In these unprecedented and challenging times, having to social distance and isolate oneself from family and friends, living with stress and uncertainty regarding jobs and financial security, and, the fear of contracting COVID-19 has resulted in an array of mental health issues. Technology, while connecting people, has also turned people into islands and added to their loneliness, stress and anxiety. Mental health needs to be addressed with a sense of urgency. We need to act now, and we need to act together.' Several Indian companies have set up call-in lines for mental health and appointed counsellors for employees.

Since 2020, a large proportion of corporate spending has gone towards helping communities manage the pandemic impact. Several companies shifted the nature of their work, transformed themselves by manufacturing things that were urgently needed. Ambuja Cement Foundation helped needy communities manage critical shortages and Diageo India factories made sanitisers in large quantities. In 2021, steel companies like JSW supplied oxygen to various parts of the country. Diageo pledged to create long-term public healthcare infrastructure by helping nodal government hospitals in 21 districts to set up oxygen plants and 16-bed mini hospital units. The company also donated medical equipment—oxygen concentrators, oxygen cylinders, ventilator beds etc.

7. Education for all

Education has been a primary focus for almost all top companies in India. It gets the largest amount of CSR spends and all top 100 of India's listed companies invest in school infrastructure, teacher training, content creation and teaching children and youth of all ages.

Nand Ghar is a CSR initiative undertaken by Vedanta in partnership with the Indian government's Ministry of Women and Child Development. The programme focusses on early childhood education and the empowerment of women. It aims to enhance the healthy growth of children and women by providing proper nutrition and facilitating regular healthcare check-ups. The initiative works along with the anganwadi mechanism. Anganwadi is a type of child and mother care centre in India. Anganwadi centres provide basic health care and promote the empowerment of women through skill-based training.

Vedanta worked with the government to create modern anganwadis and called these Nand Ghars. There are 2300 Nand Ghars across 11 states and 92,000 children and 69,000 women benefit from these. Nand Ghars provide hygienic, premium quality meals to children. They also train women and help them become entrepreneurs by providing access to credit and support services. Nand Ghars work extensively to improve pre-primary education through interactive learning. They have pre-loaded content on Smart TVs that help children in building cognitive abilities.

There are several other interesting initiatives around education by several corporate foundations. The SRF Foundation supports 1,240 schools covering 190,000 students in 22 districts of Haryana in developing innovation capabilities in children. The SRF Foundation's programme promotes awareness of AI through Data Fluency, Machine Learning & Deep learning, IOT/IIOT, Blockchain, etc. Exposing children at a young age to these technologies can bring about a change in areas such as agriculture, health, smart cities, mobility, infrastructure, transportation, and education. This program is aligned to the government's Atal Tinkering Labs (ATL) initiative which focuses on inculcating skills such as computational thinking, adaptive learning and physical computing

While Vedanta and SRF Foundation provide and support education at scale there are smaller efforts that provide rural children education to match high quality city education. Imagine children of a backward village where parents are mostly illiterate getting education in an English medium school. Mukul Madhav Foundation (of Finolex India Limited) has the audacity to make this happen.

The founders of Finolex saw a need for uplifting the rural communities in the villages of Ratnagiri and its surrounding areas. Finolex donated 10 acres of land in 2008 to Mukul Madhav Foundation to set up a school on the outskirts of Ratnagiri. The school, Mukul Madhav Vidyalaya, started in the village Golap in 2010. Golap is a small village near Pune consisting largely of farmers. Mukul Madhav Vidyalaya provides quality education in English while simultaneously making it affordable to the rural community. Starting with 151 students the school has grown steadily to increase in size and cover schooling up to tenth grade. Spread over 30,000 square feet the school provides adequate opportunities to students to excel in both academics and extracurricular activities. Students become skilled confident, and responsible individuals with strong fundamentals and values.

An all-round development of children is equally important. Mondelez India's Shubh Aarambh programme aims to do just that. It partners with NGOs to lead the three pillars of the project—gardening, nutrition and play, water and greening initiatives across various locations. Kitchen gardens are set up in schools and run by teachers and students to make fresh vegetables available for the nutrition programme. The nutrition programme provides good quality meals to students at supported schools. Active Play is undertaken with Magic Bus to help students gain social and leadership skills through lessons learnt while playing games.

ESG will continue to accelerate

The past decade has seen companies make incremental efforts to fix sustainability issues. Which is not to say that nothing got done. It did, but not at the scale that was needed. Today, the ESG movement is picking up strength. Led by activists, NGOs and scientists, several ground-level movements are taking shape and putting pressure on governments, companies and cities to take positive steps to reduce carbon emissions that are leading to climate change. Additionally, the spotlight is also on social risks, food, livelihoods, poverty and rising inequality which are some of the consequences of climate change that need to be addressed. Initiatives at scale are the need of the hour. ESG funds are therefore required for new projects as well as companies transitioning from fossil fuels to renewable energy.

ESG issues are increasingly being seen as a risk to a company. ESG risks include those related to climate change impacts mitigation and adaptation, environmental management practices, good work and safety conditions, respect for human rights, anti-bribery and corruption practices, and compliance with relevant laws and regulations. These risks are impacting company valuations and banks and financial institutions are now taking this into account. Many investors now look to incorporate ESG factors into the investment process alongside traditional financial analysis. As part of this process, investment firms gather ESG data on companies and use this to make decisions on valuation and the risk that a stock poses (see Technical Note 3). With investors looking at ESG as a value-based dimension of their portfolio, they increasingly want to understand ESG performance the same way they would any other traditional financial measure. This is leading to greater interest in robust ESG reporting along dimensions such as carbon intensity, controversy exposure, and overall ESG profile.

Previously, the key factor hampering the growth of ESG investments was the lack of clarity and standardisation of what the ESG factors are. With the EU coming out with the taxonomy for ESG (see Technical Note 5), there will be greater clarity in measuring ESG and ESG investments will get a boost. There are three important trends that are emerging as a result of this:

1. **Ensure capital acts for the long term:** Investors of capital will demand more from their money, using their influence to drive long-term, socially-useful value creation in the economy in the interests of their beneficiaries.

2. **Price capital according to the true costs of business activities:** Capital providers, and those who regulate them, will jointly consider how to reflect social and environmental risk factors in the cost of capital.
3. **Innovate financial structures to better serve sustainable business:** Financial intermediaries will use their influence and creativity to increase the flow of capital into business models that serve society's interests.

4

INVESTING IN CIRCULARITY

INVESTING IN THE CIRCULAR ECONOMY IS QUICKLY EMERGING AS the next gold rush. Since the beginning of 2020, assets managed through public equity funds, with the circular economy as the sole or partial investment focus, have increased six-fold from $0.3 billion to over $2 billion.[1] This is because of the increasing realisation that the circular economy is a vital part of the fight against climate change. Globally, we produce 0.74 kilograms of waste per person per day, 70 per cent of this waste is not processed at all and leads to 1.6 billion tons of CO_2 annually, or approximately 5 per cent of global emissions. Further, a circular approach in just five sectors (steel, aluminium, cement, plastic, and food) can cut annual GHG emissions by 9.3 billion tonnes of CO_2 in 2050, equivalent to the reduction that could be achieved by eliminating all transport emissions globally.

The need for a circular economy

At the moment, almost all our existing processes are linear in nature. They take in resources and change their form by concentrating, altering and synthesising them into products, many of which cannot be reused or recycled at the end of their intended use. Part of the reason for the inability to reuse or recycle is because it is often cheaper and easier to replace an article than to get it repaired. While some of these products do get recycled, this proportion is low.

One of the biggest areas of concern for people across the world is pollution and waste. Our cities are clogged with unhealthy levels of particulate matter in the air and mountains of trash, and our rivers are clogged with plastic. Between 1970 and 2015, India registered a six-fold increase from 1.18 billion to 7 billion tonnes in annual material consumption. It is expected that by 2030, India's annual material consumption would double to 14.2 billion tonnes due to population growth, urbanisation, economic mobility, and the resulting growth in per-capita resource consumption.[2] While Europe recycles 70 per cent of its consumption items, India recycles only 20 per cent. According to the estimates of India's Central Pollution Control Board (CPCB), Mumbai and Delhi alone generate about 11,000 and 8,700 tonnes of solid waste per day respectively. It is no surprise then that the cities are struggling to manage the total waste generated and have giant landfills of untreated waste. And they are not alone as this is the case in almost every major city across the world.

The pandemic has worsened the waste crisis as it has given legitimacy to the use of single use plastic for the purpose of masks, PPEs and other disposables such as straws and plastic cups. Further, there has been an unprecedented rise in the amount of biomedical waste that is now getting generated.[3] The journey towards building a circular economy needs a multi-pronged approach requiring the engaged participation of governments, industry and citizens. Governments need to create ecosystems that enable the creation of waste-free cities and while citizens need to segregate waste, they also need to understand the ecological impact of their consumption patterns. For example, meat can create upto 60 kg of GHG emissions, in contrast, the same weight of apples produces less than one kilogram of GHG emissions.[4]

Moreover, since we have finite resources, a linear model that generates so much waste cannot work in the long run. Should the global population reach 9.6 billion by 2050, the equivalent of almost three planets could be required to provide the natural resources needed to sustain current lifestyles. Hence we need to reduce the amount of materials we use and at the same time reuse materials rather than discarding them. For decades, global consumption has been built on a 'take-make-dispose' model. But now, adopting 'circular' solutions to creating a better model of production and consumption are becoming essential. The circular economy seeks to keep products and materials in use for as long as possible, minimising the amount used, extending their lifespan, and maximising reuse and recycling of waste. At the moment our world is only 8.6 per cent circular (see Technical Note 8).[5]

According to the UN Global Resources Outlook Report, 90 per cent of biodiversity loss and water stress is caused by resource extraction and processing. These same activities also contribute to about half of global GHG emissions. Economic growth which comes at the expense of our planet is simply not sustainable. A circular economy is a global economic model that aims to decouple economic growth and development from the consumption of finite resources. Circular systems reuse, share, repair, refurbish, remanufacture and recycle to create a closed-loop system. This minimises the resource inputs and reduces waste, pollution, and carbon emissions.

The scale of the problem

The current challenges are massive in scale and complex because of their connected nature. Let us try and understand this in the context of just one industry.

The fashion industry is responsible for 10 per cent of annual global carbon emissions, more than all international flights and maritime shipping combined.[6] Since 2000, global fashion production has doubled. But the number of times we wear each item has dropped by a third, leading to huge amounts of clothes reaching landfills. Most of the fashion industry today focusses on speed and low cost in order to deliver frequent new collections inspired by catwalk looks or celebrity styles. But this is bad for the environment as pressure to reduce cost and the time it takes to get a product from design to shop floor means that environmental corners are more likely to be cut. Criticisms of fast fashion include its negative environmental impact, water pollution, the use of toxic chemicals and the increasing levels of textile waste. The fashion industry also impacts biodiversity in a big way as many raw materials in clothes, shoes, bags and jewellery come from animals and plants.

The birth of the couture industry can be traced back to 1850 in Paris, when top designers held fashion shows for their most prized clients.[7] From there, it evolved into four big Fashion weeks: Paris, Milan, London and New York. Today, it has taken over the world, with Tokyo, Berlin, Madrid, Australia and India Fashion Weeks cementing their place on the world fashion stage.[8] Fashion Week began as a means for retailers to buy and incorporate the latest collections into their retail marketing, but they have progressed into 'in season shows', catering to fast fashion retailers, who 'see now, buy now' and replicate runway designs into retail stores. Now, pop-ups, capsule collections and one-off shows have completely changed the rules.

Fast fashion has become synonymous with instant gratification. This refers to designs that move rapidly from the runways to store shelves. Take brands like H&M, Zara and Primark. It is all about speed and agility—bringing the trend to the shop floor as rapidly as possible, sometimes even before the originals hit stores. With rapid design and supply chain systems in place, the pace at which the newest styles get to shop shelves is almost real-time! This means that essentially, we have moved from the biannual seasonality that defined the fashion industry to that of fast fashion brands that may have as many as 52 weekly 'micro-seasons' per year. Luxury brands, while slow to change, got caught up in the multiple seasons madness too and increased the number of collections each year. Sadly, this comes at a humungous cost to people and the environment.

Too much is being produced too often, leading to waste, environmental degradation and poor working conditions in factories and sweatshops.

Toxic chemicals

Vibrant colours, prints and fabric finishes are appealing features of fashion garments, but these are achieved with toxic chemicals. Textile dyeing is the second largest polluter of clean water globally, after agriculture. Greenpeace's Detox campaign[9] has been instrumental in pressuring fashion brands to remove toxic chemicals from their supply chains, after it tested a number of brands' products and confirmed the presence of hazardous chemicals. Many of these are banned or strictly regulated in various countries because they are toxic, bio-accumulative (meaning the substance builds up in an organism faster than the organism can excrete or metabolise it), disruptive to hormones and carcinogenic. Then, there is the dyeing process in which 1.7 million tonnes of various chemicals are used; not to mention hazardous chemicals like perfluorinated compounds (PFCs) that leave a permanent impact on our environment.

Synthetic fibres are entering our food chain

Synthetic garments are present in the form of micro-fibres in our oceans and are a huge component of non-biodegradable waste in our landfills. The production of synthetic fibres in the apparel industry accounts for as much as 10 per cent of global carbon emissions. It is estimated that twenty-three kilograms of GHGs are generated for each kilo of fabric produced.[10]

Polyester is the most popular fibre used for fashion. But when polyester garments are washed in domestic washing machines, they shed micro-fibres that add to the increasing levels of plastic in our oceans. These micro-fibres are minute and can easily pass through sewage and wastewater treatment plants into our waterways. However, because they do not biodegrade, they represent a serious threat to aquatic life. Small creatures such as plankton eat the micro-fibres, which then make their way up the food chain, to fish and shellfish eaten by humans.

Natural fibres are increasing the pressure on land

Wood-based fabrics such as modal, rayon and viscose that are in high demand, cause the destruction of thousands of hectares of forests. 70 million trees are cut down each year to make our clothes and as much as 5 per cent of the global fashion industry uses forest-based fabrics.[11] Cotton is an important raw material in textile production and research has shown that it takes 20,000 litres of water to produce a mere 1 kilogram of cotton fabric! In addition, the run off waters from cotton production are contaminated with fertilisers. Cotton growing requires high levels of water and pesticides to prevent crop failure, which can be problematic in developing countries that lack sufficient investment and are facing a drought risk. Most cotton grown worldwide is genetically modified to be resistant to the bollworm pest, thereby improving yield and reducing pesticide use. This, sadly, leads to problems further down the line, such as the emergence of 'superweeds', which are resistant to standard pesticides. They often need to be treated with more toxic pesticides that are harmful to livestock and humans. There is growing interest in organic cotton, with H&M and Inditex, the parent company of Zara, featuring among the world's top five users of organic cotton by volume. But overall use of organic cotton represents less than 1 per cent of the world's total annual cotton crop.

Waste

Textile waste is an unintended consequence of fast fashion, as more people buy more clothes than they need and do not keep them as long as they used to. The international expansion of fast fashion retailers exacerbates the problem on a global scale. Wardrobes in developed nations are saturated, so in order to sell more products, retailers must tempt shoppers with constant newness and convince them that the items they already have are no longer fashionable. Increasing disposable income levels over recent generations means there is less need to 'make do and mend', as it is often cheaper and more convenient to buy new items over having an item repaired. Busy lifestyles have made many people more time-poor than previous generations, and with the loss of sewing and mending skills over time, there is less impetus to repair garments. The rise of supermarket fashion that can be purchased alongside weekly provisions shopping and the regular occurrence of seasonal sales, make clothing seem 'disposable'. While there is interest in moving towards a more circular model of textile production which reuses materials wherever possible, current recycling rates for textiles is very low. For instance, despite a long-established national network of charity shops and increasing numbers of in-store recycling points in UK high street stores, three-quarters of Britons throw away unwanted clothing, rather than donating or recycling them. Each year over 80 billion pieces of clothing are produced worldwide, and after their short lifespan, three out of four garments will end up in landfills or be incinerated and only a quarter will be recycled.[12]

And what about the clothing that does not make it to market? An estimated 400 billion square metres of textiles are produced annually, of which 60 billion square metres are left on the cutting room floor.

Water

Water consumption in the fashion industry is off the charts! Two billion pairs of jeans are produced every year, and a typical pair takes 7,000 litres of water to produce. It takes 2,700 litres of water to make just one T-shirt—

that's the amount of water an average person drinks over the course of 900 days![13]

Untreated toxic wastewater from textile factories, that contain lead, mercury and arsenic, make their way into waterways, harming aquatic life and affecting the health of people coming in contact with the contaminated water. In fact, 20 per cent of industrial water pollution can be attributed to dye and textile treatment and as much as 200,000 tonnes of dyes are lost to effluents every year.

The fashion world wasn't always like this. According to *Plenitude: The New Economics of True Wealth* by Juliet B. Schor, Americans consume three times as much as their ancestors did fifty years ago, and they buy twice as many items of clothing as they did twenty years ago. In 1991, the average American bought thirty-four items of clothing each year. By 2007, they were buying sixty-seven items every year. That's a new piece of clothing every four to five days![14] Low-cost, low quality apparel involves the use of cheap and inexpensive material that is more often than not, laden with chemicals. According to the Environmental Protection Agency of USA, about 12.8 million tons of clothing is sent to landfills annually.[15] Social media only reinforces this dark side to fashion—creating consumer demand for cheap and affordable fashion.

Unsustainable practices like inventory burning

The industry also follows highly questionable practices, such as burning unwanted inventory. H&M burned $4.3 billion worth of inventory in 2018 because it was unsellable. While H&M claimed that the clothes were incinerated because they contained high amounts of lead or were mould-infected, here's the reality—burning clothes releases 2,988 pounds of carbon dioxide per megawatt hour, which is even more than burning coal (2,249 pounds per megawatt hour) and natural gas (1,135 pounds per megawatt hour).[16] In 2018, Burberry too burned $37 million worth of unsold goods and faced a great deal of public outrage. In September 2019, the company was compelled to announce that it was ending the practice of destroying excess clothing.

With increased inventory, and no buyers, what then, is the next best option? Offering deep discounts or clearing stocks? Well, this is not a solution either because all it does is shift unwanted inventory from a company's warehouse to the buyers' cupboard. Garments sold at a deep discount will always be seen as disposable and lacking value. Therefore it is only a matter of time before it ends up in a donation drive or in the garbage. From here, it gets transported to rural areas and eventually will end up in a landfill or incinerator a few months later. So all we are managing to do is to delay this occurrence.

Today, we are producing 100 billion clothes a year for just 7 billion humans.[17]

According to studies, clothing utilisation, or how often we wear our clothes, has dropped by 36 per cent over the past decade and a half. For the most part, many of us wear clothes only seven to ten times before they end up in a landfill. Right now, apparel companies make 53 million tons of clothes annually.[18] If the industry keeps up its exponential pace of growth, it is expected to reach 160 million tons by 2050.[19]

The apparel market today is pegged at around $1.3 trillion in retail sales globally per year and is forecasted to touch $1.4 billion by 2021.[20] If we are to look at only clothes (not footwear or jewellery), this value is bigger than the size of the Russian economy. Of this, the United States and China are the biggest markets for fashion retail, together accounting for 42 per cent of all spending on clothes. This can be attributed to both purchasing power as well as the sheer number of people purchasing clothes. There is, however, a noteworthy change that is happening. France, Germany, Japan and Italy are predicted to reduce their market share by 2021. In contrast, India is expected to grow at an average annual rate of 5.2 per cent. This growth is powered by an India on the development curve—in terms of a rising manufacturing sector, rising tech knowledge, as well as a growing middle class population.

In India, the fashion industry is on an upward surge. The segment is pegged at $100 billion and predicted to grow by 15–20 per cent over the next five years.[21] Consumers are increasingly gaining confidence in online experiences and what better way to relieve stress than to shop while you wait in a queue or when you are heading back home from work! While the coronavirus pandemic has certainly been a dampener for the consumption treadmill with retail sales falling by 50 per cent and clothing alone showing a

35 per cent reduction so far, it is expected that once we are over the pandemic, clothing sales will pick up again.

The circularity transition has started

The opposite to a linear system is a circular one, where everything is interconnected to everything else in some way. One person's waste is another's resource, the same way that it is engineered in natural systems. Cities, factories, governments and industrial food production function in a linear way and therefore generate waste. We need to redesign these as interconnected and interdependent systems that are part of the whole. Hence, the transition towards a circular economy is not an easy one. This requires developing systems thinking skills and also understanding sustainability sciences (see Figure 4.1). After this is needed a full mapping of the natural, industrial, and social systems, and then impacting them to facilitate circular and regenerative outcomes.

However, the realisation that a linear economy is unsustainable is driving a number of changes in how business is operating. To begin the move towards circularity, companies are building resource efficiency in their operations. This is the use of less materials and energy to achieve the same output. They are also making changes in the types of materials they use and switching to less resource intensive, recyclable or bio-degradable materials. Decentralised activities are also a growing trend in the circular economy

FIGURE 4.1
SYSTEMS THINKING FOR A CIRCULAR ECONOMY

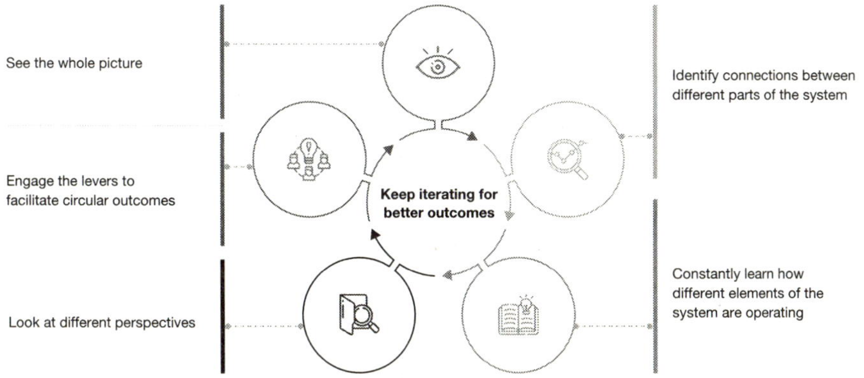
See the whole picture
Identify connections between different parts of the system
Engage the levers to facilitate circular outcomes
Keep iterating for better outcomes
Constantly learn how different elements of the system are operating
Look at different perspectives

because they support the efficient management of material flows locally. Decentralisation also contributes to resilience by bringing governance systems closer to their communities and providing local stakeholders with opportunities to actively engage in a more diverse range of activities. These changes are therefore changing the structure of supply chains, production processes and metrics of success.

We earlier discussed the scale of the problem in the fashion industry, let's take a look at how the fashion industry is transforming towards a circular economy. The movement towards this has already started with leading fashion brands investing in this sustainability led transformation.

Gucci

The fashion brand Gucci is abandoning the traditional fashion calendar. Gucci wants to make its offerings timeless and do away with seasonal collections. To begin with, it has reduced the number of yearly fashion shows it stages from five to two. The brand has also launched a new sustainability focussed collection made of recycled materials. The 'Off The Grid' collection launched in May 2020 uses only recycled, organic, and sustainably sourced materials. A large part of the collection is designed using econyl—a regenerated nylon made from abandoned fishing nets and gear salvaged from the oceans—which the brand first began to use in 2016. The company also makes sure that all its fashion shows are carbon neutral. Beyond the use of sustainable raw materials, the brand has also incorporated low-impact alternatives to sourcing, manufacturing and distribution to reduce carbon emissions as part of its annual carbon-neutral commitment.

Kering

The French Luxury Group, Kering, manages the development of a series of renowned houses in fashion, in leather goods, jewellery and watches. Gucci, Saint Laurent and Bottega Veneta are just some of the brands they own. The sustainability report of Kering reveals a strategy that is looking at transforming the entire supply chain, right from material sourcing to post-consumer waste.

First, their sustainability strategy rests on the three pillars of caring for the planet, collaborating with people and creating new business models. Second, Kering has created an Environmental Profit and Loss (EP&L) accounting system to measure, monetise and manage environmental impacts in operations and across the entire supply chain.[22] The data collated and standards are all open source and can be downloaded by anyone.[23] This twofold approach of sound intent with ongoing measurement is possibly what sets Kering apart from many others who simply highlight intent.

The EP&L measures carbon emissions, water consumption, air and water pollution, land use, and waste production along the entire supply chain, thereby making the various environmental impacts of the group's activities visible, quantifiable, and comparable. These impacts are then converted into monetary values to quantify the use of natural resources. Kering can thus use the EP&L to guide its sustainability strategy, improve its processes and supply sources, choose the best-adapted technologies and innovate new solutions.

There are three steps to an EP&L:

1. Quantifying the environmental footprint: The six impact areas group across 62 indicators that cover different types of emissions and resource use.
2. Estimating the likely environmental changes that result from these emissions or resource use are estimated based on the local environmental context.
3. Valuing the change in wellbeing: The consequences of these environmental changes for people's wellbeing are then valued in monetary terms. This valuation approach is consistent with policy recommendations of the European Commission and is increasingly used by policy makers across the world.

As per their analysis, Kering found that raw material production had the largest impact across the board. The Kering sustainability strategy therefore emphasises transformation of the supply chain to achieve sustainability. The company also announced that it was collecting data in order to extend the EP&L methodology to account for a circular, full life-cycle for products. Currently, it covers raw materials through distribution and retail; the data collection will add consumer use and product end-of-life.

Nike

Nike is now using recycled polyester for most of its products. Yarn, soles and basketball courts are a few examples of the many products Nike creates by transforming plastic bottles, manufacturing scraps and used product into new materials. But this is not enough to take Nike to net zero. Since design is an integral part of the Nike philosophy, the company has created a Circular Design Guide to enable a deep-rooted transformation in the company. This includes important themes such as new service and business models, circular packaging, low impact materials and making products that can easily be taken apart.

Several other brands are also looking to follow suit. But will fewer fashion seasons and sustainability targets that extend well into 2050 transform the fashion industry from a highly damaging one, into a force for good? We need to ask if the change is fast enough.

In the rush to realise the promise of a circular economy, we need to think through the possibility of unintended consequences. Will the jobs generated by circular innovations be better jobs? Who will get them? Circularity could reduce material extraction and waste through reuse—but at the cost of what other resources? Will circularity reduce consumption, or just maximise use of existing products? The circular economy is not a silver bullet for employment, sustainability and prosperity. Companies and governments must carefully measure the anticipated and actual impact of these actions and ensure they take us in the right direction.

Circularity needs a social context

India is a downstream supplier to many global brands in chemicals, pharmaceuticals, textiles and automobiles. Sustainability targets set by global automotive brands that focus on recycled metals versus virgin materials can have many implications. Large textile companies that focus on old methods of manufacturing will need to shift to new manufacturing standards and will need reskilling of employees. Hence the circularity transition needs a nuanced view from a social perspective. The fashion industry is notorious for not paying its downstream suppliers even a living wage. Further, the margins for manufacturing are wafer thin.[24] Sustainability led green manufacturing technologies can only be funded by the large well-funded companies and not by the marginal, small and under-funded ones.

The three R's (reduce, reuse and recycle) were once a popular theme, but have been undone by the recent era of excess where one just used and threw away the product. Going back to this philosophy is a key theme of transforming our current linear model into one that is circular. The rise of the circular economy, where resources flow continuously and safely, has jumpstarted the forgotten culture of reuse. A new generation of materials, products and services is coming, reviving business models that would be instantly recognisable to our parents and grandparents, albeit with a distinctly 21st-century overlay. That's a start, but the fact is that an entirely circular system is impossible to create.

For instance your water bottle, which is made of PET can be converted into polyester fibre, but this process will involve some usage of energy and some wastage. This is because the PET bottle also has labels and caps that can't really be recycled into fibres. There are also losses in the process of conversion, dust, waste and energy. Further, the logistics of picking up thrown away bottles, also involves emissions due to transportation and cost. Take any other product, be it your iPad, smartphone, refrigerator or air conditioner. Most of these products are complex mixtures of metals, materials, plastics, and glass. Fully recycling and recovering components from these is an equally complicated task. It is about as difficult as recycling a cup of tea into water, sugar, milk, and tea. Recycling also doesn't end when you convert it into something else. The end product then once again needs to go through this cycle. The inconvenient truth is that closing the loop is impossible!

What if we designed things differently? What if a product is manufactured smartly in different modules? For example, the raw materials could be distributed in such a way that each module could be directly processed with suitable technology when metallurgically processed. This would render the recycling of many valuable metals easier, while also maximising energy efficiency. In an economy that values refurbishment over mass production, work may move closer to the consumer, potentially causing dislocation in regions that can least afford the job losses. Measuring impact is a first step to addressing potential repercussions for those who lose from the transition.

But as much as quantification is a challenge in environmental topics, in social issues it is even more complex and often subjective. The jobs created by the circular economy may be different from existing jobs in scope and location. Such topics are hard if not impossible to capture in a single metric, but that shouldn't keep companies and governments from assessing the consequences of these actions.[25]

Sustainability today is no longer a unique value proposition for many brands, but an inherent expectation that a product will be ethically made and will not harm the environment or the community. When the Unilever CEO announced in June 2019 that they would henceforth have only brands with purpose, their share price jumped.[26]

Construction, agriculture, energy and airlines have large carbon footprints and are rapidly moving towards new low-carbon technologies. Their actions matter, but it won't be enough by itself to create a low-carbon economy. For customers to trust brands, there needs to be genuine change through the creation of products and services that are truly responsible. But customer trust in brands is at an all-time low. This is not by accident! In May 2019, more than 1.5 million children of all ages in over 125 countries walked out of schools, colleges and universities in the biggest day of global climate action ever.[27] Consumer groups were up in arms too. Protests against plastic waste in the seas, air pollution, saving wildlife and forests are emerging almost everywhere. These protests reflect the very narrow window of opportunity left to make positive change and the very real concerns about deteriorating quality of life in cities, destructive storms and extreme world temperatures. And the risks are indeed mounting.

Companies must measure their impact on resources and set science-based targets that bound corporate actions within the confines of the planet's resources. This will lead to new business models for growth and the associated change in consumer thinking that is not predicated on selling more new stuff. 'We now want to look at sustainability. We are waiting for the sustainability team to revert with a plan.' We have been hearing this phrase in corporate circles for several years and the number of people saying it is increasing. While it is great that many have begun thinking about sustainability, it also points to the siloed approach that most companies have had. A company might never really be able to come up with the 'perfect plan' for circularity, because social contexts are forever changing.

About a decade ago, sustainability in business was understood as reducing carbon emissions. Today, sustainability has evolved to encompass business responsibility and come to mean not just reducing and eliminating environmental impacts but also being 'good' for society. This includes privacy by design, transparent and trustworthy policies, positive health impacts, high safety standards at offices and factories, reduced plastic packaging, looking at biodiversity, sustainable farming and much more. The road to sustainability across all sectors is long and arduous because it needed not just innovation, but new business models. Lower consumption will only be realised if we value longevity and reuse over the purchase of virgin material-based goods. That message has not yet been fully adopted by businesses, even those that are starting to understand the appeal of circular economy. No matter how responsibly products are made, unless business models move towards sustainable consumption, we will not be able to move towards a green economy. This also means changing wasteful consumer habits that have become part of our world economy.

Financing Circularity

Circular economy requires a change in mindsets. Behavioural economists talk of nudging to change behaviours. These nudges come from government, society and stakeholders. With business leaders nudged into appropriate actions, there will be a need for alternative measurement. Share price and EPS are not enough. The financial statements need to be retooled. The balance sheets and profit and loss statements need to capture economic, social and governance (ESG) elements. Each ESG action can be seen as either a positive externality or a negative externality. Take the case of emissions (CO_2, SOx, NOx etc.). Although difficult to measure, the potential harm due to emissions can be captured on the balance sheet as an expense. Similarly, estimates of lack of diversity (gender, colour, religion, etc.) will appear on the income statement as an expense. These measurements are similar to those used for valuing externalities. Essentially, there is a need for a framework that generates an 'ESG' profit or loss (as distinct from EP&L that looks at only environmental impacts). The idea of ESG profits or EPS may sound radical but will help align the interests of all stakeholders and will help promote circularity and ESG actions.

The global financial system has a tremendous opportunity to scale up financing of solutions to enable the circular economy transition. Around half-a-trillion dollars worth of India's GDP value could be created through Circular Economy business models by 2030 in India and $4.5 trillion globally.[28] Several sectors could benefit exponentially from creating systems that enable this. For instance, just recycling of steel from end-of-life vehicles could potentially represent a $2.7 billion opportunity in India by 2025.

The United Nations Environment Programme Finance Initiative (UNEP FI) works with more than 350 members—banks, insurers, and investors—and over 100 supporting institutions—to help create a financial sector that serves people and planet while delivering positive impacts. They have identified some important areas that need to be considered carefully while financing. This includes finance for chemicals that are benign, circular systems in mining, buildings that use green construction and materials, as well as factoring pollution liability coverage in the manufacture of materials. These recommendations are also gaining ground across the financial sector and are being supported by a host of frameworks for disclosure, indicators and metrics that can be integrated into financial products and services to allocate financing for the transition to circularity. Principles for Responsible Banking, Principles for Sustainable Insurance and Principles for Responsible Investment are just some of the standards that are guiding this transformation.[29]

On the financing side are the green bonds that are tied to sustainable actions by companies. While green bonds focus on decarbonisation on land, there is a strong need to focus on oceans as well. Here blue bonds come into play. Blue bonds are an innovative ocean financing instrument whereby funds raised are earmarked exclusively for projects deemed ocean-friendly. Blue bonds can be used to promote blue carbon, protect shorelines, promote ocean energy and offshore wind power, sustainable fishing, sustainable shipping, support medicinal products that come from the ocean, and reduce harmful effects of oil and gas platforms.

Then there are sustainability-linked bonds that pay interest based on performance achieved and transition bonds that help companies move from 'brown' to 'green'. Social impact bonds are raised for social causes and like sustainability-linked bonds are a pay-for-performance security. Green bonds seem to be the instrument of choice of the fashion industry to fund the sustainability transition. Prada SpA raised EU 50 million and EU 75 million sustainability-linked loans in 2020. Similarly, Chanel has raised $700 million, Burberry has raised $387 million and H&M has raised $500 million. For Prada, interest rate could be reduced following the achievement of targets related to various factors that include amount of training hours for the employees and the use of Prada Re-Nylon (regenerated nylon) for the production of goods. Burberry on the other hand will use the funds it has raised for green buildings, natural resources, and land use, and circular economy-adapted products, technologies and processes.

On the investing side, the most popular approach is exclusionary screening. Here banks and fund houses stop investing in companies that are involved in businesses that are not considered good for society. This is the most common approach. Investors also look at ESG factors before they make investments. Several forays into this area are being made by large funds and investors. For instance, in October 2020, the BlackRock Circular Economy Fund[30] that focusses on addressing climate change, biodiversity loss and plastic pollution had raised more than $900 million in its first year since launch. At launch, the fund identified three groups of companies that drive the circular economy and their focus for investments:

- **Enablers:** Companies that deliver new, innovative solutions directly aimed at enabling the adoption of circularity by businesses and consumers.
- **Adopters:** Companies that adopt the principles of the circular economy in a manner that has a meaningful and positive impact on their value.
- **Beneficiaries**: Companies that supply alternative materials or services that contribute to a circular economy.

A report released by the fund highlights that the shift to a circular economy is likely to be driven by the confluence of three key factors: increasing regulation, changing consumer preferences favouring sustainable alternatives and corporate responses to focus on circular practices. The number of funds with a focus on the circular economy has increased ten-fold since 2016. Meanwhile, these funds' total assets under management jumped six-fold, from $300 million in 2016 to over $2 billion in early 2020.[31]

New business models for circularity

There are many ways to adopt circular economy principles. Some companies focus on recycling their own or other companies' waste materials. For instance, different types of wastes/by products of other industries are being utilised as alternative fuels and raw materials for cement production in India. McDonald's is collecting the waste cooking oil from its restaurants and turning it into biodiesel for its delivery trucks.

Carmakers in the EU now have to recycle or recover 95 per cent of the material in the cars they make under the End-of-Life Vehicles Directive.[32] India has also announced a vehicle scrappage policy.[33] Companies are now therefore starting to take account of what happens to their products at the end of their lives, right from the start of the design process. The need for alternative solutions has also led to the launch of the Circular Cars Initiative at the World Economic Forum. The initiative includes material suppliers, fleet operators, re-manufacturers, recyclers, data platforms and regulators, and will create a roadmap for a more circular car industry so that cars remain longer in use, are easier to disassemble at end-of-life and their parts can be reused.

EU's CE Finance Expert Group published a generic, sector-agnostic circular economy categorisation system that defines four distinct models contributing to a circular economy (see Figure 4.2).[34]

Given the challenges that they face, car companies are now making huge investments and transitioning to new business models. Mobility-as-a-service models are already affecting the traditional car industry, with the rise of Uber and Lyft and schemes such as Karshare's and Renault Mobility in France, which allows drivers to hire cars by the hour or by the day through a self-service phone app. Another example is Wagonex's pioneering 'just in time' approach to car accessibility, which uses a monthly subscription model rather than traditional outright car ownership.[35] While the overall sustainability impacts of subscription and sharing models are yet to be determined, there is hope that over time these will ensure that producers

FIGURE 4.2
4 MODELS CONTRIBUTING TO A CIRCULAR ECONOMY

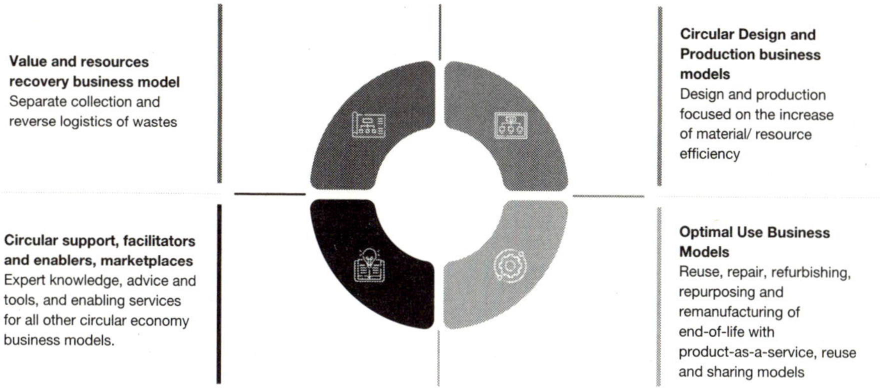

take responsibility of their own products and manufacture them in ways that they are easy to reuse and recycle.

Value and resources recovery business model
Separate collection and reverse logistics of wastes
Circular Design and Production business models
Design and production focused on the increase of material/ resource efficiency
Circular support, facilitators and enablers, marketplaces
Expert knowledge, advice and tools, and enabling services for all other circular economy business models.
Optimal Use Business Models
Reuse, repair, refurbishing, repurposing and remanufacturing of end-of-life with product-as-a-service, reuse and sharing models

Some sectors are focussing on extending the life of products or giving them a second life—medical equipment is a good example, where companies such as Philips and Siemens take back equipment such as MRI scanners at the end of their life, refurbish them and sell them in a thriving second-hand market to customers that need the scanners but cannot afford the latest equipment.

There is also a shift from selling products to selling services. So where lighting manufacturers used to sell lightbulbs, now they sell lighting, while carmakers sell mobility rather than cars. The idea is even being extended to clothing, with brands such as Mud Jeans leasing its products to clients.

Another feature of the circular economy is that the line between business and consumer is becoming blurred thanks to the advent of the sharing economy, which sees private citizens renting out their rooms or space in their cars through platforms such as AirBnB and BlaBlaCar.

These changes provide a challenge to traditional models of business. Can I trust you? Where do my products come from and what do they contain? Questions like these are increasingly becoming important to consumers as well who want transparency so that they can trust the brands they are committing their money to. These questions are equally important to brands who now need to take responsibility for the entire use, reuse and recycling of the product and its packaging. As the demand for 'green products' picks up, systems that build transparency into supply chains and help customers and brands prove the provenance of their products are now becoming absolutely critical to the conversation. Technologies like blockchain to determine traceability, spectrometers to determine quality and content and cloud based applications are picking up.

Consumer consciousness is increasing: There is growing concern about sustainability and awareness about what customers can do to alleviate the impact of their choices on the environment. The world over, trends such as healthy living, organic food, plant-based diets and so on are on the rise. This is impacting fashion, food, transportation and almost every other category. For instance, in India, health issues, such as respiratory disorders, skin diseases, food and water-borne diseases are on the rise as a result of growing air pollution and the quality of food and water. This is driving Indian consumers to become more conscious of what they eat. In the past, checking the fine print on packages was not a common practice. Now, more and more consumers have begun to give equal importance to the quality and source of ingredients used in the food.[36] Today, faced with increasing globalisation and environmental challenges, plus the pandemic, consumers are moving local. Some of the things they are doing are buying local produce and taking domestic holidays to reduce the environmental costs of air transport (of both people and goods). As this trend is picking up, cultural storytelling, authenticity and craftsmanship are increasingly in demand as we return to local sourcing and manufacturing.

Traceability, innovation, and social responsibility irrespective of the location of the manufacturing facility will be key: Sustainable behaviour that is both good for the planet and consumers will now become a core component of brands. Hence, even outsourced supply chains will need to be accountable for following corporate standards on emissions, responsibility, ethics, human rights and more. Brands will no longer be able to escape scrutiny by claiming that they are only responsible for what they do within their corporate premises.

According to MeiLin Wan of Applied DNA Sciences, at the heart of all the talk about sustainability is: can you prove it? Can the brands and manufacturers prove that if they say they are using a sustainable fibre or material, that they can demonstrate with transparency, that that fibre is in fact in the product that they are marketing and selling to the consumer? The consumer hasn't quite figured out that many of these claims are based on 'paper-based' certifications that can be circumvented, and materials used can be substituted by lesser quality items. Even the word 'carbon footprint' is not necessarily understood by the consumer—not all consumers are the same and therefore the potential for misinterpretation can greatly vary. Does reducing the carbon footprint do anything to affect the consumer to buy more? This idea of perception versus reality in the mind of the consumer is quite important, especially if companies are expecting quick returns when in fact, it is not clear if or when the alignment will happen. The question is whether brands and manufacturers are willing and committed enough to stay the course.

Products will be made to last: Planned obsolescence is a policy of designing a product with an artificially limited useful life, so that it becomes obsolete (i.e., unfashionable, or no longer functional) after a certain period of time. This is why your phones and electronic gadgets last only a few years now. However, this process is extraordinarily wasteful because older gadgets reach landfills and newer ones emit more carbon in the process of being made and shipped to customers. This practice, which largely began with the computer industry has also entered other sectors such as fashion, where clothes only last a few washes, shoes disintegrate after a season and home textiles run colour because they use substandard materials and dyes. The cycle though is turning. With companies being forced to report emissions and take back products, they are beginning to make high quality products that last longer, can easily be upgraded and are made from recycled and reusable materials.

Take back what you ship out: Our cities and oceans are now overstretched with the sheer quantum of waste being generated and their inability to manage it. Plastic packaging and bottles don't biodegrade. Neither do electronics. For the last few decades, the onus of waste management has been on municipalities. Regulation the world over is now forcing companies to design products with better materials that can be assimilated into the environment or to take back products that cannot. Responsibility is now being redefined not just for the emissions generated during production, but for the entire life cycle. Extended Producer Responsibility (EPR) is now becoming mandatory across products and countries.

Doing more with less

Each year, more and more sustainable products hit the market. Not all of these are perfect zero waste solutions, but entrepreneurs are beginning to think harder about their products. The market's idea of sustainability is slowly expanding to include waste-free packaging and more transparency. PATCH, a compostable and vegan alternative to traditional band-aids, is an example of where sustainable products are headed. PATCH strips are 100 per cent compostable, and the company is 100 per cent transparent about what goes into them. Large retailers like Walmart are also incentivising zero waste products. Walmart has a 2025 target to achieve 'Zero Waste' in its own operations and work with suppliers and customers to prevent products and materials from becoming waste upstream and downstream in pursuit of a more circular economy.[37]

The demand for sustainable waste disposal solutions increases every day, so entrepreneurs, engineers and inventive people everywhere are coming up with new creative ways to tackle these environmental problems.

Hence companies, instead of just relying on their internal teams, are asking the larger community for help. For instance, Natura, the Brazilian cosmetics brand organised an open innovation challenge for zero waste packaging that attracted entrepreneurs, start-ups, researchers, universities and companies from 35 countries.

The big debate, of course, is around who should push the sustainability agenda. At one level, the onus lies with the government to ensure that pollution norms are met, and ecological destruction abated. At another level, companies need to take it upon themselves to educate consumers about the repercussions of their actions.

The concept of circularity is simply about doing more with less. About smart design of not just products but ecosystems where one person's waste can be a resource for someone else. This also points to the need for collaborations and scientific insights on how to use and make things. In future, net zero pledges need to be turned into concrete actions and the circularity transition will play an important role in this. While existing pledges account for 15 per cent of the emissions that need to be reduced, the remaining 85 per cent will come from circularity.

5

ADDRESSING FOOD, WATER AND ENERGY

AGRICULTURE USES 70 PER CENT OF THE WORLD'S FRESHWATER resources, and more than one-quarter of the energy used globally is expended on food production and supply. Hence, water, food and energy are tightly interconnected. While energy is used to grow food, plants can also be used as biofuels. While water is needed for food production it is also needed for electricity generation. Energy, in turn, is needed to transport and fertilise crops.

Globally, there is sufficient water to produce food for everyone, but food and nutritional insecurity remains widespread. 462 million people across the world are underweight. The problem of malnourishment is more acute for India. Almost 15 per cent of the population is undernourished. 195 million people go hungry every day.[1] The impact on children is even worse. 21 per cent of children under the age of five are underweight.[2] 38.4 per cent of children under the age of five are stunted and one in four children are malnourished.[3] Furthermore, where people have limited or no access to safe water or sanitation, the prevalence of diarrhoeal diseases is a major factor in high child mortality rates, malnourishment and loss of productivity. In water-scarce regions, there needs to be robust strategies to protect water availability to maintain agricultural production and avoid food price volatility.

The water-food-energy nexus is therefore central to sustainable development.[4] Demand for all three is increasing, driven by a rising global population, rapid urbanisation, changing diets and economic growth. In

2050, it is expected that there will be a 70 per cent increase in demand for food and a 40 per cent rise in demand for energy. By 2030, the world will have to confront a water supply shortage of about 40 per cent.

The inextricable linkages between these critical domains require a suitably integrated approach to ensuring water and food security, and sustainable agriculture and energy production worldwide.

Higher yields on the same land in harsher weather

In many parts of the world farmers smell the soil to decide if it is ready for sowing. For people who live off the land, taking these decisions based on gut instinct and traditions is common. Farming, the main source of livelihood for millions across the world, changed significantly after the Second World War. This was termed as the 'green revolution'. The first green revolution, attributed to Norman Borlaug, was a series of rapid technological and agronomic advances that increased crop yields significantly, saving more than a billion people from starvation. The agricultural revolution brought phenomenal growth in food production around the world. At the same time, it became a victim of its own success. Some of the unintended consequences impacting the agricultural landscape were increased water use for irrigation, soil degradation, and chemical runoff. Since the mid-1980s there has been a slowdown in growth of yields and we are facing difficulties in growing food due to adverse climatic conditions and soil quality. We are now faced with a situation where about one-third of the world's topsoil is already acutely degraded, and the United Nations estimates a complete degradation within sixty years if current practices continue.[5]

The health and vitality of soil everywhere plays an integral role in food production—this is threatened by the climate crisis. Rising temperatures are changing where and how things can be grown and the climate crisis has altered the water cycle around the world. The result is shifting precipitation patterns and increased evaporation that causes more-frequent powerful rainfall events and more severe droughts. In many areas, rainfall has become either increasingly abundant or in desperately short supply. So, when it comes to agriculture, climate change is doing what it does best: exacerbating existing problems to the point of crisis.

This is also perhaps an opportunity to look deeper and transform the agricultural ecosystem which three quarters of the world's poorest depend upon. If small farmers can be made more productive and enabled to grow resilient crops it can have a huge global impact on nutrition and poverty.

We basically need higher yields on the same land in harsher weather! Experts are therefore calling for the need for a second green revolution which uses the vast technological prowess we have developed and focusses on regenerating the soil and agrarian ecosystems. Each 1 per cent increase in soil organic matter helps soil hold 20,000[6] gallons more water per acre. Heightened water holding capacity means crops are more resilient through times of drought or heavy rain. By maintaining surface residues, roots, and soil structure with better aggregation and pores, soil organic matter reduces nutrient runoff and erosion. And the healthier the soil, the healthier the crop. When plants have the nutrients and roots systems they need to thrive, they build compounds to help protect against insects and disease. There is also growing evidence that a healthy soil microbiome full of necessary bacteria, fungi, and nematodes is more likely to produce nutrient-dense food, promoting better human health.

While the need for the second green revolution is critical, we first need to understand that all over the world agriculture is a high-risk business. First, it is significantly dependent on nature. Floods and droughts can wipe out crops. So can extreme weather conditions. Or bugs and pests can destroy crops. Even with the right inputs, the output is never guaranteed. Even if all goes well and the farmer produces a good crop, (s)he may not find remunerative prices. Second, agriculture is prone to capacity cycles just like any cement manufacturer. For instance, when the onion production is low, onion farmers receive a good price for their products. Seeing this other farmers think they can do better by planting more onions and less of, say, potatoes. With everyone producing more onions there is an oversupply of onions and the price of onions drops—making onions unremunerative. Third, the high risk makes financing agriculture expensive too as banks impose high interest rates to cover for the higher risk.[7] The result is the much talked about agrarian crisis.

In India, many farmers now have started talking to scientists and experts who are from agricultural research universities and are frequently sent to the villages either by the government or by companies who want to source quality products from them. The experts give them knowledge about what to grow, how to protect produce from pests and more importantly, how to maximise yields on their land parcels. Experts are now advocating regenerative farming practices too. Regenerative methods build organic matter in the soil so they can increase water-holding capacity and make farms more resilient. Advocates claim a triple win: climate change mitigation, increased profit for farmers and greater resilience to a changing climate.

With the world population estimated to grow to 9.7 billion by 2050,[8] this represents an increase in agricultural demand of approximately 70 per cent.[9] To meet this number another agricultural revolution is necessary. The first green revolution relied on new seeds, new fertilisers and new methods of production. The second green revolution will revolve around new technologies that will enable the farmer to make better decisions through connected devices (internet of things).This is also called smart agriculture. It will be aided by the thought that genetic engineering of new crops and foods will take the lead in producing increased crop yield and nutrition.

ITC Climate Smart Agriculture

Several organisations, like ITC, have taken steps to focus on advanced technologies and new farming practices to create agricultural value chains. ITC is one of India's foremost private sector companies with a diversified presence in several sectors including fast moving consumer goods and agriculture based businesses. ITC's businesses and value chains create sustainable livelihoods for more than 6 million people, a majority of whom represent the poorest in rural India.

In 2016 ITC Limited partnered with Climate Change and Food Security Programme (CCAFS) of Consultative Group for International Agricultural Research to develop Climate Smart Villages. The main objective was to make villages more productive and more resilient through an Adaptation Prioritisation Toolkit. The toolkit included a range of climate smart interventions categorised into six major categories:

- Weather-smart (e.g. ICT-based agro-advisories, agriculture insurance, and water stress tolerant crop varieties)
- Water-smart (e.g. rainwater harvesting, demand-side efficiency, laser land levelling, micro-irrigation, raised bed planting, and change in crop establishment methods)

- Seed/breed-smart (e.g. adapted crop varieties, adapted animal breeds and seed banks)
- Carbon and nutrient-smart (e.g. site-specific nutrient management, precision fertilizers and residue management, legume catch-cropping, agroforestry, conservation tillage and livestock management)
- Institutional/market-smart (e.g. local institutions, community-based custom hiring centres and cooperatives, market information and off-farm risk management)

In the first phase, 15,000 farmers were directly covered under this programme in 594 villages of Madhya Pradesh, Rajasthan and Maharashtra. The interventions around these initiatives led to an increase in yield up to 15 per cent, with income improvement up to 37 per cent, and reduction in GHG emissions in a range of 36 to 45 per cent. Based on the learnings in the first phase, ITC has expanded the Climate Smart Village programme to 1618 villages in 14 states with a plan to cover 10,000 villages and benefit 3 million acres eventually.

ITC has further developed this framework to include other initiatives as well. Its strategies and key interventions include transferring knowledge to women farmers and building robust community institutions (see Figure 5.1).

FIGURE 5.1

ITC STRATEGIES AND KEY INTERVENTIONS

Transferring knowledge & technology to farmers (Women Agriculturalists)	**Promoting climate-smart agricultural practices**	**Building robust community institutions**
Demonstration Plots	Micro-irrigation Organic Inputs	Agri-business Centres
Farmer Field Schools	Farm Mechanisation Mulching	Custom Hire Centres
	Agro-forestry	Women-managed Agri-enterprises

Source: ITC Sustainability Report [10]

Mondelez transforms Cocoa Farming

Mondelez International, Inc. is one of the world's largest snack food and beverage products company. It operates in over 150 countries and owns some of the most well-known brands such as Cadbury Dairy Milk, Bournvita, Oreo and Tang powdered beverages. The Indian arm of the company, Mondelez India, is the largest chocolate company in India and has been present in the country for the past seventy years.

The company's activities are aligned to its ESG goals of building a sustainable snacking company. It has a focus on climate, ingredients, packaging, social impact and wellbeing amongst others.

For Mondelez India, this journey began in the '70s, when the company decided to grow cocoa in India to supplement the import from Ghana and the Ivory Coast. While the company had experimented with growing cocoa as far back as the '60s, the cocoa-growing farms had not really scaled. Till the '90s, there were very few farms where cocoa was grown. It was largely considered a foreign crop with fluctuating prices and Indian farmers were wary of investing time and energy in something where returns would fluctuate. Additionally, the company had not been sure if cocoa farming could be done to scale in India given the climatic conditions. However, new research revealed that the climate and soil conditions in the southern part of the country were best suited to growing cocoa.

This was when the organisation began an intensive process of transforming the global supply chain into a local one. This potentially had twin benefits, the ready availability of high-quality cocoa at a reasonable price and reduction of the company's carbon footprint. Today, India has reached a cocoa production level of about 20,000 metric tonnes. However, it was not easy to convince farmers to take the first step. The company followed a five-step approach to achieve this transformation. This consisted of 1) regular meetings with farmers to educate them about the benefits of cocoa and convincing them to plant cocoa, (2) partnering with agricultural universities to develop local suitable cocoa hybrids, (3) creating large scale nurseries to provide quality cocoa seedlings at competitive cost to farmers, (4) engaging with farmers to educate and train them on good agricultural practices by providing best in class technical knowhow on cocoa cultivation and processing of cocoa beans, (5) providing a ready market for cocoa beans and a remunerative farm-gate price to the farmers. This process ensured that farmers adopted the most environmentally suitable farm practices that were sustainable and nature friendly. At Mondelez, this is known as the Cocoa Life Programme.

Cocoa production requires a significant amount of patience from the farmers. After planting the cocoa tree, it takes three to four years till it starts bearing fruit. After 3-4 years, the cocoa tree will be in its productive stage for twenty-five to thirty years assuring the farmer of regular income. Some farmers replace the tree much earlier to benefit from newer varieties which are higher yield and resistant to pest & diseases. One of the key benefits of the Cocoa Life programme is that farmers receive a good competitive price for their products. Due to the company's direct farm sourcing model, farmers get lucrative prices compared to other agricultural produce. Moreover, the company has introduced a unique model of growing cocoa as an intercrop to coconut, arecanut and oil palm gardens which enables the farmers to nearly double their income per unit land area. Being an 'intercrop' and non-competitive with the existing crops, cocoa not only helps in increasing income but also in improving micro-climate and soil fertility that benefits the farmer. Furthermore, government has been encouraging farmers to take-up cocoa farming by supporting them through subsidies for new planting and agriculture inputs via local government schemes. Cocoa being a women friendly crop, Mondelez India also encourages women farmers to take up cocoa production through specialised women farmer engagement programmes. To further extend support and inspire marginalised tribal farmers, in remote locations within the four southern states, to adopt good practices in agriculture, the Cocoa Life team has identified tribal communities and trained them in cocoa farming.

Not only has Mondelez been at the forefront of starting and growing cocoa farming in India, it has improved the livelihoods of the farmers and brought about improvements in other areas. By undertaking camps at farms, the villagers learn about things like health and nutrition. The company works with government schools in these areas to improve the education of children by providing infrastructure and working with a foundation to help inculcate in children life-skills through sports. To deliver on its mission, Mondelez has five principles that guide all its actions:

1. Increase transparency, by connecting consumers to cocoa growers;

2. Promote self-sufficiency by building knowledge and skills within cocoa communities and tribal farmers.;
3. Make greater impact through transformative partnerships;
4. Respect human rights, focussing on child rights and promoting women's empowerment; and,
5. Increase business advantage by ensuring a sustainable supply of cocoa for Mondelēz International's much loved brands.

According to Deepak Iyer, President, India, Mondelēz International, 'We started the Cocoa Life programme over fifty years back. Through this programme we intended to transform the cocoa supply chain. Today, the programme supports 100,000 farmers. If you see a cocoa tree in India, there is a good chance that it came from the Cocoa Life programme.'

Managing water for all

Globally, countries are facing a water crisis because of depleting groundwater aquifers. This is due to over-extraction to support expanding cities, industries and food production. Also, there is seepage of untreated water into water bodies which is making it unfit for use, causing various waterborne diseases. Some scientists predict that India, China and the Middle East will run out of fresh water by 2030 due to over-extraction. The water crisis therefore needs urgent attention!

India has 4 per cent of the world's fresh water resources and a whopping 16 per cent of the world's population, and we are ranked a dismal 120th out of 122 nations, in terms of its quality, according to a UN report.[11] It is predicted that by 2030, 40 per cent of the people in India will not have water to drink. Although rivers are considered sacred and holy in India, the Central Pollution Control Board estimates that almost half of India's 445 rivers are unsafe for consumption on account of pollution, and there is not even one river in India whose water can be consumed without extensive treatment. Of the total water available in India, 85 per cent [12] is dependent on rains and the rest is fed by melting snow. Shifting rainfall patterns have meant that India is either coping with drought or dealing with floods at any given point of time. The India Meteorological Department points to changes in rainfall trends in India. There have been a greater number of incidents of excess rain such as the one in the north Indian state of Uttarakhand in 2015 and the severe floods that affected the south Indian state of Kerala 2018. Because of these incidents, there is loss of life, infrastructure and widespread damage and moreover water replenishment happens in a very haphazard manner leading to inadequate water in the dry season. Moreover, with increased temperatures overall, due to climate change, both crops and human population need more water than before, to cope with the heat. It is believed that a rise in sea levels will eventually contaminate both fresh surface water as well as groundwater supplies.

Water scarcity and water quality are predicted to be one of the largest economic and health concerns in the coming decade, meaning that businesses will need to take into account an area's water resources before developing a region. Hence water scarcity is being increasingly featured as a corporate risk. This risk needs to be addressed for all water-intensive companies. This is a major worry for industries belonging to the sectors like agriculture, steel, thermal power plants, chemicals, textiles, cement and manufacturing. The business risks of water scarcity are many. These include decreased water supply for business activities, higher water costs, operational disruptions and associated financial losses, impacts on future growth and license to operate, regulatory caps for water use and conflicts with local communities and other large-scale water users. Large corporate campuses, manufacturing plants and office complexes are a huge drain on community water resources too.

Since water is difficult to transport, its scarcity tends to be a serious local or regional phenomenon. Collection of water is left to women and children who need to trade time spent on this with earning their livelihoods or going to school. Thus, unavailability of adequate potable water pushes these groups further into poverty and never allows them to come out of the vicious circle.

Recognising growing concerns about water around the globe, companies across the world are attempting to manage water, not just within the corporate boundaries but even for communities. This means reducing the amount of water used to produce goods and recycling water used for manufacturing processes so that it can be returned safely to the environment, and replenishing water in communities and nature through locally relevant projects. Companies are increasingly talking of being water-positive or water-neutral. Like 'carbon neutrality', the tactic of 'water neutrality' relies

FIGURE 5.2
WATER MANAGEMENT PROGRAMMES

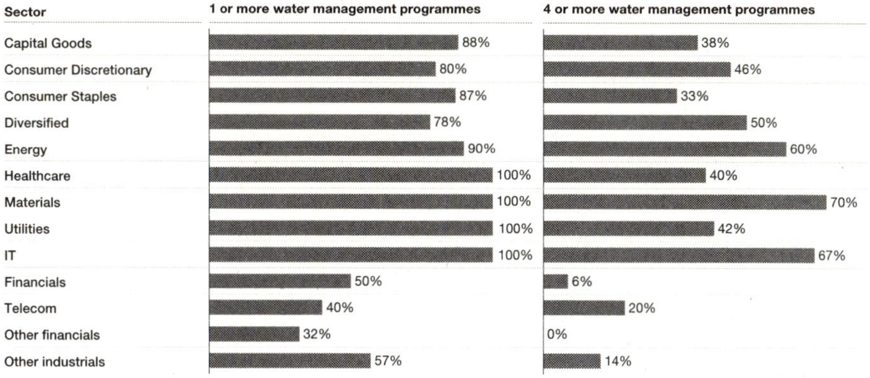

Source: Responsible Business Rankings

upon a kind of offsetting of one's water consumption, a balancing of water accounts.

By supporting healthy watersheds and sponsoring clean-water projects in communities, as well as continuing to implement technological solutions at its factories, the companies say that they will theoretically be able to save or replenish the amount of water they use. Water is a finite resource, but water neutrality is a complex term. Hence, taking water from one place and replacing it in another doesn't exactly balance accounts in the first location, but it certainly helps local communities. Which is why, besides operations, Indian companies focus on provision of safe drinking water, and rainwater collection and storage as part of their social responsibility programs. Also a significant number of companies have 4 or more water management programmes (see Figure 5.2).

Diageo's framework for water security

Diageo India is a leading beverage alcohol company that has fifty manufacturing facilities across states and union territories in India. It is incorporated in India as United Spirits Limited (USL). The company also has a large agricultural supply chain and works with farmers for sourcing a variety of agricultural produce for its drinks.

One of the regions the company works in is Rajasthan. Rajasthan is

India's largest state by area, but with only 1.1 per cent surface water, making it almost completely dependent on groundwater which is fast depleting. The dry and arid state almost entirely depends on the annual monsoon rains and groundwater. Traditional water harvesting structures in Rajasthan are called taanka. These are made in or near homes to store water for families during the dry season. Balesar Panchayat Samiti in Jodhpur District in western Rajasthan is one of the worst affected areas due to scanty rainfall and poor ground water quality. The area is also affected by fluoride concentration in groundwater beyond the permissible limit of 1.5 mg per litre. Stone mining activity is widespread in the areas and due to over exposure of silica, silicosis is a major health problem among a vast majority of the population. Silicosis coupled with intake of fluoride contaminated water has led to health concerns in the area. Mostly children and women spend a substantial duration of the day in travelling to distant sources for bringing water which hampers time they could have invested in education and livelihood respectively.

Diageo decided to help the local community in Jodhpur district by building a taanka for sixty households. In addition, awareness drives were organised in the project villages. The villagers were made aware of the need for water harvesting along with knowledge about traditional sources of water harvesting. Awareness was also created around important topics such as safe drinking water and personal health and hygiene, so that prevalence of waterborne diseases could be reduced. The company has implemented several other water projects in the areas that it operates. For instance, in Rajnandgaon district, ponds are the source of potable water for the villages as the community uses them for daily work and agriculture. Here Diageo has repaired thirty ponds, enabling them to store rainwater. Twenty-three thousand people from thirty villages have benefitted from the project.

According to Abanti Sankaranarayanan, Chief Strategy and Corporate Affairs Officer, Diageo India, 'We believe that water is an essential lifeforce for a vibrant, healthy and prosperous India. Our commitment to the country and to this resource stands firm as we use science, indigenous knowledge and modern processes to go beyond our own operation and replenish the amount of water used in our final product in water-stressed areas through various water replenishment projects.'

These projects are part of Diageo's social responsibility framework, under which, by 2030, every drink the company makes will use 30 per cent less water than today. Further, the company will replenish more water than it uses in all water-stressed areas. This is not all, Diageo aims to achieve net zero carbon emissions in India by 2025, deliver over 150 community water projects across the world, and support over 150,000 smallholder farmers with farming techniques to regenerate the land and build biodiversity.

Dalmia's community water projects

Companies like Dalmia Bharat, a sugar and cement conglomerate, are aware of the challenges that water brings. For them soil and water conservation is a key component of their social responsibility activities. While making ponds, managing watersheds and dams are key, a clear long-term vision is formed by them to enable water sufficiency in communities. Take the case of the Jhunjhunu district also located in the arid state of Rajasthan where the company took on a massive water conservation project when a study revealed that with the present rate of use the region would have groundwater only for the next ten years. However, this was in 2018. Today, the district has transformed after the Dalmia Bharat Foundation took up intensive water-based initiatives in the area. At the first stage, the foundation took stock of water resources in the villages of Chirawa Block, Jhunjhunu. District resource mapping was undertaken and it was observed that serious interventions in controlling the groundwater overdraft was needed. At the same time, recharging of groundwater related activities had to be undertaken to save people from this manmade catastrophe. The foundation then involved the community as sustainable water resource management is impossible without community participation. This included public consultations to active participation in the design and delivery of projects.

Reducing agricultural emissions

What we eat and grow makes up around $10 trillion of global GDP and employs up to 40 per cent of the global workforce. Nature-positive solutions can create 191 million new jobs and $3.6 trillion of additional revenue or cost savings by 2030.[13] The World Resources Institute (WRI) has identified a five-step framework to increase agricultural yields and reduce carbon emissions caused by agriculture : (1) reduce growth in demand for food and other agricultural products; (2) increase food production without expanding agricultural land; (3) protect and restore natural ecosystems; (4) sustainably increase fish supply; and (5) reduce GHG emissions from agricultural production. There is a limited role for soil carbon sequestration and a much larger role for reducing emissions from cattle, manure, fertilisers, rice cultivation and energy use.

Technology and Renewable Energy for modern agriculture

Agriculture and energy are the two pillars of transformation that can give a huge fillip to the Indian economy. 70 per cent of India's rural households work in agriculture and energy is the fuel that empowers the $3 trillion Indian economy. But both these sectors are going through transformative changes. The need to shift to renewable energy means that the energy sector is in transition. Similarly, Indian agriculture, which has been plagued by low yields and small farm sizes is looking at innovative technology led solutions for a much needed overhaul.

The pervasive problem of Indian agriculture has been the one of water. Either too much water, due to flooding and excessive rainfall or too little water due to droughts or location of the land. Over time, these issues are expected to exacerbate due to the impacts of climate change. Either way, many technology-based solutions exist to solve this perennial problem. Improving agricultural yields by providing water and using new technologies implies an increase in the use of electricity. In the last few years, a significant part of rural India has been electrified, but grid-based electricity for agricultural use is still a big gap. In the absence of grid-based electricity and water, Indian farmers draw ground water using diesel and kerosene based water pumps to irrigate their lands. By some estimates 6 to 7 million pumps run on diesel and about a million run on kerosene.[14] Not only are these fuels harmful to the environment as they release noxious fumes, they are also expensive to run with farmers spending between Rs 50,000 to Rs 80,000 a year on this.

To improve agricultural yields there is also movement towards precision agriculture. Started in the 1990s, precision agriculture aims to leverage state-of-the-art technologies to bring more accuracy and control crop production. It focusses on boosting yields and curbing waste. Companies like Google are being enlisted to help farmers improve yields and optimise production through artificial intelligence.[15] How does this work? By using Geographical Information Systems (GIS), farmers can view their crops through heat maps. For instance, patches in red may indicate dead fields while patches in green would indicate healthy fields. The green areas would require more fertilisers or pesticides. The red areas may not worked on by the framers. Machine learning is bringing new advances to these heat maps. With the terrain getting mapped in greater detail, a farmer can place his reliance on real time responses. Companies are increasingly providing technologies that promote precision agriculture. To manage all this, IoT technologies will likely take centre stage on the farm of the future. Sensor-controlled rooms are already growing altered lettuce and the all-important bee is getting a boost from automated heaters.[16] The use of IoT has the potential to cut costs and boost food production by 70 per cent by 2050.[17] The use of sensors can also improve animal welfare and reduce the use of resources such as water.[18] While these developments look really exciting, they need large amounts of energy to function.

Renewable energy can provide the impetus for this transition towards a modernised, high productivity agricultural system. Well-managed, precise irrigation can increase crop yields to up to four times that of rain-fed agriculture and renewable energy based solutions such as solar water pumps can achieve this by providing easy access to water at substantially reduced costs. The transition to renewable energy has been understood by the government of India as well. Government schemes[19] are propagating and incentivising the use of solar water pumps. However, the transition requires grassroot level pull too. Organisations such as the Schneider Electric Foundation are working to enable this transition. The foundation provided several solar water pumps to the villagers in Nabarangapur, which is a district in south-west Odisha bordering Chhattisgarh and Andhra Pradesh. The rain-dependent region is in a hard-to-reach terrain where grid electricity is not easily available. Even though the land is fertile, male members have migrated outside as they are unable to eke out a living in the absence of regular water supply. Once the villagers started using solar water pumps, land productivity improved significantly. For instance, just seven solar water pumps were able to help irrigate over 80 acres of land.

While this was a significant impact, the villagers realised that their solar water pumps were utilised for only 50 per cent of the total time and asked the Schneider team to help them in other areas such as harvesting their fields and processing the harvest. The Schneider engineering team then observed all the processes that the villagers undertook and realised that they could setup a microgrid that could power harvesting and food processing. But this was just the beginning, a single source of energy meant that its usage needed to be monitored and equitably distributed. Collaborative operation and management of the microgrid was enabled through the formation of solar user groups that were tasked with ensuring that things ran smoothly.

Local and Traceable

Food needs to be farmed, harvested or caught, transported, processed, packaged, distributed and cooked, and the residuals disposed of. Each of these steps causes emissions. While you and I may have cut down on our travels in the last year, our food has continued to travel long distances. In many parts of the world, temperate crops, such as wheat, can be obtained mostly within a radius of 500 kms. In comparison, the global average is about 3,800 kms. Which essentially means that the carbon emissions caused by transporting food are higher than the emissions caused by growing food! Aalto University dissertation researcher Pekka Kinnunen, modelled the minimum distance between crop production and consumption that humans around the world would need to be able to meet their food demand. The study factored in six key crop groups for humans: temperate cereals (wheat, barley, rye), rice, corn, tropical grains (millet, sorghum), tropical roots (cassava) and pulses. The researchers modelled globally the distances between production and the consumer for both normal production conditions and scenarios where production chains become more efficient due to reduced food waste and improved farming methods. They found that 27 per cent of the world's population could get their temperate cereal grains within a radius of fewer than 100 kms. The share was 22 per cent for tropical cereals, 28 per cent for rice and 27 per cent for pulses. In the case of maize and tropical roots, the proportion was only 11–16 per cent.

Then, there is another big issue of food safety. Consumers want to know where their food comes from, what it contains and how safe it is. Tracking and tracing where everything comes from is highly complex, but this is an increasing demand from customers. Knowing the origin of food products can also help reduce emissions and help understand the true impact of global food supply chains. Companies like Nestle and ITC are now paying heed to this growing trend. Nestle is expanding its use of blockchain technology, through the IBM Food Trust Blockchain Initiative, to the company's luxury coffee brand Zoégas. Nestlé's select editions of Zoégas whole beans and roast and ground coffee is a 100 per cent Rainforest Alliance certified blend of arabica coffee beans from three origins—Brazil, Rwanda and Colombia. Through blockchain-recorded data, buyers of the coffee will now be able to trace their coffee back to the different origins.

Significant transformations are also happening in the farm supply chains where customers are directly buying from farmers. ITC has initiated a direct-to-consumers initiative in Guntur District in Andhra Pradesh. In Guntur district, farmers face numerous challenges such as small land holdings, lack of finance, lower yields, water shortage and finally, over-reliance on natural occurrences such as rainfall, to produce their crop. The farmers under the guidance of ITC and financial support from India's National Horticultural Mission have set up shade nets for producing vegetables—the first of its kind in the Vinukonda region.

The technology controls the micro climate partially or fully as per the requirement of the crop. This technique of growing vegetables reduces reliance on rainfall and makes optimum use of land and water resources. The shade nets enable farmers to grow multiple commercial/cash crops and vegetables (cucumber, capsicum, chilli, tomato etc.) throughout the year, thereby increasing their income levels significantly. The farmers are provided with constant guidance on best practices and diverse technologies are demonstrated so that they can produce vegetables with better yield and quality.

Besides supporting the farmers with region/crop-specific package of practices, the programme focussed on establishing a market-linked production system. The ultimate objective is to produce vegetables based on market demand and directly connect the produce to consumers, thereby eliminating middlemen and generating more value for farmers. Under this model, ITC has created a post-harvest infrastructure where the vegetables are cleaned, sorted, packed and distributed directly to consumers under the Farm2home brand and other retail outlets. Through this, ITC has developed farmer entrepreneurs in villages, thereby generating more employment opportunities.

The transformation of agriculture

About $44 trillion of economic value generation—more than half the world's GDP—is moderately or highly dependent on nature and its services.[20] Land transformation for the production of agricultural commodities is a key driver of impacts on nature. However, changing land use transforms the ecosystem and impacts biodiversity. This is why, experts such as Shiv Sivakumar, Group Head - Agri Businesses at ITC Limited are saying, 'to create a sustainable Net Zero world, agriculture needs to go back to its basics'.

The current mainstream practice of cultivating individual crops in large tracts of land is unsustainable. We need to shift towards poly-cropping and integrated farms. Before the advent of industrial farming, integrated farms were the norm. In these integrated farms, pisciculture, animal husbandry, beekeeping and other activities were practised in tandem with cultivating a variety of crops. Various types of plants, livestock, mushroom, aquaculture and other aquatic flora and fauna were managed for maximum productivity in such a way that one complemented the other. The waste generated from one component was recycled and used as a resource for the other. This was a system to protect and conserve land and water resources from depletion. In countries like India, where majority of farmers holding less than two hectares of land practise subsistence farming, risks are heightened through mono-cropping. The benefit of integrated farms is that the ecosystem becomes self-sufficient and costs and risks go down in the long run. However, the challenge is that farmers running integrated farms need to have an in-depth understanding of multiple disciplines, which isn't easy. But there is an enormous opportunity for technology to support farmers.

We are at an inflection point in the agri-tech space in India. There is access to affordable technology, large-scale public data sets and an openness among the farmers to embrace new solutions. Multiple start-ups and corporates are also working to narrow the divide between farmers and end consumers, so that the entire ecosystem flourishes.

6

LEAVE NO ONE BEHIND

MODERN ECONOMICS HAS RUN COUNTER TO THE BASIC RULE OF humanity—do unto others as you would have done unto yourself. It propounds the practice of profit above everything else, going so far as to say that human beings must pursue their self-interests, and that it is 'rational' to do so. The belief is that if everyone looks after himself then markets will ensure that everyone will be better off. This hasn't really happened anywhere in the world as inequality has reached new highs. The ratio between wages and profit is increasingly and dangerously imbalanced and people are questioning the fairness of the current economic system, calling for changes towards more sustainable prosperity. This has resulted in some increasingly dysfunctional trends in financial markets, economic systems and job markets. Further, the prioritisation of profit over everything else has fuelled unsustainable consumption and climate change. All in all, we are in the middle of a massive mess which is being exacerbated by the things we ignored for the last thirty years—inequality and climate change.

Also, the pandemic has cost us a functional economy and left the economically marginal sector unemployed and fending for basic needs such as food and shelter. Inequality means that people need to work even when they are sick, and they then spread the disease to others. Lack of ecological management means that there are large masses of land in our cities and villages that have been degraded due to overuse, waste and poor management. These impact quality of water and air, leading to worsening of health conditions in which the poor suffer disproportionately. Inequality and climate change need urgent reform. Perhaps this is the impetus we need to reimagine and emerge stronger.

The pandemic shift

The pandemic has worsened several challenges and shone a spotlight on others. Its impact is felt across all countries and all sectors of business. Changes that we are seeing have a direct bearing on achieving sustainable development goals and companies and governments will need to adjust their strategies to cope with these changes.

Healthcare for all

The pandemic has exposed chinks in healthcare systems across the world. Even the developed nations have been found wanting in the availability of beds and doctors. At the same time, focus has shifted to telemedicine and remote healthcare. This is a positive development for people in remote areas so that they can have access to basic healthcare. At the same time, governments and the healthcare industry are being spurred ahead to broaden the base of the hospital network and ensure universal healthcare.

People are also becoming more health-conscious and focussing on remaining fit, which is giving an impetus to the wellness industry and healthy foods. This is emerging in almost every category—packaged food, fruits and vegetables, drinks, cosmetics, home care and personal care. Consequently, investing in local communities, volunteering, buying from local suppliers and supporting local causes is becoming important for companies.

In the case of food, indigenous immunity boosters have become part of daily rituals furthering the local industry. People are also realising the importance of quality fruits and vegetables. Both the growth in immunity boosters and the need for high quality produce is likely to spur sustainable farming—reducing reliance on water usage and pesticides.

Clean air

During the 2020 lockdown, people across the world experienced clear skies and fresh air—something they had never experienced in their lifetime. With vehicles off the road, pollution levels dropped. This experience is likely to have a profound impact on the way people are going to think about their commuting preferences. This is an opportune moment for a policy shift towards sustainable transportation. There are massive efforts on for cleaner mobility solutions. The trajectory of the shift to sustainable transport will become steeper than what was anticipated earlier. Dealerships are now seeing enquiries for electric vehicles, and the trend is only likely to grow. With the right policy initiatives, fiscal benefits, joint production and R&D efforts by automakers, sustainable mobility will take off.

Consumers are adopting environmentally friendly lifestyles

For consumers, environmentally friendly lifestyles are becoming the new theme as environmental and health concerns are taking increasing mindshare.

Electric vehicles and plant-based meats seem to be the important areas of consumer focus in several parts of the world.

- Electric vehicles (EV) will account for 40 per cent of global new car sales by 2030. 2020 was a pivotal year in EV purchases and this will only accelerate in 2021. [1]
- The global plant-based meat market will reach $51 billion by 2025, implying a threefold increase in penetration from 2019 levels. Also, interest in veganism is surging. If Google searches are any guide, interest in the plant-based diet has surged in recent years across much of the rich world.[2]

Consumers who purchase EV's and plant-based meat see themselves as 'doing something good' for the causes they believe in—climate change and animal welfare. Further, they believe that these positive consumption choices also contribute to better health—EVs reduce pollution and plant-based meats have lower cholesterol. Consumers are also turning vegan due to growing concerns about their health and for the climate.

Technology acceleration

Due to the disruption caused by COVID-19, we experienced more digital transformation than we have seen in the last twenty years. While many businesses suffered closure, telecom, online grocery, pharmaceuticals, telemedicine and healthcare innovated and grew. The internet is now even more crucial as it has helped provide a continuity of services in a world that was locked down. The pandemic massively accelerated some long-predicted technology trends and businesses that once mapped digital strategy in one- to three-year phases had to scale their initiatives in a matter of days or weeks. The effect of lockdowns across the world ensured that online shopping from a nice-to-have became a must-have around the world. Spurred by this shift to digitisation, Indian ecommerce is expected to grow from $64 billion in 2020 to $200 billion in 2027.[3]

This has had two important impacts on education and work.

Quality education

Providing quality education has been a massive problem for all developing countries. Large resources are required for providing school infrastructure and training of quality schoolteachers. During the pandemic, 191 countries announced or implemented school or university closures, impacting 1.57 billion students.[4] Teachers, students and schools had to get on a digital fast forward to adapt to online learning. The pandemic has shown how this can be bridged by online education and remote education through television shows. It is now proven that high-quality education can be provided at scale. Schools and technology providers are finding many configurations through which education can be provided.

This will significantly aid in the achievement of the SDG of quality education, provided technology can reach the remote and rural areas of the world. In Indian rural households, only 10 per cent of students were able to operate computers or mobile phones against 32.4 per cent of students in urban households. Only 15 per cent of rural Indian households have access to internet as against 42 per cent of urban households.[5] The digital divide will impact education in a big way.

The transformation of workplaces

Workplaces transformed as a result of office closures and social distancing during the pandemic. Work from home became a reality. Now, while many companies are shutting offices or reducing office space, many others want their staff back in offices. Among employees, opinion is divided as well. While no one really knows how this will pan out in the long run, it will certainly change how companies are organized. At the same time, companies are realising the potential gains from digitisation and automation. Digital skills will increasingly become the must-have for any form of employment.

Measuring the S in ESG

The underlying principle of the SDGs is to leave no one behind, which is why they offer us an integrated perspective to combat this crisis. In the 2030 Agenda we have a holistic framework that brings the global economic, environmental and development agendas together for the first time. Because they are so broad and complex—the very thing they are often criticised for—the SDGs can help us understand and respond to the wide-ranging impacts of COVID-19. The Sustainable Development Goals are a framework that bring these diverse aspects together—from poverty rates, to economic growth, education and health. The 17 Goals, and their 169 targets and 232 indicators, are a unique tool to help governments, businesses and NGOs understand the full scope of complex policy challenges like COVID-19.

The first impact of the pandemic was felt on supply chains with supplies from China drying up. Slowly bottlenecks from other countries started showing up. Until COVID-19 showed up, most of the procurement activities were centred around cost savings. The mantra appeared to be 'buy from wherever the materials are cheapest, subject to quality parameters'. This is now changing with risk of supply disruption being factored into the cost. At the same time, many companies and countries are considering near-sourcing or planning to become self-sufficient. This is likely to have a profound impact on supply chains. This re-jigging of supply chains gives companies an opportunity to build green or sustainable supply chains. There is also a lot of attention on fair wages, safe working conditions and quality healthcare in external supply chains. In the past, companies have frequently focussed on the offices and factories they own when they cite adherence to the SDGs and other statutory compliances. The external supply chains that are largely part of their outsourced businesses have been ignored. Several instances have come to light where the people who work with outsourced partners of global brands have been poorly treated. Extending the fairness and equality to everyone the brand touches is now an expectation.

The pandemic has also created a focus on ESG (environmental, social, and governance) based investments. As mentioned in Chapter 1, investors are increasingly investing in ESG funds, and the volumes of these funds have skyrocketed. Child labour, diversity in the workplace, health and safety of employees—all these and more are part of the 'social' parameters that ESG seeks to cover. But measuring these parameters is extremely difficult. For instance, take the case of child labour—with diverse global supply chains with contractors and sub contractors, it's hard for companies to know who actually makes their products. They rely on paper-based certificates provided by contractors to prove that no child labour was used. While things have certainly improved over the last ten years in terms of reduction of child labour, gaps remain. Respect for human rights across the supply chain is an increasing ask from investors worldwide and companies today are attempting to go deeper into this area. But above everything else 'social' just means—doing the right thing, all the time. If you have the right intent, metrics and processes will follow. There is increased scrutiny and emphasis on how companies are impacting society and this is likely to intensify.

Creating balance in society

The tussle between private profit and public good is emerging everywhere. The tentacles of corporate power strengthened by technology seem weak as company after company has teetered in the face of a small virus. For society to flourish, for hope and optimism to hold sway we need a radical redesign and for this radical redesign—a moral core that holds true in the eye of a storm and helps create a foundation for a better society.

In the face of global pandemics and the fragility of current economic systems, the rosy hue of capitalism has abated and people are asking why capitalism isn't solving problems and whether exponential, unfettered growth really leads to long-term prosperity. Alternative models that propagate regenerative capitalism are now emerging which state that a perpetually growing economy would eventually come into conflict with a finite biosphere, and would impose limits for economies and how we live our lives. They go on to highlight the core principles to achieve this need empowered participation. Which essentially means that, the whole is greater than the sum of its parts; the active participation of every element powers the health of the whole. Each unique contribution spells a better future than those operating in isolation ever can.[6]

Regenerative systems also propagate balance. The regenerative economic system calls for a middle ground everywhere, be it between nature and technology or present and future. Central to this approach is a focus on gender equality, well-being and inclusiveness. Inequality is worsened by people being unable to access knowledge, jobs and digital skills. Inequality in all forms, therefore, needs to be addressed.

Bridging the gender divide

When climate change causes natural resources to become scarce, traditional gender roles intensify—as does violence against women. Such abuse can prevent women from pursuing work, education and other opportunities.[7] Female labour force participation rates demonstrate the potential for a country to grow more rapidly[8] and the rates vary across developing countries and emerging economies. In the Middle East, North Africa and South Asia, less than one-third of women of working-age participate, while the proportion reaches around two-thirds in East Asia and sub-Saharan Africa.[9] This rate is influenced by social factors and economic factors such as economic growth, education levels, fertility rates, gender roles, stereotypes and social norms. The pandemic has reversed global progress in achieving equality between men and women and the fallout could be long lasting.[10] More women lost their jobs during the pandemic as compared to men or bore a disproportionate burden in terms of managing home and work. Going at the current rate of progress, the World Economic Forum estimates that it will take 133.4 years to achieve global parity between men and women in terms of equal pay, health and education.

What has been most noticeable is the falling rate of engagement of women in the Indian labour force, despite strong economic growth and rising wages before 2020. According to a report of the International Labour Organisation (ILO), India's female labour force participation rate (LFPR) fell from 35.8 per cent in 1994 to merely 20.7 per cent in 2019.[11] In comparison, the LFPR in Sweden, is as high as 88 per cent! However, if one is to consider specific areas, India is ahead. For instance, India has the distinction of having 11.7 per cent of its pilots as women, against a global average of 3 per cent. Similarly, over half of India's banking sector in terms of asset size, had female chiefs, until recently. However, with the global share of women in the workforce placed at 40 per cent, India lags behind in female workforce participation, being ranked 11th from the bottom among 131 countries.

Also, 71 per cent of female workers in India are employed in agriculture.[12] Research shows that if women farmers were to have equal access to the same resources (such as trainings, financing, and property rights) as their male counterparts, they could increase their crop yields by 20 to 30 per cent, strengthening their livelihoods and their households. When women are able to earn their own wages, they typically reinvest 90 per cent of those earnings back into their families and communities.[13] The education of girls is therefore one of the ten most powerful ways to reduce GHG emissions.[14] Women form a substantial part of the economy and if female workforce participation were to increase by 10 per cent, it would add $770 billion to India's GDP by 2025.[15] Further, if participation of women in the workforce was the same as men, India's economy would see a 27 per cent increase in GDP, a bigger impact than in any other region in the world. Moreover many problems with societal imbalances can be corrected by empowering women—financial empowerment, legal empowerment, balance in society and more.

Companies, non-profits and other stakeholders have taken the lead in driving change in India. Since one of the reasons women do not head back to work is because they need to stay at home and care for their children, organisations like SEWA Federation run childcare centres, allowing women to take up jobs and stay for longer hours at work. Pratham Institute has been working with women in villages since 2016 to bring digital devices into villages. With digital devices, women can gain access to content and acquire new learning skills. Women also further impart their knowledge within their communities and through this, we see the rise of women owning beauty parlours, tailoring stations and many of them even working as mechanics in cities. Recognising the need to foster self-employment, companies like Godrej Consumer Products Ltd (GCPL) have partnered with several non-profits and set up the GCPL Salon-i programme. The programme has reached out to 1300 salon micro-entrepreneurs who are in turn reaching out to 90,000 women, building their capacity in technical skills and financial literacy.[16]

Some other organisations have undertaken long-term programmes to build a diverse and inclusive work force. A study by the Indian School of Business and Hero MotoCorp on skilling gave insights on opportunities for women in employment and entrepreneurship. The study showed that women, when provided vocational training opportunities, performed well, even better than men in terms of certification, grade and employment. Women in the programme were more likely to take to self-employment after certification than men (22.58 per cent women versus 7.14 per cent men). Yet there was a consistent difference between the salaries of men and women, with men earning higher salaries than women. The wage gap was about 17 per cent and spread across all categories—apprenticeship, self-employment and wage-employment. Recognising the need for urgent action, Hero MotoCorp started two projects called. Tejaswini and Jeevika.

Project Tejaswini (Tejaswini roughly translates to someone who radiates energy) focussed on increasing the women workforce in Hero MotoCorp's manufacturing operations. Project Tejaswini was started in October 2016, by welcoming twenty-one woman associates to the shop floor. From 2016 to 2019, Hero MotoCorp recruited around 100 girls trained from the Industrial Training Institutes and placed them on the shop floor. The girls were employed in roles as diverse as fitter, welder, electrician, electronic mechanic, machinist and turner. To make the girls comfortable on the shop floor, the company undertook several measures. Since most of the shop floors were populated with men, toilets needed to be constructed for women. For encouraging the participation and strengthening of interpersonal relationships, the plant teams organised sports and cultural events. Some ergonomic changes were also made in the work area for women. Female nurses were appointed to provide healthcare to female workers and creches were started to enable the female workers to leave their child in a safe manner. The project outcomes were seen in terms of improved product quality, timely product delivery, innovative work culture and building of an inclusive mindset at the plant level.

The second programme that Hero MotoCorp undertook was Project Jeevika (meaning livelihood) that focussed on providing livelihood and skills training to girls and women from marginalised socio-economic backgrounds. The training programmes equipped them to become auto mechanics (very much a male bastion until recent times), computer operators, tailors, beauticians, and so on. As part of the programme, the focus was not just on skill enhancement but also on getting jobs for the trainees. The company has trained 19,119 young women till 2020, of which more than 60 per cent got jobs or became entrepreneurs with substantial monthly earnings.

ITC's Women's Economic Empowerment Programme aims to provide women with opportunities to earn independent income, helping to strengthen their position as decision-makers in their families and in their communities. There is a special focus on women living in extreme poverty who are the only earning members of their families and have no assets or regular incomes. With training and financial support, women can take-up self-employment activities, set up small businesses or join together to form self-help groups or micro-enterprises. Over 27,000 poor women have been covered till now with more than 75 per cent of them tripling their annual incomes. Their earnings and savings mean better education, nutrition and health for their children—a vital investment in the future of their communities. Equally important, the confidence they gain along the way is helping to break gender inequalities and build a more equal society.

Data indicates that companies with greater gender diversity outperform those with less, often by as much as 30 per cent. Yet, the participation of women in critical decision-making forums, Boards of Directors and at the CXO level, is not where it should be. It is only when there are diverse voices at the workplace that we will allow for different perspectives and better choices.[17] Gender bias begins at the hiring stage. Some roles are considered better suited for women—sales executives, shop floor assistants etc., while others, such as those in manufacturing, are considered better for men. This stereotyping needs to be done away with. Candidate skill is the only thing that needs to match with the job requirement and not the hiring managers' preferences, assumptions and presumptions. Equal pay for equal work is a fundamental right. A report by the Ministry of Statistics and Programme Implementation, however, indicates that women in urban areas with a graduate or higher degree earn 24 per cent less than their male counterparts! Pay must be aligned to match employee performance and not be based on gender.

Then there is the urgent need of preparing the women workforce for the jobs of the future. As computing advances gather speed and processing power, intelligent machines will soon be able to do our jobs at a fraction of the cost and in far lesser time. Some sectors are already going through this transformation and others will soon follow. Some of the breakthroughs in AI and machine learning are truly remarkable. Today, robots can be taught complex tasks by showing them a single demonstration. Documents and audio recordings in multiple languages can be easily translated with remarkable speed and accuracy. AI-based diagnostics of health scans are equally accurate and fast. And, this is just the beginning of the mega tech revolution that will unfold in the coming years.[18] This kind of automation will enable businesses to improve performance and over time will also exceed human capabilities. By some estimates, about a third of human activity will get automated in the next twenty years. This essentially means that we need to build up the women workforce for the jobs of the future that will be accelerated by the digital revolution.

TABLE 6.1: TOP EMERGING AND DECLINING JOBS

Top Emerging Jobs	Top Declining Jobs
1. Data Analysts, Scientists	1. Data entry
2. Big Data specialists	2. Secretarial services
3. AI and Machine Learning	3. Factory workers
4. Operations Management	4. Customer Service
5. Software development	5. Stock keeping
6. Sales and Marketing	6. Record keeping
7. Digital Transformation specialists	7. Postal services

UNESCO Director-General Irina Bokova said, 'Whether based on education, gender, jobs, health or resources, inequality is one of the gravest threats to our common future. In the face of polarisation, fragmentation and exclusion, we must respond with human-centred policies that empower all women and men, strengthen the capacity of governments and rally the multilateral system around shared narratives, solidarity and understanding to protect what is common to us all—our culture, our humanity, our planet .... This begins with education and skills and calls for a special focus on narrowing the gender gap, especially in the growth sector constituted by professions requiring a background in science, technology, engineering and mathematics.

This is our message in Davos—the Fourth Industrial Revolution must be a development revolution.'[19]

Reinvigorating the creative economy

Creative industries have their origin in individual creativity, skill, and talent. They have potential for job creation through the generation and exploitation of ideas or imagination. Using this broad definition, creative industries range from advertising and social media to the likes of agribusiness, design, and handicrafts. Creative industries provide a platform to support the sustained empowerment of women. In communities across the world, rich cultural value and traditional designs have been protected and nurtured by women through creative industries. Women are economically empowered by being able to develop their skills, find jobs, and earn money. As a result of this economic empowerment, women often find the path to social and political empowerment within their communities as well. Creative industries also make a significant contribution to the larger economy. In the EU for example, these industries contribute around 3 per cent to regional GDP, equivalent to approximately €500 billion annually, and provide employment for over 6 million people.[20] Creative industries play a dual role: first as an important area for investment in the knowledge economy, and second as a means of reinforcing values and cultural identity. This is why organisations like UNIDO, UNESCO, and UNCTAD promote creative industries to maximise economic contribution of women and facilitate culturally inclusive development.

India has had a large creative community from time immemorial. Every village and every community had artists and artisans that preserved cultural heritage through craft and local designs. With issues such as large-scale urbanisation, climate change and sustainability being at the forefront, there is a crying need to build self-sustaining rural livelihoods to prevent mass migration to urban hubs. At the same time, giving impetus to traditional crafts and making them more current can enable and fuel the creative, local and sustainable ecosystems that have been languishing after the industrial revolution. After agriculture, handicrafts is the largest source of income among rural populations—an estimated 17.79 million Indians will be engaged in craft production by 2022. What is even more important is that many

Indian crafts are the sole domain of the women in the household. With the right kind of inputs the craft sector can be developed into a powerhouse of rural skill and enterprise.[21]

Production estimates indicate the size of the sector as roughly Rs 302.57 billion, with Rs 168.58 billion generated through exports of Indian handicraft and handloom products. There is a growing demand both internationally and domestically for handicraft and handloom products and a growing consumer consciousness around organic and fair trade practices that create value for marginalised populations.[22] However, the status of craft in India needs to be elevated for it to scale, as currently the sector is besieged by poor design, lack of working capital and a disregard for the quantum of efforts highly skilled master craftsmen and women put into creating seminal pieces.

Corporate India has realised that this is an untapped opportunity to empower women and several are attempting to focus on local crafts for livelihood generation. Antaran is a key intervention of the Tata Trusts' Craft-based Livelihood Programme, initiated to bring seminal changes in craft development. It aims at rejuvenating ailing handloom clusters through an end-to-end programme. In the first year, three handloom clusters have been chosen, one each in Odisha, Assam and Nagaland.[23]

Dalmia Bharat Foundation and MonAmi Foundation are working to create a new range of products based on local skills in Sitapur, Uttar Pradesh (see Figure 6.1). Moonj is a wild grass that grows along the seasonal ponds or larger water sources that is harvested by hand usually during the monsoons. The women of Sitapur travel long distances from their villages to harvest this grass, a time-consuming task, as only the central stem of the grass needs to be gathered rather than the whole grass itself. After a few days of sun-drying, the grass is lighter in colour and then the actual processing begins. Moonj is cut, shaved and dyed in different colours and left out to dry again. Only after this initial preparation which spans a few days and involves a lot of hard work, is the grass ready to be woven into gorgeous baskets, wall displays and many other extremely efficient and handy products. While the project began before the pandemic, it came to a standstill during the pandemic induced lockdowns in 2020. Unfazed by their inability to travel, the team at MonAmi decided to train the women via Zoom sessions. Even though there was initial resistance and training needed to be adapted, they

FIGURE 6.1
MonAmi ASSESSMENT FRAMEWORK

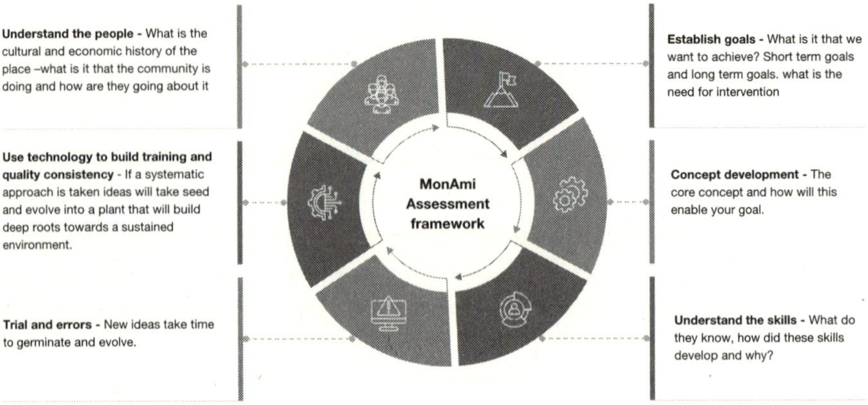

persevered and a stunning collection of wall decorations was created. When asked for reasons for their success, Anurag Rana, Managing Trustee, Mon Ami Foundation, said, 'A vast body of traditional knowledge exists in rural India as part of their everyday lives. This is overlooked by most organisations trying to provide rural livelihoods. To plan an intervention, a system cannot be broken, as there are age-old processes in our society and villages that have their cultural bearings.' The team therefore undertook a detailed skill assessment to understand what is desirable and valuable for a sustainable future for the community. This assessment was then adapted to modern technology and training interventions.

Understand the people - What is the cultural and economic history of the place –what is it that the community is doing and how are they going about it
Establish goals - What is it that we want to achieve? Short term goals and long term goals. what is the need for intervention
Use technology to build training and quality consistency - If a systematic approach is taken ideas will take seed and evolve into a plant that will build deep roots towards a sustained environment.
MonAmi Assessment framework
Concept development - The core concept and how will this enable your goal.
Trial and errors - New ideas take time to germinate and evolve.
Understand the skills - What do they know, how did these skills develop and why?

Including Persons with Disabilities

The conversation around diversity and inclusion is incomplete without the inclusion of people with disabilities in the workforce. Bengaluru-based software solutions provider Mindtree not only employs persons with disabilities, but it has also initiated several welfare programmes. The Mindtree Foundation states helping people with disabilities as its most important charter.

However, organisations such as Mindtree are rare, because for many companies, diversity and inclusion policies do not include employing 15 per cent of the world's population of people with disabilities. Further, disability is invariably restricted to hiring, and there are seldom any efforts made on skilling people for the jobs they can do, or modifying job roles to meet the capabilities of people with disabilities. According to Arman Ali of National Centre for Promotion of Employment for Disabled People (NCPEDP), 'Sometimes companies exclude people unknowingly by following mechanical recruitment processes. For example, when companies reject resumes solely on the ground of qualifications (rather than looking more closely at skills and capabilities), the result is exclusion.'

What is needed is a holistic conversation on people with disabilities to make organisations aware of their actions and the steps needed to bring grassroots level changes. NCPEDP instituted the Helen Keller Awards in 1999 as a result of the findings of a survey conducted wherein the results showed that the average percentage of employment of people with disabilities was 0.54 per cent in the public sector and 0.28 per cent in the private sector. While the situation has improved to some extent in terms of private companies, only 34 lakh of the 1.35 crore people with disabilities in the employable age have a job in India, taking the unemployment rate to more than 70 per cent.[24]. Also, only a few sectors employ these people. For instance, a meagre 0.6–1 per cent of the IT sector workforce comprises of people with disabilities. This indicates that inclusive employment opportunities, even after so many years, remain limited to a few sectors and geographies.

The pandemic has further worsened the situation with job losses across the board and work from home situations which may not work well for everyone. 26.8 million people with disabilities (PWD) in India are being overlooked during the pandemic recovery, stuck at home without therapy or social programmes, and struggling to book COVID-19 vaccinations. PWD are disproportionately affected by COVID-19 and suffer a higher mortality rate than the general population.

A research conducted by NCPEDP and Oxfam talks of six important steps that companies need to take to build an inclusive workforce:

- Creating an inclusive culture by building awareness in employees about their colleagues with special needs
- Upskilling and reskilling employees with disabilities on an ongoing basis
- Building a pipeline of potential employees through skill development programmes
- Mapping skills of people with different types of disabilities with job roles

- Creating special budgets to help employees with disabilities
- Helping people with disabilities solve problems related to travel, access and special tools

Providing access to technology and knowledge

Knowledge can be a great advantage. But this also means that people who don't have this knowledge or don't have the ability to access it can be at a significant disadvantage. Knowledge and digital inclusion is now interlinked as the internet is everywhere. We are connected through our devices with permanent flows of information all around us. Technology is needed for everything—remote working, ecommerce, online classes for kids, delivery of essential public services, digital finance that includes basic banking, mobile money, e-wallets, crowdfunding, alternative credit scoring, and cross-border remittances. The digitally disadvantaged, either because of lack of access, language issues or literacy, face huge, disproportionate challenges. There are other challenges too such as the challenge of partial information, fake news, search engines favouring certain types of results and so on. Wherever information access is partial, denied or incorrect, it gives rise to inequality.

Technology is changing society

Since the time the printing press was invented, or even the wheel, technological innovation has always lead to higher growth, an improvement in the quality of life and better jobs. For instance, in 1830, it took 250–300 hours for a farmer to produce a hundred bushels of wheat. By 1975, with large tractors and combines, a farmer could produce a hundred bushels of wheat in only three to four hours. Technology therefore helped produce more crops while keeping the cost of inputs such as seeds, water, electricity under control. The Green Revolution undertaken by the Indian government in the seventies using new technology helped generate surplus crops that were distributed to the poor, improving their life span, better health enabled them to work more. Also, the farmers made more money, which they invested in buying more goods and services, educating their children better and improving their quality of life.

The vast majority of people in almost all countries rely solely on the value of their labour to sustain themselves as the number of people who have capital assets is very small. The earlier technologies complemented labour. This continued during the early days of computing as well. For instance, word processors, spreadsheets and databases helped office workers do their jobs more efficiently and this led to a boom in the services economy as things like accounting, office services could be done faster and more efficiently. But the new technologies that consist of artificial intelligence, robotics and machine learning are different. These technologies can substitute labour. Advancing artificial intelligence and robotics is devaluing that labour because technology is going to be able to do a lot of the routine, repetitive, predictable type of jobs and tasks that people are now paid to do.

Technological progress is also showing no signs of halting. In fact, 5G will only accelerate this shift. 5G isn't just able to transport more data at much faster data transfer rates than 4G, it will support a huge number of devices at the same time in a specific range with a connection density that is about 500 times as high as 4G. This will bring instantaneous high-powered connectivity to billions of devices and enable real time services, new business models and almost instant interactions. For instance, it can facilitate holographic conference calls, instant access to medical treatment, reliably connecting patients and doctors all over the globe. 5G will enable richer, smarter and more convenient living and working, new jobs will therefore emerge, but others may decline. The spread of automation is already changing the face of India's manufacturing. Robots are far more visible in manufacturing plants, and as a result, the number of people needed are fewer and time to market faster. Take the case of Thermax, L&T, Ashok Leyland, Mahindra and Mahindra[25] who have traditionally been large employers. Their factories are now increasingly being automated, resulting in fewer jobs and at the same time, new skills are needed to manage this automation.

Workers will now need to be skilled to meet the challenges that digital disruption will bring. The digitally included will be able to pick up new skills faster and will be able to access knowledge on an ongoing basis. Dr Shefaly Yogendra, on UK Research & Innovation's AI Review external advisory group, said, 'There is understandable fear of automation related job losses. What history tells us is that jobs change. Some jobs that exist today will not exist tomorrow, but new jobs will be created. This means the real challenge is re-skilling and constant learning and easy access to ways to update skills.' Automation therefore is likely to change the very fabric of society. [26]

Digital inclusion

The measures taken to tackle the COVID-19 pandemic placed digitally excluded people in a precarious situation. The marginalised sections of society, the elderly and the differently abled did not have access to digital devices or the required skills to use digital technologies. It is proving to be particularly challenging for such people to access essential services, which rapidly moved online. Children were unable to join digital classes, the elderly struggled to use e-commerce apps to get groceries and medicines and more.

Digital inclusion is also complicated by gender issues. In 2012, a study in a semi-urban area found that mobile phones were largely owned by men in small income homes. In most of these homes, both husbands and wives were daily wagers, doing a variety of jobs in an industrial hub near Delhi. As part of a social experiment free mobile phones were given to the women. The women were trained to use the phones and the phone interface was converted into the local language, Hindi. Within two months another survey was conducted which found that almost 90 per cent of the phones had been taken away by brothers, sons or husbands. Even though the phones helped women get information about jobs and helped them stay connected, the men felt that giving them a phone was futile for social reasons. In some cases, they even sold off their phones. Globally, in 2019, only 48 per cent of women used the Internet, compared to 58 per cent of men; this gender gap ranges from 3 per cent in developed countries, to 43 per cent in less developed countries.[27] Digital technologies and the Internet offer 'leapfrog' opportunities and empower women and girls by building their confidence, increasing their economic power and independence, and improving access to knowledge. The digital gender gap is thwarting opportunities and risks and exacerbating inequalities between men and women.[28]

Given the intrinsic interconnectedness between the digital divide and existing socio-economic inequality, it is imperative to enhance efforts to promote digital inclusion. The United Nations Secretary-General António Guterres has put forward a comprehensive and holistic vision towards achieving this in his Roadmap for Digital Cooperation.[29] This includes five sets of recommendations on how the international community could work together to optimise the use of digital technologies and mitigate the risks:

1. Build an inclusive digital economy and society;
2. Develop human and institutional capacity;
3. Protect human rights and human agency;
4. Promote digital trust, security and stability;
5. Foster global digital cooperation.

We need a plan to include the disadvantaged, the people who will be left out. Technology will reinforce inequality by twisting information access and creating a parallel reality. Fake news is one example of that. Interested parties with terabytes of data can practice micro-targeting to achieve their purposes. In many parts of the world such as Latin America and Africa, large parts have no access to broadband. And it is not only about access. In the UK alone, over 12 million adults lack digital skills to manage the digital world. Access to technology is not the only answer to bringing equity, it is equally about education and empowerment.

Artificial Intelligence (AI) and emerging digital challenges

There is a joke going around in social media asking people the question as to—who was responsible for the digital transformation of their organisation—the CEO, CFO, CTO or the COVID-19 pandemic. And the answer was the pandemic, which accelerated the digital transformation of a few years into a few months. This digital transformation cut across industries, consumer types and demographics and appears to be here to stay. While the outcomes will vary significantly by industry, a few common themes are emerging across sectors and raising responsibility and ethical questions.

In April 2019, Google dissolved its external advisory board designed to monitor its use of artificial intelligence (AI).[30] The advisory board included a number of prominent academics in diverse fields ranging from AI, philosophy, psychology and robotics. It also included some members with controversial views on various topics. After a public outcry against the belief systems of some board members, the board was disbanded. So, why did Google need to form this advisory board? Possibly because AI-based decision making has many nuances that are not entirely black and white. With AI becoming pervasive, businesses, communities and governments will use it to automate tasks, take decisions and optimise resources. In everyday life, we take decisions based on many things such as our moral values, rules and regulations in a region and domain and belief systems. When decisions are made by humans, many of these factors play a role in deciding what to do. When decision-making is done by machines, algorithms are created that help define situations and the machine's responses. Moreover, the machine needs to learn from these situations and continuously redefine the algorithm, just as we do in everyday work. While everyone seems to know about AI playing chess and self-driving cars, there are many more uses, both good and bad. AI-based systems can be used to strengthen airport security by recognising faces and suspicious behaviour. It can help scan medical records and identify problem areas as well as suggest medication and interventions. In fact, the largest users of AI are now the mining and the agricultural sectors.

A lot of what AI can do depends on how it is used and how it is designed. For instance, while China is the world leader in facial recognition technology, the country is using it to monitor and target its ethnic minorities.[31] AI can also generate fake news, fake videos and imitate human voice. Computer games, apps and websites can be made more addictive and manipulative. Scientists have argued that a goals-driven system like AI which is taught to maximise revenue and increase compliance would increasingly become more and more efficient and therefore less empathetic and more controlling. This means that business responsibility will also include issues around the design of algorithms. Experts warn that the frameworks governing AI need to be capable of ensuring accountability over the long term. What may seem unbiased and ethical could develop unconscious biases over time and replicate them to scale. Efficiencies and optimisation is great when you want machines to run in a certain way. But within AI it has different connotations. For instance, to improve commercial outcomes, the AI system may sack employees or indulge in unethical practices. Recently, a company stated that it wanted to aggregate health data of all school children in India. While that's a laudable ambition, one could correspondingly ask, 'What is the consent mechanism used to aggregate kids data? How will the data be used? Who will you give it to? What other data sets will you use for your machine learning algorithm over time? How secure will that be?'

The important question is that at what stage do you get a sense that safeguards are in place? Mostly people have not been blindsided by AI. They have been blindsided because safeguards have not been put in at the right time and AI was not closely monitored. The European Union brought into force the General Data Protection Regulation (GDPR) in 2019[32]. GDPR requires that companies rethink the way they approach data privacy. They need to ask customers explicitly to opt in to receive information. Consent must be granted in a 'freely given, specific, informed, and unambiguous' way through a 'clear affirmative action'. As the regulation states, 'silence, pre-ticked boxes or inactivity should not therefore constitute consent'. Then, there is the 'right to be forgotten'. Under this concept, codified in the GDPR, personal data must be erased when the data is no longer needed for its original purpose, when the data subject has withdrawn his or her consent, or when the data no longer complies with the regulation. The GDPR and India's draft privacy laws are only a beginning to rein in malpractices and dubious techniques. We need to be aware that in the game of marketing, intent matters more than the tool. So, while monitoring data is key, who will regulate the people who use this data? As artificial intelligence and deep learning become pervasive, we will need to be more vigilant towards digital technologies. Algorithms only reflect the biases and the intentions of the creators, and we need to balance the ability to do something with the ethics of should we be allowing this at all?

Data beyond borders: The growing footprint of the corporation that transcends geographical boundaries means that ground rules too need a refresh or a new articulation. Data and infrastructure that extends beyond social and national boundaries cannot be left hanging. Data is the new oil is a capitalist's statement. Data for good is a social intent. There should be a societal contract around data and very large companies must factor in intent, rapid change, the changing role of government and oversight. In a data-driven world, if trust holds the key to everything, what does it really mean to see that you 'trust' the company with your data? Also with several companies launching satellites, our data could now literally be residing in space, without any kind of oversight from regulators and governments. Whom then do we trust? As you read this there are about 2,000 satellites orbiting above our heads, and apart from an occasional glimpse in the night sky, they're pretty much invisible. But they have become a huge part of everyday life on Earth. By 2025 as many as 1,100 satellites could be launching each year—up from 365 in 2018. Just one project, SpaceX's ambitious Starlink, aims to fly 12,000 small satellites by 2027. This and similar projects aren't just crowding the skies—they're delivering a host of technological upgrades meant to improve life.

Brain Stimulation and Genetic Modification: There is a growing belief that improving memory and attention is possible through interfaces and stimulation. Simultaneously, there is growing concern about the possible impact of this research and experimentation. Should there be some kind of oversight, or should we let people do whatever they want to their brains or genes? What about parents who let their children use such a device in the hopes of boosting their grades?

The datafication of children: Ultrasound photos on Facebook and live updates from the delivery room mean children now have digital footprints before they're even born. And because any data that can be hacked will be hacked, we have already seen children and their families being blackmailed for money as a result. The FBI recently warned that kids are at risk in schools as hackers have already stolen academic and behavioural data from thousands of schools. What does this mean for your child's future, especially in an era when background checks are ubiquitous and all knowing?

Behavioural Analysis through digital and mixed reality interfaces: More institutions are now using hand-eye coordination, the angle at which you hold your device, finger pressure, hand tremors, navigation patterns, and other hand movements to judge whether you're really you when you log into an app. We all want to be protected from hackers, but we might also want to think about how this information is being collected, stored, and used. What is the individual's response to such large scale analysis and, in some cases, without the person fully understanding the implications?

Genetic Modification: DARPA's Insect Allies Project has been around for a while, the goal is to create genetically modified insects that can deliver viruses to plants. The viruses deliver new genes to the plants in an effort to make them more resistant to climate change and human interference. But it's easy to argue that they can just as easily be used to decimate crops and wipe out the food supply of millions of people.

To build equity, we first need to build trust

The last decade was the age of connections enabled by social media platforms, collaboration via cloud computing and enablement of distributed work via the gig economy. The next decade will be different.

As the pandemic and economic crises have laid bare the inequalities in our societies, three themes have consistently emerged in discussions about the post pandemic recovery. First, how can we create an inclusive society. Second, the urgent need to rebuild a sustainable and livable planet. Third, the need to build trust. The urgent necessity to address these three important areas will transform society and business. To manage these transitions and emerge on top will require a deeper understanding of trends and strategies that can unlock newer opportunities. Some of the emerging trends reflect the need for economic aspirations, a need for better living and new frameworks to build trust.

Everything about our economy is based on trust. Scientific enquiry and the values upon which science rests, sustain democratic systems. Democracy prospers only when it encourages vigorous debate based on 'reason, coherent argument, rigorous standards of evidence and honesty'. It is no coincidence that it is the most populist, often authoritarian, leaders who think they can do without expert input, relying instead, purely on emotional appeal. However, managing the pandemic has also heighted the importance of building trust. Should we wear a mask? Should children go to school? Should we socially distance? These, and a thousand other questions emerged when the pandemic struck. The response of countries, people and businesses rested on how much they trusted the emerging news and information from governments and experts. At the begining of the pandemic, in certain parts of the world, epidemiologists after being discredited or dismissed as superfluous, later on became leading faces in the fight against the pandemic.

Information is now produced and distributed as much by major tech companies and the networks they create as it is by TV or newspapers. News has proliferated over the past decade and so has fake information. Increasingly people have lost faith in experts, instead several have switched to believing people in their own social network. This has led to some radical shifts with groups believing that climate change is a conspiracy and more. The London School of Economics Truth, Trust and Technology (T3) Commission deals with the crisis in public information.[33] Their report said that 'trust' was socially constructed. It is a product of our economic and political environment and current circumstances.

The massive scale and multifaceted effects of the pandemic have caused a significant reversal of this trend. It has drawn attention to the need for scientists, doctors, epidemiologists, economists and experts of every type. Results from both Germany and the UK suggest that public trust in science and researchers appears to have soared during the coronavirus pandemic. The proportion of Germans who said that they trust science and research 'wholeheartedly' shot up to 36 per cent in mid-April 2020.[34] This is four times the proportion recorded in the same survey in 2019. An overwhelming eight in ten respondents said that political decisions should be based on scientific evidence. Similarly in the UK, a survey commissioned by the Open Knowledge Foundation, found that nearly two-thirds of respondents said the pandemic had made them more likely to listen to expert advice from qualified scientists and researchers.[35] This is a significant about turn from the last few years when trust in experts had dropped significantly.

Similarly, climate science has also been beset by fake news that has boded ill for the move towards a carbon free transition. For instance, at the end of 2019 the raging Australian bushfires led to a massive debate. One side believed the primary cause of the fires to be the climate crisis which created the conditions for the devastation. The other side believed the primary cause of the fires was arson, perhaps even by climate activists looking to dial up fear around climate change. Misleading data even made its way into the British parliament, prompting a group of scientists to write, 'The claim that arson is a primary cause of this season's bushfires has been comprehensively debunked: fire officers report that the majority of blazes were started by dry lightning storms. Nevertheless, social media is awash with false claims about the role of arson, obscuring the link between climate change and bushfires.'[36]

At the simplest level, trust is a contract of faith between two parties. The individual shares information with a company that then provides access to information and services. At one level, there is a barter between the company and the individual where both parties trade in information. The individual knowingly or unknowingly gives the company access to data about themselves and trusts that the information shared will not be used to harm the owner of the information. The software platform or company gives access to information or a platform with the belief that it will be used appropriately. The more a person uses the software or platform, the more information they end up sharing and then the relationship becomes an unequal one after a point where the company knows more and more about how the person operates and how they can be influenced. The flow of information between the company and its customers and the company's ability to use it implies a deeper more fundamental relationship at work: the one of trust. The world in 2030 will see the proliferation of artificial intelligence and connected devices.[37] Businesses will automate complicated tasks, reduce production costs and reach new markets. Continued growth in internet access will further accelerate change.

Since business is part of society, business needs to be part of the solution to stay relevant and build trust. Proactively shaping critical societal issues and helping address the many things that are important can strengthen the social contract between business and society. In the modern world trust is the new currency, and equity the by-product.

To create a world that is free, fair and inclusive we need to bridge the gender and the knowledge divide through trust. Hence, we need more than just long-term policy decisions, behaviour change and business transformation to create a better world. We need a philosophical core that helps people lead better lives while we create a new economy. A vision for a better world where trust is the currency of change, is the need of the hour.

7

GREEN JOBS FOR A GREEN ECONOMY

TO ASSUME THAT THE PRIVATE SECTOR'S ESG-BASED EFFORTS ALONE will solve the problems of social justice, inequality and environmental degradation is at best, wishful thinking and at worst, delusional. This is because we need two additional components to start enabling the massive change that is needed. The first is that the financial markets, the most important part of the global economic system, need to start factoring environmental issues into decision making and further, they need to start financing the change if they don't already do so. Second, public policy across the world needs to enable the transition towards sustainable markets[1] that account for carbon, social factors and the enabling building blocks such as innovation, R&D and the removal of perverse subsidies. This needs to be done while keeping three core principles in mind: playing the long game, looking at proactive responsibility rather than just fixing the current problems, and lastly by creating global networks that enable public good.

This holistic change can also be termed as the transition towards a green economy. A green economy is defined as low-carbon, resource-efficient and socially inclusive. In a green economy, growth in employment and income are driven by public and private investment into such economic activities, infrastructure and assets that allow reduced carbon emissions and pollution, enhanced energy and resource efficiency, prevention of the loss of biodiversity and ecosystem services.[2] Such a shift won't be easy, because it will need a fundamental redesign of finance, policy, business, governance and energy.

Green technology transition

Across the world, the move to clean energy is the number one priority for everyone as it accounts for 55 per cent of global emissions. However, meeting climate targets will also require tackling the remaining 45 per cent of emissions associated with making products. This is because the shift towards net zero needs new forms of energy and therefore new skills. These skills will relate to emerging areas such as hydrogen and carbon capture but many of them will also be about deploying clean energy into existing sectors. For instance, architects and environmental consultants will need new skills when creating low energy buildings. Similarly, electricians now need to be taught how to install and maintain solar panels in homes or set up a solar water pump in villages. Petrol pump attendants will need to understand how electric charging stations for EVs work.

By the end of 2020, around 800 municipal governments across the world had in place regulatory policies, fiscal and financial incentives, as well as indirect support policies which enable the uptake of renewables in buildings and transport city-wide. In some cases, city targets and policies are more ambitious than those set by higher levels of government. The implication is a huge shift in jobs and skills.[3]

The Sundarbans, a designated world UNESCO heritage site, is an archipelago of 102 islands located in the state of West Bengal in eastern India, in the Ganges Delta, stretching into southern Bangladesh. It forms the largest estuarine mangrove forest in the world and is also home to the Royal Bengal tiger. As the frequency and intensity of extreme weather events are expected to increase in the future, it is very important to conserve the mangroves of the Sundarbans. At the same time, about 4 million people live in the Sunderbans and need livelihoods to support themselves; they therefore need energy too. However, it is difficult to provide grid electricity in many parts of this ecologically sensitive and hard-to-reach region. In 2015, when the World Wildlife Fund reached out to Schneider Electric Foundation[4] programme with this problem, the company's engineers proposed that they provide solar-powered electricity to 1000 households through micro-solar power stations. A community solar microgrid is a small energy system planned, designed and installed to provide reliable and clean energy for vital community facilities and assets within a defined area.

In 2020, when one of the decade's severest cyclones, Amphan, hit West Bengal and Bangladesh, it breached embankments, uprooted trees, and destroyed homes, tearing electric poles, snapping wires and plunged major parts of the Sundarbans into darkness. However, the Satjelia Island in the Sundarbans with approximately 8,293 households stood out as an exception where the community solar microgrids set up by WWF India in partnership with Schneider Electric held the fort and continued to serve communities in an important life-supporting way. The standalone solar PV systems/micro grids proved to be a viable option for sustainable energy solutions for island-based communities in the Sundarbans.

After Schneider Electric Foundation provided lighting in homes, the local community came to them with another big problem, the one of reducing human–tiger conflict. The local villagers need land to eke out their livelihoods as woodcutters, fisherfolk, honey gatherers, leaves and grass gatherers. As the population of humans has increased, so has encroachment on land that the tigers hunt in. The foundation then collaborated with several NGOs to create local home-run business opportunities and wealth creation. Solar lights were installed along the village areas bordering the forests and this has prevented tigers straying into villages. The latest estimation of tiger numbers in the Indian Sunderbans indicates an increase in the population of big cats and a big improvement in the health and wellbeing of the local community.

While clean energy has been a great solution for people and the planet, the biggest reason for this project's success has been the way the local community worked together to manage energy requirements.

Schneider Electric Foundation trained local people as electricians with the necessary skills in managing the solar installations. According to Abhimanyu Sahu, Director, Schneider Electric and CEO, Schneider Electric India Foundation, 'Energy is life, and new age energy skills are the key to creating a transformative rural landscape.'

Ten broad areas of economic activity will make a significant contribution to the net zero transition.

Photovoltaic solar is one of the cheapest and most scalable renewable energy technologies available today. Its applications range from grid-scale generation through to individual panels and everything in between.

Wind energy provides clean, sustainable and predictable energy at scale. This at-scale deployment has quickly brought down costs and enabled new innovations that drive up efficiency and reduce maintenance. Offshore wind is an excellent choice for large-scale renewable energy generation.

Hydrogen can be converted to various forms of energy, such as power, heat and transport fuels. It has a wide range of potential decarbonisation uses across the whole energy system—in electricity storage, industry, residential and commercial heat and transport.

Carbon Capture, Utilisation and Storage (CCUS) offers a sustainable solution to dealing with significant GHG emissions. Through mechanical, chemical or other means, carbon can be captured from a range of industrial processes and energy generation plants before reaching the atmosphere. This carbon can then be used in other processes or stored in geological formations.

Bioenergy is renewable energy derived from biomass. The energy in biomass can be converted to transport fuels, heat, power or gas; making bioenergy a flexible energy resource. Furthermore, bioenergy has great potential to produce negative carbon emissions when used in combination with carbon capture and storage technologies.

Energy from waste is a highly scalable solution to two problems—managing residual waste and generating sustainable energy. There are technologies that can address all types of waste ranging from agricultural by-products to household waste, generating electricity, heat and biofuels. The size of the facility can be adapted to everything from individual farm waste management to grid-scale electricity generation.

Smart grid technologies allow for the more efficient and automated running of electrical grid systems at any scale. A range of baseload and intermittent generation technologies can be integrated and managed as an integral system, alongside demand side response mechanisms, automated fault location, management, remote monitoring and operation. With integrated storage, smart grid technologies and services can significantly improve the stability, reliability and quality of any electrical grid system.

Agri Tech offers a broad range of technologies, innovations and approaches that help increase agricultural output whilst using less resources and having a lower environmental impact.

EVs and green transport technologies are picking up. Transport is a large contributor to global GHG emissions. Technologies to compete with internal combustion engines are increasing and include Battery Electric Vehicles, Plug-in Hybrid Vehicles and Hybrid Electric Vehicles. Costs for these new technologies are also falling, making them viable alternatives.

Energy-efficient buildings and construction can result in lower operating costs and reducing the carbon footprint, benefitting all structures from domestic dwellings to large-scale commercial facilities. Smart technologies can take these benefits even further.

Building back better with Green Jobs

The pandemic has devastated the world of work, causing massive human suffering and laying bare the extreme vulnerability of many millions of workers and enterprises.

The global COVID-19 pandemic has caused unprecedented job losses and economic uncertainty. Estimates say that 300 million people across the world will likely fall into poverty.[5] While social media has been abuzz with memes that say, 'we are all in this together', the reality is that the rich have managed during the lockdowns far better than the poor, who had no place to stay and no regular supply of food. Reports have repeatedly pointed out that for millions of poor people, the spectre of hunger is a far greater threat than the fear of an illness due to a virus. In normal circumstances, with no financial reserves to fall back on, all it takes is a small misfortune—an accident or an illness—to tip people into destitution. Mostly such disasters are visited upon individuals and their families but remain invisible to the larger world. It took an unprecedented calamity to give us an undeniable demonstration of the precarious existence of millions of migrants in urban India. This is not just India's story but that of almost every poor citizen who depended on daily earnings to eke out a living. With factories and stores shut and desolate roads there are no opportunities to earn or work harder to recover what has been lost.

No work means no pay and no food.

The current and potential impacts of COVID-19 in less developed countries highlights the inequality between wealthier and poorer nations, as well as inequalities within less developed countries. Latin America is arguably the most unequal region in the world; many people there live in overcrowded conditions, sometimes lack sufficient access to handwashing facilities, and are vulnerable to the virus's spread. In Latin America, Africa and parts of Asia, many people work in the informal economy, with no protections if they are sick or told to stay at home. Many cannot afford access to health care. In countries like India, migrant workforce and daily wagers who have been hard hit by the absence of money and a complete loss of dignity are worried too. The pandemic-related lockdowns led to food shortages and a mass exodus at the borders of big cities.

In general, developed countries are better equipped to manage the pandemic, but COVID-19 has nonetheless reinforced inequalities within developed countries too. In Europe and the US, the less affluent often have a reduced ability to work from home and practice social distancing. Many essential workers—including custodial staff, grocery clerks, delivery workers, and some health care workers—are dependent on hourly wages, must work and, therefore, are more exposed to the virus. Many self-employed and gig economy workers who lacked paid sick leave were the first to be laid off in the pandemic. The pandemic has also highlighted other inequalities, such as unequal access to the internet, which limits people's ability to work from home and take part in distance learning.

Various thought leaders and experts across the world are now calling on governments to make policy changes that can speed up the efforts to adapt to the imperatives of climate change. One such initiative is the Global Commission on Adaptation (see Figure 7.1).[6] It is led by Ban Ki-moon, Bill Gates and Kristalina Georgieva, and includes 35 Commissioners and 23 convening countries. The Global Commission on Adaptation has called for accelerated progress in seven areas: locally-led adaptation, urban resilience, water resources management, social safety nets, food security, nature-based solutions and disaster prevention. These recommendations align with and

FIGURE 7.1

ACCELERATED PROGRESS IN SEVEN AREAS

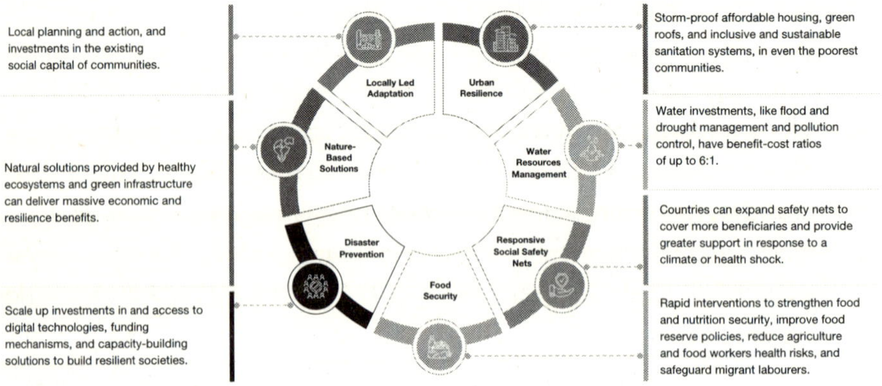

Local planning and action, and investments in the existing social capital of communities.
Natural solutions provided by healthy ecosystems and green infrastructure can deliver massive economic and resilience benefits.
Scale up investments in and access to digital technologies, funding mechanisms, and capacity-building solutions to build resilient societies.
Locally Led Adaptation
Urban Resilience
Nature-Based Solutions
Water Resources Management
Disaster Prevention
Responsive Social Safety Nets
Food Security
Storm-proof affordable housing, green roofs, and inclusive and sustainable sanitation systems, in even the poorest communities.
Water investments, like flood and drought management and pollution control, have benefit-cost ratios of up to 6:1.
Countries can expand safety nets to cover more beneficiaries and provide greater support in response to a climate or health shock.
Rapid interventions to strengthen food and nutrition security, improve food reserve policies, reduce agriculture and food workers health risks, and safeguard migrant labourers.

Source: The Global Commission on Adaptation

support internationally agreed frameworks, including the 2030 Agenda for Sustainable Development, the Paris Agreement on climate change, and the Sendai Framework on Disaster Risk Reduction, while prioritising an equitable and resilient recovery.

As governments and businesses look to stimulate growth, a new study found that net zero solutions can create 395 million jobs by 2030—jobs that have a direct, positive impact on the planet traditionally involve renewable energy, electric transport, energy efficiency or nature conservation. But right now, as more sectors transition to low-carbon models, every job has the potential to become 'green'. As per the ILO, green jobs are jobs that contribute to preserving or restoring the environment, be they in traditional sectors such as manufacturing and construction, or in new, emerging green sectors such as renewable energy and energy efficiency.[7] Green jobs, according to the ILO, help:

- Improve energy and raw materials efficiency
- Limit GHG emissions
- Minimise waste and pollution
- Protect and restore ecosystems
- Support adaptation to the effects of climate change

There are active efforts from governments and policy makers all across the world to transition to a green economy and incentivise the ecosystem to create green jobs. A green economy, built around sustainability, will enable environmental stability and financial growth. Seizing these opportunities will need a workforce with the right skills so that business is in the strongest position possible to take advantage of opportunities in the future. Governments can do the following things to set the framework for a green economy:

1. **Measure the right things, set the right targets:** Governments can set bold targets for social and environmental progress, and adopt new measures to track how well the economy is delivering them.
2. **Align incentives to support better outcomes:** Governments can use regulation and fiscal policy to pursue environmental and social goals and support sustainable business models.
3. **Drive socially useful innovation:** Governments can use every opportunity to create drivers and incentives for innovation aligned with core sustainability goals, and should exemplify and enable sustainable business.
4. **Create green jobs:** The shift from the coal, oil and gas-led economies will need a huge reskilling of the workforce that can work with technologies based on renewables and zero waste.

India's Green Transition

For economies struggling with the shocks caused by the COVID-19 crisis there is an urgent need to move towards the path of recovery. However, the economic recovery must be durable and resilient, a return to 'business as usual' and environmentally destructive investment patterns and activities must be avoided. On World Environment Day 2020, global institutions[8] working on development, labour and environment united around key actions for spurring a green, just and transformative recovery. They released a statement that highlighted the importance of a green recovery from the COVID crisis. A just transition is one that leaves no one behind, upholds human rights, protects the most vulnerable in our societies and creates new, green jobs. Underpinning these principles is the recognition that the participation of all stakeholders is core to a transformative recovery and the diverse visions, values and priorities of women, youth, and indigenous peoples are considered.

While India has been on a steady growth trajectory, the pandemic has impacted its ambition to be a $10 trillion economy by 2030. Given the limited resources of a developing economy, integrating principles of green recovery can ensure that growth and environmental protection, can both be addressed. The focus needs to be on priority sectors that can be good for the economy as well as for the environment.

Clean Energy

The move towards decarbonisation through clean energy is changing the way companies and people look at energy. People are installing solar panels on rooftops, thereby reducing the need for accessing coal-based power from the grid. Improvements in storage technologies and lowering prices of solar panels will induce more people towards rooftop power generation. There is a growing trend globally toward 'electrifying everything', from cars, buses and trains to food production, heating and air conditioning—using electricity instead of fossil fuel to power their uses. But electrification of all sectors will see an increased demand for electricity unless it is matched with efficient use and electricity from renewable sources. Energy optimisation means using less energy in existing environments, but also means managing demand efficiently and switching to green fuels.

- Energy Efficiency: Expanding energy savings primarily in existing buildings and homes[9]
- Demand Response: Helping customers to use energy in concert with a dynamic power grid
- Fuel Switching: Stop burning fossil fuels indoors and switching to electricity

India has set itself an ambitious target of 175GW of renewable energy by 2022 and has raised the 2030 ambition by committing to having 450GW of installed capacity.[10] 60 per cent of India's energy generation is likely to come from renewable and non-fossil fuel sources by 2030.

A growing economy needs energy. India's energy sector and its extensive grid network is the backbone of the Indian economy. This now needs an upgrade so that the rapidly scaling renewable energy infrastructure can be integrated. The current model of regional and national grids is likely to be replaced by individual ownership and local and micro-grids.

FIGURE 7.2

THE SKILLS TRANSITION

Clean Energy	New Skills needed
Offgrid energy	Microgrid installation, servicing and monitoring
Energy management	Installation of wind and solar energy solutions e.g. solar water pumps
Conversion / Retrofit to renewables	Power quality monitoring
Energy Storage	Understanding current systems
Storage (battery)	Installation and Maintenance
Battery recycling	Handling and recycling of lead-acid, Lithium Ion Batteries

Managing demand and supply gaps will be crucial, and technologies like smart metering, blockchain and artificial intelligence will be required to ensure the balance between demand and supply. During the transition phase (from fossil fuels to renewables) extreme care needs to be taken to ensure that disruptions do not occur.

The Clean Energy transition consisting of a decentralised model of renewable energy and a rapid acceleration towards the target of 160GW can create more than a million jobs by 2022. Jobs in the energy sector can actually be doubled by 2030, should India continue on this trajectory. The estimates for job creation through this sector are even more impressive if one looks at the 2050 horizon. Up to 3.5 million people can be employed in the Indian power sector by 2050 and more than 3.2 million people can be employed in the renewable energy sector by 2050 (see Figure 7.2).[11]

Electric Mobility

Apart from business operations, transportation is another significant contributor to climate change. Hence, across the world, we see a growing impetus on moving towards e-mobility which utilises clean energy. In India too, we find that the industry is taking some steps in this important sector which contributes to half of the manufacturing GDP and seven per cent of the overall GDP in India. The Indian government has formulated the National Electric Mobility Mission Plan 2020 and the Automotive Mission Plan 2026. These provide the vision and roadmap for faster adoption of electric vehicles and their manufacturing in the country so that by 2030, 30 per cent of cars on Indian roads are electric. A vehicle scrappage policy has also been formulated.

From our study of leading auto and component makers in the country, we find that over the last five years, companies have been undertaking research and development of EVs of all kinds—two-wheelers to commercial buses. For instance, Tata Motors is developing a hybrid version of passenger cars, in addition to working on an electric bus. Collaborative projects and interesting partnerships are also emerging. Mahindra deployed EVs in partnership with on-demand ridesharing company Uber in Hyderabad. Wipro, a member of EV100, encourages its employees to use EVs and has launched corporate vehicle ownership, lease programmes and installed charging points across all its major facilities in India. Foreign investment is also picking up in this sector as companies like Tesla and Ather Energy have announced plans to set up EV manufacturing facilities in India.

Charging infrastructure is slowly expanding in the country with leading public energy and utility companies, viz. BPCL, HPCL, IOCL, NTPC and Power Grid setting up EV charging facilities at their retail outlets across India. NTPC's charging infrastructure has provision for battery swapping too. Amongst the private companies, Tata Power and Cisco Systems India offer charging infrastructure. The former has expanded its EV mobility infrastructure across the country adding sixty-five charging points in eight cities. The company has also tied up with HPCL, IGL and IOCL for setting up commercial-scale EV charging stations at retail outlets and other locations across the country. Separately, BHEL has developed a 50 kW DC fast charger for EVs to address the wayside charging infrastructure business.

The automotive sector currently employs over 35 million of India's workforce both directly and indirectly, attesting to the huge footprint it has in livelihood creation. By giving an impetus to Electric Vehicle manufacturing, use and infrastructure, India is creating jobs too. The Ministry of Skill Development and Entrepreneurship is preparing a programme to provide adequate manpower to the electric mobility industry. The blueprint for EV-based skills aims at generating 10 million jobs. This consists of re-skilling existing workers.[12]

Green Cities

The coronavirus pandemic was an unprecedented global challenge for both health and economic well-being. In India, about 40 per cent of the urban population lives in informal housing. These are the only areas where most service providers of our economy can afford to live. It appears that practising distancing for service takers and service providers are not the same, with it being the city's responsibility to provide for all.

Today, everyone talks about social distancing as a key to break the spread of the disease. However, is social distancing affordable? Millions who make the urban ecosystem tick, live as squatters, in dense lanes and single rooms. Dense settlements like these, the world over, have been COVID-19 hotspots. Delhi alone has around 3,000 such settlements, housing 5.8 million people. Despite drastic steps taken during the early stages of the outbreak, a large section of people tested positive in Delhi and an assessment revealed 73 per cent of the 84 identified containment zones were in dense settlements.

Space, traffic, pollution, that were a city's concern for decades, have taken on a new dimension now. People also don't want to use public transport because of the fear of the spread of disease. Hence, personal transportation has now picked up. This is unsustainable as it will again lead to congestion and poor air quality which are terrible for human health. Cities therefore need to be designed keeping in mind open spaces, affordable housing for all and the ability to earn a living within a 15-minute walking distance. Other ideas to improve the quality of life in cities centre around promoting urban farming and improving energy and resource management.

Urban redesign can therefore yield jobs, improvement in quality of life and better health. Sameh Wahba, Global Director for the World Bank's Urban, Disaster Risk Management, Resilience and Land Global Practice says, 'If urban areas are where COVID-19 impacts have been the most severe, it also means that interventions in cities and towns can have the biggest impact. Cities are vulnerable to climate shocks and produce an outsized share of carbon emissions. But that also means they are the key to climate sustainability and where green investments will have the biggest outcomes.'[13]

Preserving the environment

Land degradation is one of the most significant contemporary environmental issues facing India today. As a result of this there are multiple first-, second- and even third-order effects that occur. Land loses the ability to grow food, biodiversity is impacted and this increases migration and poverty. Protection of our most valuable ecosystems, which provide habitat resilience as well as carbon sequestration, needs to be an important priority. Today, every dollar spent on restoring the landscape has the potential to generate at least $9 in economic benefits. In the US alone, ecological restoration is a $9.5 billion industry, employing 126,000 people and indirectly generating $15 billion and another 95,000 jobs.[14]

Thriving forests can benefit agriculture by helping control erosion, improving the quality of soil, water and air, preventing landslides, preserving biodiversity, reviving pastures, recharging aquifers, and providing food, fodder and medicines. They can therefore provide livelihoods to rural and tribal populations. Similarly, forests can benefit cities too. India has launched a scheme that aims to create urban forest cover in 200 cities across the country.

Lakes and canals can be rehabilitated to increase natural cleansing of polluted water while also recharging groundwater aquifers. Such an integrated approach can create new jobs and at the same time improve quality of life. Climate change is fundamentally about water. In 2020, while Chennai was praying for rain, Mumbai was facing a deluge. As discussed in the earlier chapters, India's ground water situation is dire. Twenty-one Indian urban communities, including Delhi, Bengaluru and Hyderabad are probably going to run out of groundwater in the next few years. Water harvesting and consequently groundwater revival, are critical to ensuring water security.

India is also home to 21 of the world's 30 most polluted cities. The pandemic has unequivocally shown that human activity causes air pollution and not just geography. Air pollution cleared up in all Indian cities during the 2020 lockdown, but if we continue to produce, consume and power our lives the way we do right now, food shortages, water scarcity and the quality of the air we breathe, all of them will worsen. Alongside the technological revolution, what we need is an equally unprecedented cultural revolution in the way we connect with the planet. Since clean air and good health are directly correlated, a number of opportunities are opening up in measuring, monitoring and improving air quality.

While governments play a critical part in the attainment of sustainable development, the extensive capabilities of the private sector—particularly in relation to technology development and technology transfer—also have a key role in preserving the environment. Industry is developing technologies to restore, protect, and manage natural ecosystems. These are also advancing rapidly with the help of machine learning, Big Data, 5G, 3D printing, IoT and many more technologies that are taking centre stage. These technologies help us in guiding the green recovery in the following ways:

- **Connect** better and faster
- **Provide traceability** so that interventions can be targeted
- **Predict better** by using AI's capability to analyse big data
- **Monitor & Track** the world around us
- **Augment** human abilities
- **Optimise** scarce resources to reduce our footprint

Technology can play a powerful role in preserving natural systems and protecting them from damage (see Figure 7.3). Remote sensing technologies, IoT, blockchain have an important role to play. WRI has developed Global Forest Watch, an online forest monitoring and alert system that uses crowdsourcing, to allow anyone to create custom maps, analyse forest trends, subscribe to alerts, or download data for their local area or the entire world. The WWF in Australia, Fiji and New Zealand has attempted to stamp out illegal fishing and slave labour in the tuna fishing industry using blockchain technology. 'From bait to plate', the advances in blockchain technology can help consumers track the entire journey of their tuna—and potentially other agricultural commodities and fish—revolutionising systems of certification and traceability. We can also use satellite data and cost-effective GPS tracking devices to 'see' and understand global fishing and global vessel traffic.[15]

Bridging the skills divide

In times of great shifts, perspectives change and so do processes and systems. This is in part, because of necessity and partly because of a re-prioritisation of what matters more. To navigate this new world of shifting priorities and systems, new skills are needed. The methods of imparting knowledge also need to scale and adapt to new realities. Pushed by the new realities, businesses are going digital at an unprecedented rate. They are also prioritising safety, remote monitoring and digital knowledge. The nature of jobs is therefore changing. For instance, infrastructure and construction sectors won't just need electricians, masons and plumbers, they will also need operators who can fly a drone to monitor the project site. Project managers will need staff who can take the temperature of the workers and add it into the health and safety mobile app. Basic knowledge of data entry, scanning, digital photography and remote maintenance will be needed.

Pushed by the new realities, businesses are going digital at an unprecedented rate. They are also prioritising safety, remote monitoring and digital knowledge. The nature of jobs is therefore changing. The pandemic and resulting shocks have caused years of progress in moving towards digital technologies to happen within months.

This has also meant that for people to get back to work, new skills are needed. While countries have launched skills initiatives and companies have spoken about the need for new skills, nothing quite matches up to the scale of actual requirements.

The pandemic has accelerated the shift towards online learning in the education system. Schools and colleges have almost instantly moved to e-learning, while the vocational skills environment needs to catch up. Getting people together to learn vocational skills for any sector mostly involves classroom training and practical application of the learned skill. But how do you teach new skills in a post COVID-19 world, which needs social distancing, safety precautions and constant monitoring?

Microsoft is launching a global skills initiative aimed at bringing more digital skills to 25 million people worldwide. This initiative will bring together every part of the company, combining existing and new resources from LinkedIn, GitHub, and Microsoft.[16] Over the next five years, Microsoft estimates that the global workforce can absorb around 149 million new

FIGURE 7.3

NEW SKILLS AND TECHNOLOGY FOR PRESERVING THE ENVIRONMENT

	Technology	New Skills needed
Air Quality	• Air quality monitoring in cities and various external locations • Air purification devices • Monitoring air quality data in Smart Buildings • Linking air quality data to Digital Apps and wearable devices • Air quality monitoring to preserve biodiversity • Air quality monitoring in seed banks, healthcare	• Installation of IOT sensors and devices • Monitoring IOT sensors and devices • Maintaining IOT sensors and Devices • Using Mobile Apps via smartphone / tabs • Understanding maps • Imaging
Water	• Smart Water systems • Water ATMs • Water conservation structures • Water quality management and testing • Water leakages	• Installation of IOT sensors and devices • Monitoring IOT sensors • Maintaining IOT sensors • Using Mobile Apps • Smart Metering • Reporting on water quality
Biodiversity, wildlife and natural systems management	• Utilising Real-time Data to Stop Deforestation • Tracking wildlife • Early warning systems for flooding, landslides or avalanche hazards in mountain areas	• Data analysis • Systems understanding • Installation of devices • Flying drones for monitoring, search and mapping

Source: Collated by authors

technology-oriented jobs. Software development accounts for the largest single share of this forecast, but roles in related fields like data analysis, cybersecurity, and privacy protection are also poised to grow substantially. Microsoft's skilling project will be grounded in three areas of activity:

(1) The use of data to identify in-demand jobs and the skills needed to fill them;
(2) Free access to learning paths and content to help people develop the skills these positions require;
(3) Low-cost certifications and free job-seeking tools to help people who develop these skills pursue new jobs.

Navigating these challenges requires a collaborative approach across the public, private, and non-profit sectors which the Microsoft initiative seeks to address by giving grants to various non-profits and involving other stakeholders. In these dark times, the Microsoft initiative offers a ray of hope to people across the world who are seeing jobs disappear and don't have the funds to adapt to the rapidly changing, digitising work environment. This is how responsibility is done at scale. But the world needs more than just one company teaching digital skills. The ways of imparting knowledge needs to scale and adapt to new realities. E-learning is possible when people have smart phones, great connectivity and curriculum that adapts to digital. In India, vocational skills such as plumbing, wiring, carpentry and masonry are largely done by people who don't have this kind of technology access nor the money to afford it.

However, with unemployment at an all-time high and industry wanting workers with different or enhanced capabilities, this is the time to scale skilling infrastructure in the country and rapidly match it to industry needs. KPMG's COVID-19 skills sector impact report speaks of reprioritising the skills sector and technology interventions for continuous learning.[17] Says Debabrata Ghosh, Director of KPMG India's Education and Skill Practice, 'We need to re-examine skilling from the lens of effective learning, evaluation and monitoring. Simply translating classroom curriculum assumes that learners are ready to learn online, the learning will be effective and that teachers know what needs to be done. We need significantly more efforts than that!'

The digital transformation of vocational skilling is now the need of the hour. This digital transformation can give us the opportunity to scale current efforts into something that can be useful and just the thing that millions of unemployed Indians need, to skill fast, get certified and reach employers who need their skills. But we need to do this in a methodical, innovative way while understanding three clear things.

First, for digital skilling, we first need to think digital inclusion.

Digital inclusion at one level means helping people with the digital hardware such as access to phones, electricity, data access and delivery. Stipends given to trainees under government schemes and in private institutions need to include device and data access for the duration of the vocational training. In addition, programmes need to be mindful of accessibility best practices for special needs trainees.

Second, training needs to be done with relevant content and in local languages.

Classroom learning enables the instructor to modify courses in local languages or dialects. Digital can enable this at scale, but efforts are needed to get away from the 'English only' mindset of those developing the content. Digital content in the language of the customer or the trainee is actually the need of the hour. Teachers themselves need to be reskilled even as they deliver something very different for a new world.

Third, effective use of digital tools.

Digital learning is not about setting up Zoom classes or PowerPoint presentations. It is far more than that. Using simplistic, software-driven approaches can lead to digitisation of content but may fail to actually teach anything. We need research that examines the multifaceted digital tools that can be used to enhance learning. When should videos be used? When should simulators be used? When should assessments be done? We need to move from omnibus terms like Augmented Reality (AR) and Virtual Reality (VR) towards simulation labs and learning platforms that help people learn well.

In this fast changing world, we need the skills sector to pivot fast for the jobs that are just around the corner and the methodologies to best deliver what is needed. Accelerated learning, quick turnarounds and deep insight from the various business sectors can have a transformational impact. Green jobs linked to digital skills could benefit both the economy and the environment, and include everything from alternative fuels to tasty foods. However, significant work needs to be done at the policy level to enable new kinds of jobs that are good for people and the planet.

8

BRANDS WE TRUST

CLIMATE DISCLOSURES AND STRINGENT ESG COMPLIANCES IS WHAT lies ahead for the big companies the world over. While the EU has been leading the way, there have been interesting developments in the US, New Zealand, Russia and India as well. This shift is being led by public policy, disclosure requirements, compliances and investor requirements. 57 per cent of investors in the Asia-Pacific region expect to have incorporated ESG issues into their investment analysis and decision-processes by the end of 2021. 36 per cent want social issues to comprise a larger proportion of the mix in 2021.[1] Sustainable business practices are no longer niche. As they break into mainstream markets, brands will need to find new ways to compete, and to demonstrate their sustainable credentials. Broad claims about being green aren't enough anymore.

Customers want responsible brands

There are also shifts happening in customer expectations. Studies across the world reveal a clear, unmet consumer demand for sustainable products. Consumers also want to know what they can do to alleviate the impact of their choices on the environment. In fashion, consumers are looking for increased transparency in supply chains, while at the same time demanding seamless fulfilment from mobile shopping to drone delivery[2]. In other consumer categories too, more than two-thirds of respondents consider sustainability when making a purchase and are willing to pay more for sustainable products.[3] For instance, in Singapore sustainability is a key concern for customers as four out of five consumers say they care about the environment. A third of consumers would make most purchasing decisions based on product sustainability and environmental impact.[4] Similar consumer trends exist in India too within certain socio-economic profiles.

Shifting consumer values are leading to growth in newer markets, innovative new products and emerging categories. Etihad Airways piloted its first Greenliner flight to test eco-friendly initiatives in support of sustainable aviation. These consist of a variety of measures to reduce waste and offset emissions and will subsequently include offering guests carbon offset options for their journey.[5] Zara has created the Join Life label which has the most sustainable raw materials and/or processes.[6] Canadian entrepreneurs Mike Medicoff and Damien Vince have created a toothpaste that comes in the form of a tablet called the Change Toothpaste to eliminate the plastic waste generated from toothpaste tubes. Colgate-Palmolive has launched recyclable toothpaste tubes.

Companies are therefore shifting their mindsets and ambitions to re-invent who they are and what they offer. Only by fundamentally rethinking what kind of business they are in, can they thrive in a low-carbon future. Once this shift has been adopted, organisations are either transforming existing product portfolios or creating new ones. 'Sustainable brands' are emerging that take the promise of responsibility to customers. Sustainable packaging, environmentally friendly and healthy ingredients, responsible supply chains, cruelty free formulations with no animal testing are just some of the product attributes that are being built into the brand. One such initiative has been by GHCL's textile division.[7] Incorporated in 1983, GHCL is a well-diversified group operating in chemicals, textiles, and consumer products segments. GHCL's target customers were largely young millennials, who were concerned about the environment. A dipstick survey[8] found that they wanted to contribute to creating a better environment by negating the effects of climate change, further they wanted quality, originality and constant improvement in products. Hence, innovation was the name of the game.

GHCL produced a range of bedding products under the brand name Rekoop. Rekoop bedding was made by recycling PET[9] bottles into an eco-friendly polyester fibre. The polyester fibre was manufactured by Reliance and was then spun by GHCL into yarn and processed into ultra-soft fabric.

The bedding made from this fabric was sustainable and free of any hazardous chemicals. The biggest problem stemmed around building trust. How could a customer be certain that Rekoop was actually made out of recycled PET? Traceability of the fibre, from the beginning to the end, was crucial to inculcate loyalty and trust among buyers.

Fortunately, technology helped solve the issues with traceability. In order to authenticate that the bedding came from recycled fibre, molecular tagging was undertaken. Applied DNA Sciences, Inc. is a provider of molecular technologies that enables supply chain security, anti-counterfeiting and anti-theft technology. For instance, through this technology one can tag, test, and track the originally recycled PET (polyester) fibre from the place of origin to the point of sale. This inherent traceability 'signature' is introduced at the stage when the polyester pellets are produced. The customers then have the power to verify that the material is safe and authentic.

The Rekoop brand campaign spoke of two prominent product features: (a) use of recycled PET bottles to produce yarn, providing it with a sustainable status; and (b) molecular tagging to certify the sustainable nature of the bedding. However, when Rekoop was launched, and the company felt proud about its contributions to the environment, it was surprised by the reactions from many online bloggers. The critics maintained that there was no big deal in using recycled plastic in a bedsheet, if it went back as waste after thirty to fifty washes. Once it was discarded, unlike the PET bottle, it couldn't be reused. So, the only thing that GHCL achieved through its process was to postpone the inevitable.

Clearly, recycling was not an end in itself. It was only one step in the right direction. The company had to close the recycling loop. For this GHCL spoke to a Japanese company that had the technology to de-polymerise the polyester from blended fabrics. The polyester could then be reused again, and the cycle could go on. The plastic would never enter the waste chain again. Obviously, this threw up a new challenge—how would the company collect used bedspreads from the consumers from all across the world? GHCL managers then started talking to global retailers to figure out ways so that the used products could be returned through a viable and practical mechanism.

Just like GHCL, any company can innovate to be more sustainable either by transforming an existing brand, or creating a new brand for a select category or business model. Sustainable behaviour that is both good for the planet and consumers is a challenge which may take time to work its way through. But the implication is that brands need to have a wider sense of responsibility.

Brand purpose needs to do much more

Typical marketing strategies consist of online, outdoor, print and television campaigns to create mass demand, and thus economies of scale for manufacturers and lower prices for consumers. If one were to ask for the most iconic marketing campaigns of all time, Nike, De Beers and Bajaj Scooters brands would most definitely feature as favourites. Nike's 'Just Do It' campaign was launched in 1998 and is still working wonders thirty years on![10] De Beers, a Diamond is Forever, has been running for over seventy years! Bajaj Scooters, Hamara Bajaj campaign convinced Indians to buy two-wheelers and is still remembered after thirty years.

And therein lies the power of marketing! Brands and the values they represent have had a lasting impression hence marketers are powerful influencers of consumption patterns. Over time, marketing has been blamed for creating the consumption economy, where customers buy an unending array of products they may or may not need. Other observers have also pointed to the exploitation of human emotions that has remained a strong force in the creative departments of advertising agencies. It's easy to cite examples of ads that play upon fear, sexuality, pride, and social acceptance. When ads are analysed in this way, we need to think whether they just mirror society or manipulate it?

One of the most important findings from a recent research is the fact that brand trust is one of the biggest considerations for consumers when making a purchase. About 85 per cent say that the ability to trust a brand to do what is right can be a deciding factor or deal-breaker.[11] However, customers, trust in brands is dipping. Most don't really believe the advertisements they see or the claims made by marketers unless they see real, on ground action. Glamorous advertising, lip service to feel-good causes are now being called out for what they are: the playbook to win awards, get great PR and book celebrities. This is why marketers and advertisers are doubling down on the belief that a successful brand requires an overarching brand purpose. What it essentially means is that by aligning a company with a social cause or a pressing environmental concern, a company can aspire to a higher standard than a traditional brand mission or brand positioning.

Hero MotoCorp sells two-wheelers whose primary function is to take people from one place to another. Yet, two-wheelers also feature predominantly in accidents. India's road network is the second longest in the world. Its transport sector is the key to its economic growth. Urban centres are congested, and the road network is constantly being upgraded. At the same time, there has been a general lack of awareness among people about basic traffic rules, traffic signage and lights, and safety precautions to be taken while driving in dangerous road conditions. In India, according to the Ministry of Road Transport and Highways (Government of India), 480,652 accidents were reported, and 150,785 persons were killed in India during 2016.[12] In August 2016, timed with the Rio Olympics, Hero launched the 'Hero Come Home Safe' campaign. The campaign featured anxious family members from young children to grandparents, waiting for their loved ones to return home safe. The minute-long spot was part of a CSR initiative, 'Ride Safe India'. It was aimed at sensitising consumers by linking road safety to family bonds. The campaign generated close to 15 million views on social media platforms.

The promotional series aimed to sensitise people to safety. Although safety is intrinsic to the vehicle, by helping people drive safely it is adding to safety—a prime concern among drivers and their families. Hero MotoCorp added value to its two-wheelers by addressing safety in totality rather than just as a feature of the vehicle. It built an emotional connect between the brand and the consumer which in turn helps boost sales and increase brand loyalty. Hero's strategy to take on road safety issues hinged on behaviour change, road safety training and building awareness through media reach.

Behavioural change: This was attempted to be brought about through the creation of traffic training parks where not only adults learnt about road safety but also safety habits were inculcated in children. Children were seen as significant influencers. If a child asked the parent to wear a seat belt or wear a helmet, the parent had little option but to comply.

Formal education: This involved conducting road safety classes for children and influencers. The programme was also expanded to colleges and universities. Street plays and mobile vans where trainers travelled with audio visual equipment also featured in the campaign.

Awareness: Given that behavioural change and formal education had limited reach, the company also reached out through social media and television. Having built awareness about road safety, the company engaged in ground-level activities to give road safety a push.

Capitalism and Brands

The cornerstone of the capitalist economy has been the desire for growth and therefore more and more consumption. Successful marketing campaigns have sparked rampant and unsustainable consumption patterns. Indiscriminate consumption is not a recent phenomenon. It is arguably a by-product of our rapidly globalising world, which has made goods and services cheaper and quicker to access. This is evident in our culture of 'fast fashion' and 'disposable gadgets', with a disregard for the true environmental cost of these goods. Consumers are locked into the endless cycle of buying clothes that align with currents trends, hooked on festival deals and sales. Consumerism and over-consumerism are buzzwords today and with it comes excessive waste.

The large-scale transformation in the energy ecosystem is raising new demands on people and resources worldwide. To reach net zero we need the coming together of business, society and government, by no means an easy ask. Further, the rise of the global middle class, with roughly 3 billion new entrants between now and 2030,[13] will likely lead to an explosion of demand for goods and services and food. This growth is most likely to come from thedeveloping world—China, India, Nigeria, Indonesia, Bangladesh and a few other countries, mostly in Asia and Africa. This has major implications for climate change as this will lead to a huge spurt in emissions. To ensure that efforts to decarbonise achieve the desired results we therefore need better models of consumption and newer sustainable designs for cities, offices and homes. At the same time, the demands and aspirations of the developing world cannot be undermined. Marketing therefore needs to play a strong, positive role in defining aspirations and providing solutions to solve them.

Sadly, as we have seen in the earlier chapters, there are limits to our physical world as our resources are infinitely finite. What has been established is that excessive consumption is a big part of the problem and marketing is a big part of this trend towards heightened consumerism. Then again, if marketing can impact consumer behaviour, can it not be effectively deployed to change the here and now? We need to reinvent the way we market to consumers; marketing can't just be about getting consumers to buy more of everything!

Today, billions of people are hyper-connected to each other, allowing for an instantaneous spread of new ideas and innovations. Issues like climate change demand our immediate attention, as water and soil stress, extreme weather, pollution indices and food insecurities disrupt everyday lives. Consumers are more conscientious than ever before about what they buy, wanting to know how it was produced and who produced it. However, companies do not make it easy to discern this information and this is what needs to change as we move forward. As things stand, large corporations control the world. 'Greenwashing', where changes are made at the surface level, while they do not really impact anything, are common. For instance, barely 5 per cent of the consumer electronic brands make it easy for customers to recycle products. While most fashion brands speak of recycling as part of one-off campaigns, almost none of them make recycling a part of retail processes.[14]

One of the biggest trends in the last few years has been the one of brands addressing plastic pollution. Consumer goods companies, food and beverage, beauty, toys and every other sector that uses plastic has doubled down on reducing plastic use.

Brands move towards Zero Plastic

In August 1955, *Life* magazine published an article titled 'Throwaway Living' which celebrated the idea of mankind entering a golden age of buying products and then throwing them away when not needed.[15] Modern day life has extended this concept much further than what anyone possibly ever imagined. Single use plastics, garments, electronics and so on. Almost everything around is part of the use and throw economy. This has been aided in a large part by plastic, the miracle material that is light, versatile and easy to convert into almost anything.

Plastic production took off around 1950. Of the 9.2 billion tons of plastic that has been produced, a staggering 6.9 billion tons qualifies as waste. An astounding 6.3 billion tons has never even made it to a recycling bin![16] Plastic is being dumped carelessly on land and in rivers, and since plastic is lightweight, it gets blown by the wind, carried by the river waters and eventually washes out to the seas. 'Great garbage patches', a term coined by oceanographer Curtis Ebbesmeyer, have taken over our oceans. Of the eight garbage patches, the largest is three times the size of France, and contains some 79,000 tonnes of waste![17] Nearly half the plastic in circulation has been produced over the past fifteen years, and at this rate, we are set to hit 34 billion tons by 2050![18] What is even more alarming is that no one is clear on how long it will take for the plastic to biodegrade completely. Some estimates say 450 years and others say, never. Meanwhile, plastic waste that has reached the oceans affects nearly 700 species of marine life—either through strangulation or by the ingestion of small bits of plastic.

Most of the plastic produced is used for packaging, something that is intended to be discarded within minutes after purchase. Between all the beverage and consumer goods companies, the number of bottles, tubes and boxes produced every year is mind-boggling. What has compounded the problem is the many Stock Keeping Units (SKUs) that brands have for each product. Take the case of shampoo—besides a large size, each brand has smaller bottles as well and then to make things more convenient and affordable, there are sachets or tear-off packets that are being sold. All of these make their way to the trashcans around the world. E-commerce and online food delivery companies are culprits too, with many products being supplied with either excess packaging and/ or non-biodegradable packaging.

The river Pasig in Manila, the Philippines, was declared biologically dead in 1990, as 72,000 tons of plastic flows downstream in it every year. Efforts are now being made to revive the river. The Yamuna in Delhi faces the same fate as the Pasig. At less than eleven kilograms, India's per capita plastic consumption is nearly a tenth of the US, at 109 kilograms, but this is steadily rising and nearly half of this is single use plastic. Since India lacks an organised system for management of plastic waste, there is widespread littering across towns and now even in rural areas.

Consumers are becoming more and more aware and have started saying no to plastic. They are willing to say no to plastic straws, bring reusable bags while shopping, recycle their trash and compost their wet waste. In 2019, a group of schoolgirls in India collected all the food wrappers they generated during a two-week period. The students collected a whopping 20,244 wrappers, a majority of which could be attributed to two manufacturers. They then mailed the wrappers to the companies with a note: 'We are happy with the taste and quality of your products, but unhappy with the plastic packaging. We want to ensure a safe environment for our future generations and minimise our plastic footprint. We have decided to collect used plastic wrappers of your products and send them to you for safe disposal. Please help us savour your products without guilt, by introducing eco-friendly packaging.'

In 2016, a Greenpeace petition for a UK-wide plastic microbead ban hit 365,000 signatures in just four months. The past few years have seen protestors from the US to South Korea dump excessive plastic packaging waste back at supermarkets. Irate customers in the UK overwhelmed the postal department by mailing crisp packets back to their manufacturers as they are not recyclable. The 'no-straw' movement has seen a huge following the world over. The United Nations has declared a 'war' on single-use plastic. BBC's Blue Planet II struck an emotional chord with viewers as its series dedicated six minutes of the final episode of the series to how plastic is affecting sea life. Visuals of a helpless turtle tangled in plastic netting and an albatross dead because of shards of plastic lodged in her gut really hit home and people wanted to fix things and take action.

One of the reasons the fight for plastic has taken centre stage and overtaken even issues of climate change, is perhaps the fact that this problem is tangible and we are witnessing its ill-effects in the here and now. Awareness and exposure of the ill effects of plastic has meant there are now serious efforts to address the issue. Kenya, France, the European Union and even India are starting to ban plastics. The UK has committed its government to a twenty-five-year plan phasing out disposable packaging by 2042. India has announced that it will do the same by 2022. Alongside, corporations are exploring new ways to becoming more sustainable.

Walmart

Walmart has announced it is trying to achieve 100 per cent recyclable, reusable or compostable packaging for its private brand packaging by 2025. It will further encourage other brands that it sells to set similar goals.

Nestle

Swiss food giant Nestle has said it would invest $2.1 billion over the next five years to cut its use of virgin plastics in favour of food-grade recycled plastics.[19]

Mattel

Toy manufacturer Mattel, in its recent commitment, wants to use 100 per cent recycled, recyclable or bio-based plastic materials in its products as well as packaging by 2030.

Unilever

Food and cosmetics giant Unilever has also stated that it will cut its use of new plastic in packaging by half by 2025.[20]

But overall, large scale action is needed in several industries to make a genuine, grassroots level change. With the increased awareness of making the environment eco-friendly, renowned brands are making efforts to either stop or minimise the usage of plastic for their products. From toy manufacturers to hotels, these companies claim to be stepping up by introducing greener means for their products. The United Nations[21] has outlined a path which intends to cut plastic pollution by at least 50 per cent.

Cosmetics and the plastic clean-up

Moisturiser, foundation, shampoo, eye shadow, lipstick, aftershave, shaving creams, beard products and perfume have three things in common. They are all part of the beauty industry, use plastic as part of their packaging and have a large number of chemical ingredients. Customers on the other hand are demanding 'natural, clean, and sustainable beauty'; they are even willing to switch brands given this value proposition.

Plastic waste and chemicals that harm the environment and people are a big part of the challenges that the $532 billion beauty industry needs to solve.[22] The cut back on plastic packaging and the shift to natural ingredients is not that easy. Light, cheap and flexible plastic packing has given the industry the ability to manufacture and distribute at scale. Chemicals used in the industry perform the same purpose. The supply chains consisting of the ingredients industry and plastic packaging manufacturers are huge, complex and multi-billion dollar industries in themselves; reconfiguring them is no easy task. But this massive shift has now become essential.

Scientists calculate that the top 200 metres of ocean alone contains up to 21 million metric tons of plastic, and the beauty and personal care industry has contributed a significant amount of this plastic waste. [23] This is because a typical lipstick or eye liner is encased in plastic containers that is almost never recycled. These products reach landfills or become part of the humungous plastic waste in the oceans. Moreover, when it comes to expensive makeup and perfumes, they are often sold with external packaging consisting of layers of cellophane, plastic and cardboard in an effort to make them look premium. It is estimated that more than 120 billion units of packaging are produced every year by the global cosmetics industry, most of which are not recyclable.[24]

Some popular beauty products like make-up remover wipes are made from non-biodegradable plastic fibres. The WWF has stated that in 2018 alone, the UK was projected to make its way through 10.8 billion wet wipes and 13.2 billion cotton swabs. In fact, these wipes were creating what are called 'fatbergs' in the sewer systems, blocking passageways and causing waste to resurface! [25] Many facial or body scrubs and toothpastes have microbeads in them to add 'grit' to these products. These products were banned in the US in 2015 and completely phased out in 2017. Canada, New Zealand and the UK have followed suit. Activists are continuing to push for regulation worldwide. In addition to the plastic in the products, the packaging is wrapped in cellophane and liners to ensure that the product is sealed.

Some brands are taking a stand and becoming organic, using sustainably farmed ingredients and (mostly) plastic-free packaging. Some of these brands are Tata Harper, Farmaesthetics, RMS beauty and Lush.

Terracycle has a beauty product recycling programme, where plastic shampoo bottles, caps, lip gloss tubes, hair spray cans can be donated to be cleaned, sorted and distilled into plastic pellets to make recycled products.

Sustainable packaging is the new trend with small companies like True Botanicals, Gunilla Skin Alchemy, LOLI and large corporations like Unilever and L'Oréal are joining the bandwagon too.

In 2013, L'Oréal decided to address the core of its activity: the development of beauty products with its global sustainability programme 'Sharing Beauty With All' and announced tangible sustainability goals for 2020. At its core lay an innovative tool known as SPOT (Sustainable Product Optimisation Tool), created to assess and improve the environmental and social performance of products across all brands. Sustainability is now fully integrated into the design process of the group's new products, from the earliest stages. In 2020, L'Oréal unveiled its new sustainability programme, labelled L'Oréal for the future, which speaks of accelerating its transformation towards a model respecting planetary boundaries. The company will achieve carbon neutrality across all sites by 2025. Its plastic packaging will be sourced from bio-based or recycled sources by 2030 and there will be a 50 per cent reduction compared to 2016 per finished product in GHG emissions by 2030. L'Oréal is also allocating €150 million to address urgent social and environmental issues as well as empowering its consumers to make more sustainable choices with a Product Environmental & Social Impact Labelling mechanism, which will be progressively deployed for all the French beauty giant's brands and categories.

Some beauty brands are doing away with plastic altogether. True Botanicals and Annemarie Skin Care both use a dark brown glass instead of plastic. By keeping out sunlight, it also enables the manufacturers to use fewer preservatives. However, glass makes the product more expensive and heavy, increasing shipping costs. LOLI is one of the world's first zero-waste beauty lines, with products that are 100 per cent waterless, and packaging that is glass and post-consumer recycled cardboard.[26] Lush is promoting shampoo bars and soaps, with no packaging whatsoever! Since 2005, Lush has sold more than 41 million shampoo bars, saving 124 million plastic bottles from ever being produced.[27]

The toy industry clean-up

The global toy industry is about $90 billion in size and has thrived on the constant consumption treadmill. Most toys can't be repaired, instead they are used and discarded. Further, about 90 per cent of all toys manufactured are made of plastic.[28] A poll found that more than a quarter of parents admit to throwing away toys that are in perfect working order.[29] Discarded toys make their way to landfills and oceans. As with food, parents are starting to focus on what toys are made from and where they are being manufactured.

Acting on these concerns, the big toymakers like Lego and Hasbro are now turning green. In 2016, Lego joined the Bio Plastic Feedstock Alliance and developed prototypes of next-generation bricks made from renewable materials, more specifically, a bioplastic derived from wheat. The leaves, bushes and trees of Lego are made with plastic sourced from sugarcane. This is part of the Danish company's pledge to use sustainable materials in its products and packaging by 2030. The Lego group has joined the How2Recycle® initiative to provide customers with clear guidance on how to recycle their Lego packaging responsibly. Already 100 per cent of the paper and cardboard used in Lego products and packaging is sustainably sourced and certified by the Forest Stewardship Council. Since 2014, the company's products come in smaller boxes, saving approximately six thousand tons of cardboard a year and improving transport efficiency. The company has set a target to use sustainable alternatives to the current raw materials used for its Lego products by 2030.[30] Over the next few years Lego's parent company, Kirkbi, is investing $547 million to build a wind farm off the coast of Germany.

Hasbro recently announced new environmental sustainability goals to minimise waste, improve energy efficiency, reduce GHG emissions and conserve water at its owned and operated facilities around the world. The company will eliminate all plastic in the packaging of new products by the end of 2022. Additionally, Hasbro became the first in its industry to pilot the Higg Index, originally developed by the Sustainable Apparel Coalition, to further assess the environmental impact of its toy and game suppliers.

The toy majors have also realised that reuse, sharing and repair can prevent countless toys from reaching landfills. The LEGO® Replay initiative, encourages owners to donate their used Lego bricks to children's charities. The initiative is currently being piloted in the US. In countries like India, hand me down toys are common but many of these toys can't really be repaired and still end up reaching landfills. French association Rejoué[31] realised this and has been collecting, cleaning, repairing and reselling used toys since 2012, so far saving 300 tonnes of toys from landfills. Sustainable, recyclable and plant-based are now popular adjectives in the toy industry.

Supported by the EU's programme for the competitiveness of SMEs (COSME), ecoBirdy has launched its first collection of design furniture for kids made entirely from recycled plastic toys. Toys are made of ecothylene®, an innovative material that separates the recycled plastic by colour and gives every product an original and unique look. The best part about ecoBirdy is that it also works on educating kids about sustainability, using a storybook called *Journey To a New Life*, raising awareness on plastic waste and recycling. Children are then empowered to contribute to a more sustainable future by bringing old and unused toys for ecoBirdy to collect and turn into beautiful furniture. As of 2021, ecoBirdy has collected 55 per cent of the 25,000 kilogram recycling goal they set for themselves.

Sustainability has also entered the gaming industry. One of the most important lessons that educators can teach learners is that their choices matter, whether those are individual decisions or the solutions they support in their communities. To help students understand these crucial concepts, Minecraft: Education Edition has released the all-new 'Radical Recycling' lesson![32] This activity takes place in Sustainability City, a virtual world that gives students the chance to make their way through an epic Minecraft map as they explore recycling in a bustling urban setting.

Moving from spin to journeys that create trust

Proactively shaping critical societal issues and helping address the many things that are important can strengthen the social contract between business and society. While companies cannot solve many issues, there are others they can certainly influence. But is that all? Will anything really change? Will companies suddenly solve the climate crisis, the plastic waste crisis, inequality, poverty, data privacy and all the problems that exist? Responsible brands, responsible manufacturing and responsible strategies are now perhaps the need of the hour, but more so are the core values that drive business. Environmental and social concerns are becoming a priority—from the energy you use to power your servers, to your product's packaging, to how the people that make up your supply chain are treated—it's all about 360 degree brands.

These core values need to permeate marketing departments too. A sustainable fashion brand can't be promoting the use of fur and leather. Similarly, a brand that propounds zero waste can't be using single use plastic. If a company is talking about net zero targets, should the marketing department be sponsoring programmes and events that don't follow sustainability practices? In the case of Formula One car racing, Castrol stepped up to help the team it was sponsoring to reduce carbon emissions. The number of other companies that have done similar activities is abysmal.

To understand why Castrol did this, we need to understand its sustainability targets as well as the sport it sponsored. Castrol's sustainability strategy[33] sets out aims for 2030 to save waste, reduce carbon and improve lives. The company also provides carbon neutral offers to its customers. The brand values are in sharp contrast to the fact that car racing has a very high environmental impact. In 2018, Formula One calculated its total carbon emissions at 256,551 tonnes (not including fans' transport to races). Formula One teams fly 160,000 kms a year to test cars and compete and it was no surprise to see that 45 per cent came from the logistics of shifting freight around the world by road, air and sea and 0.7 per cent came from the emissions of the racing cars themselves. Formula One has announced plans to be carbon neutral by 2030 and is being supported by teams and sponsors. Six-time champion Lewis Hamilton has pledged to ensure his life and business activities are carbon-neutral by the end of the year. Teams are announcing carbon neutrality targets too. Castrol, the main sponsor, has worked with their team Roush Fenway Racing on its green goals as part of the sponsorship package, and the team has now been certified as carbon neutral.

Climate change is already impacting the sports we love. The Australian Tennis Open (2020) was disrupted by smoke from bush fires, the Rugby World Cup (2019) was disrupted by Pacific typhoons and there are many more such examples. By 2050, increased temperatures and increased humidity will reduce days you can play sport by half! Global sporting events are responsible for at least 0.6 per cent of global emissions—that makes it responsible for 300–350 million tonnes of carbon dioxide emissions. The carbon footprint of some sports are larger than country emissions.

Shouldn't more sports event sponsors be taking note? The same brands that talk sustainability and net zero are sponsoring and promoting entertainment, sports and promotional events that simply don't link up to the company's sustainability targets.

It is actions like these that make customers lose faith in what brands talk of. Having a brand purpose is great, but it needs to permeate all aspects of what a company does. A recent global survey revealed that if 77 per cent of all the brands in the world today ceased to exist tomorrow, no one would care.[34] Brands across categories have tried every trick in the book to not be part of that 77 per cent. As a result of this relentless pursuit to find 'meaningful' roles in consumers' lives, one of the biggest themes that emerged in the past decade is that of 'Brand Purpose'. For instance, almost every brand is now supporting a cause or an important customer concern. But as brand purpose began getting conflated with 'saving the world', marketers went down a slippery slope. Recent marketing history is littered with examples of brands hijacking 'trending' causes and social issues with superficial intent and then getting called out, hurting both brand and bottom-line in the process. Meanwhile, consumers are more suspicious than ever of businesses and their brands' lofty pledges to make the world a better place. Yet, reports across the world have found that people favourably perceive and become patrons of brands that share their values.

Our world has increasingly prioritised:

- **Scale over Quality:** Reach more people, do more things irrespective of genuine impact. How many likes do you have, rather than genuine feedback. Number of customers rather than actual revenue.
- **Speed over Trust**: How quickly can you get information out, regardless of authenticity.
- **Surveillance over Privacy**: Tracking customers without their knowledge and monetising data.

Trust is the variable that determines customer loyalty and credibility. What customers value is not the product but a trusted relationship and what 'surrounds' the product. When companies talk of their responsibility strategies to customers, investors and communities, some claims are easy to believe, others aren't. This is because companies that truly believe in their values decide to drive change in an arena which authentically aligns with what their organisation actually does and consistently drive this message. This is an important strategy that top Indian brands are adopting. When trust is broken, products quickly lose their perceived value and brands are seen as essentially equal. There are three reasons for this—Action and not just words, Repeatability and Consistency.

1. **Action and not just words:** Companies you trust don't just say the right thing, they do the right thing.
2. **Repeatability:** They also do the right thing again and again.
3. **Consistency:** They are also consistent in their behaviour.

Hence, building trust is a journey.

So what should marketers do with brand purpose in this new consumer age?

For starters, recognise that creating brands with purpose can't be an emotion inducing advertisement, it has to be something the brand actually does. Hence brand purpose doesn't just need a tag line, it needs process maps, a deep understanding of sustainability and measuring social impact (see Figure 8.1).

Understand sustainability targets

Chief Marketing Officers (CMO) are often asked, why they support a cause vis-a-vis another. But, beyond citing consumer research, most struggle to find genuine answers. Further, there have been several incidents where a company launched a big campaign promoting a social cause, but it stirred up anger and did more harm than good. Marketing therefore needs to understand that aligning yourself to environmental and social causes is not the same thing as genuine change. Whether a brand should align themselves to a cause or not needs more than consumer research. It needs granular, strategic insight about how a business generates value. For this to hit home, marketing managers need to do their homework by reading sustainability reports. They need to know the difference between terminlogies like CSR, ESG, SDG's and more.

Measuring social impact and not just 'likes'

While measuring ESG, environmental actions of companies are relatively easily measured. Measuring social and governance actions, on the other hand, are difficult and complex. This is marred by the fact that there are

FIGURE 8.1

TASKS TO BE DONE BY A COMPANY CREATING AN ESG STRATEGY

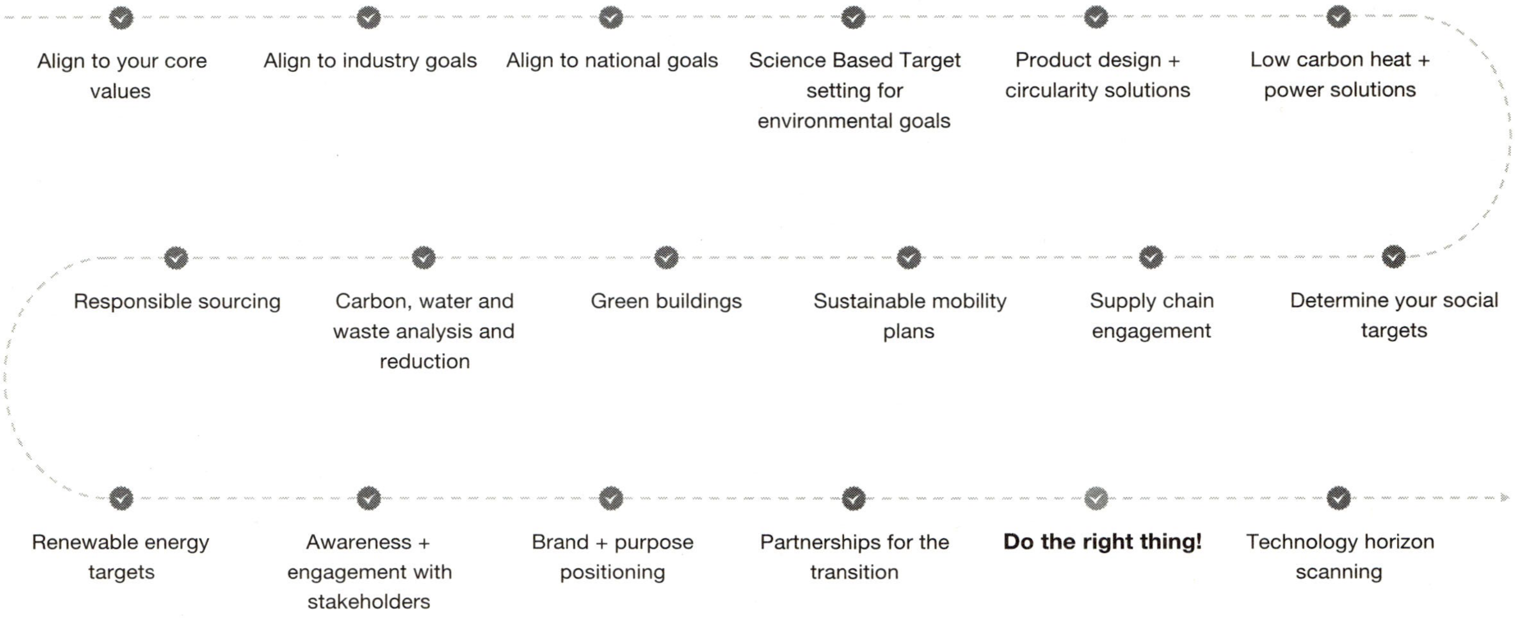

several reporting documents that, at times, don't reflect the same things. This lack of maturity makes navigation of the field complex and costly. However, the field is growing rapidly and standards are evolving. Marketing heads can also make use of reports like the Futurescape Responsible Business Rankings which reflect how top Indian companies have performed across the past few years on ESG parameters.[35]

Processes to back up the intent

When a company is started, founders typically have a point of view or a purpose in mind. Over time though, this purpose could get diminished or lost in the efforts to scale. In recent times, emerging trends are showing that trust seems to trump everything else. So, a customer, when given two brands with similar functionality and price, will pick the one they trust more. Trust however, is nebulous, and is built over time and many things contribute to it. Marketing, though, has recently started talking about brand purpose as a way of hot fixing the trust gap. The GHCL example shared earlier showcases how a brand was supported through sustainability processes, to prove the authenticity of their claims. It also highlights the fact that internal measures of sustainability may not be enough when it comes to consumer products and much more needs to be done when faced with consumer demands. Processes are therefore essential to build a brand that is trusted.

Building Trust and Traceability

Brands are adopting the low carbon economy through different approaches. Some are getting certified[36] for carbon neutrality, some are significantly transforming their product footprint and more, but others are concerned if these approaches are enough.

- How can companies be sure of the quality, origin and carbon footprint of products they are supplying if their supply chains are outsourced?
- Is anything that is produced in one country and shipped to another ever going to be carbon-neutral?
- How can companies access and transform the waste at the ends of the value chain, including end-of-life?
- How can consumers continue to have access to the products they love and yet do no damage to the environmental systems?

Large, complex and opaque supply chains means that brands don't really know what they were selling, who made it and exactly what the product contains. Traceability is a huge challenge. For instance, the provenance of a fabric very often is doubtful. Is a garment 80 per cent cotton and 20 per cent polyester, no one really knows! This is because for the longest time almost all supply chains, across industries, have relied on a paper trail to build authenticity. Certifications and certification bodies have therefore proliferated. But a paper trail authenticated via third party audits by its very nature is prone to misuse and has often proved ineffective. Only a technology-led approach, which enables materials to be tagged and traced from the farm to retail outlet, can address key social and environmental issues. There are several companies that have emerged that help in addressing this problem through a variety of technologies.

So, what can brands do? First, identify causes that are a part of the values of the company. This doesn't mean just finding a trendy issue; it means deciding to drive change in an arena which authentically aligns with what an organisation actually does. The organisation then needs to invest time and resources—and have an action plan.

And lastly, create trust metrics that need to be measured on an ongoing basis.

Setting the right targets

Terms such as ethics, CSR and sustainability have not prevented companies from behaving irresponsibly in the past. While FMCG companies have contributed to causes, they have at the same time helped in the proliferation of single use plastic. While automotive companies have talked about fuel-efficient cars, they have gone about and lied about carbon emissions. While social media platforms have made settings that expose your content only to friends, they have later changed these settings so that friends of friends could also see your content. Philanthropy, therefore, is not a cure for corporate sins, neither is creating brands that focus on social causes. For that matter, creating sustainability reports without corporate purpose just adds to the feel good factor without any genuine change.

So, should we just align everything to the SDGs and everything will be all right? Not exactly.

FIGURE 8.2

TASKS TO BE DONE FOR A COMPANY MOVING TO REDUCE CARBON EMISSIONS

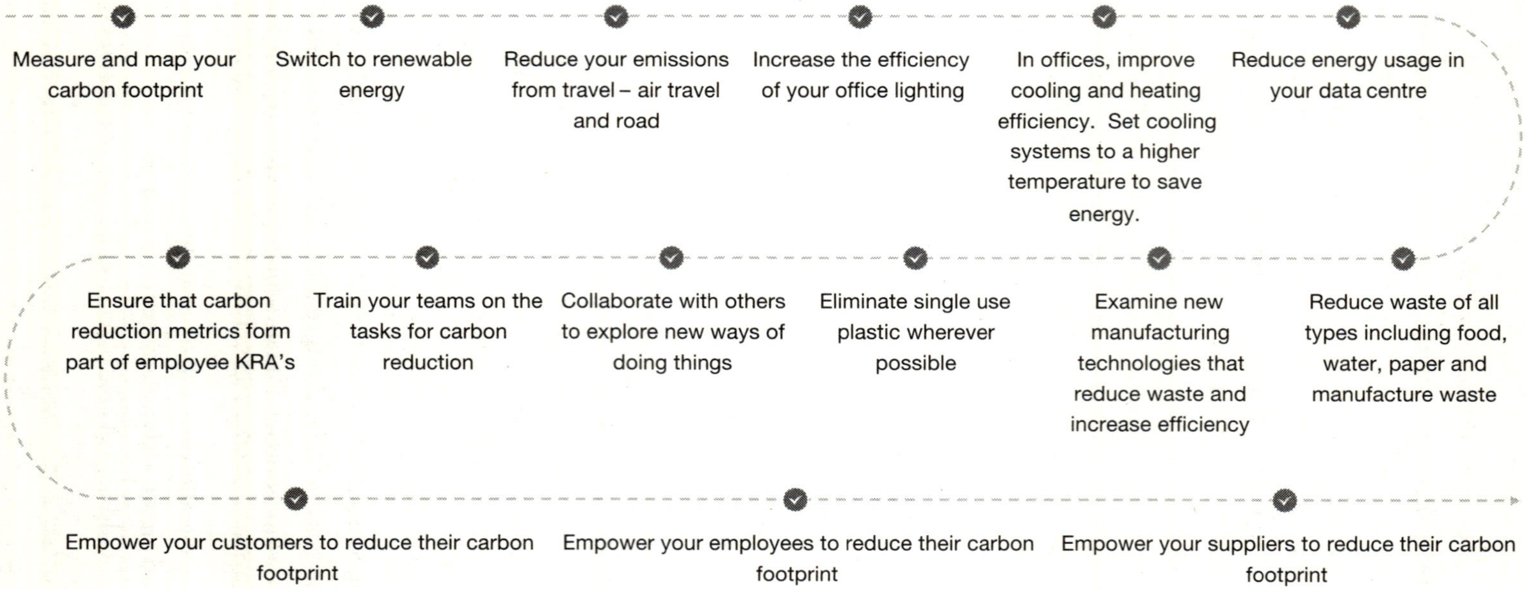
Measure and map your carbon footprint
Switch to renewable energy
Reduce your emissions from travel – air travel and road
Increase the efficiency of your office lighting
In offices, improve cooling and heating efficiency. Set cooling systems to a higher temperature to save energy.
Reduce energy usage in your data centre
Reduce waste of all types including food, water, paper and manufacture waste
Examine new manufacturing technologies that reduce waste and increase efficiency
Eliminate single use plastic wherever possible
Collaborate with others to explore new ways of doing things
Train your teams on the tasks for carbon reduction
Ensure that carbon reduction metrics form part of employee KRA's
Empower your customers to reduce their carbon footprint
Empower your employees to reduce their carbon footprint
Empower your suppliers to reduce their carbon footprint

That is because the sustainable development goals aren't economic goals. The SDGs are national ambitions and not business strategies. Organisations have a profit motive. Most companies don't have a framework that could address something like poverty, hunger or good health for all. At the same time, the way business functions impacts national goals. For instance, excessive pollution from diesel cars impacts air and thereby the well-being of people. Hence, national goals and business activities need to be aligned to achieve common goals and finance is the glue that can make this happen relatively seamlessly. On the next page, there is a checklist that could help you create a responsibility framework for your company.

Over the past few years, the climate discussion has attracted an increasing number of supporters but what has been missing is the urgency and the tools to scale up. Carbon auditing or footprinting is seen as the first step to including carbon emissions reduction in the management of supply chains. Software giants SAP and Salesforce.com and start-ups such as Tempe and Persefoni, have launched products to help firms document their emissions.

Since the impacts of these decisions are so far reaching, a move towards low carbon can then involve every aspect of the company—product design, operations, logistics, marketing, finance and everyone in between. Mapping the impact of these decisions also needs a framework that is technology enabled. This is especially true of large companies with hundreds of suppliers and consumers cutting across geographical locations (se Figure 8.2).

9

TRANSFORMATION AT SCALE

BASED ON MEASURES SUCH AS GDP, LIFESPAN AND WEALTH, LIFE has never been better for the earth's human inhabitants. Even though the pandemic has brought into stark contrast the darker side of capitalism, it has highlighted the immense power wielded by technology and how we can gather around common causes such as healthcare to scale up. At the same time, humans collectively are now changing earth systems to such an extent that it will be seen in the fossil records. This era is now being termed by scientists as the Anthropocene epoch. Microplastics everywhere, frequent wildfires and pandemics are symptoms of the Anthropocene epoch. In this era, humanity has pushed the planet to the brink of environmental collapse.[1] Climate change is amplifying the intensity and frequency of floods and wildfires and the increasing possibility of pandemics such as COVID-19. 70 per cent of cancer drugs are natural or synthetic products originally found in the environment, 75 per cent of global food crops rely on animal pollination and marine and terrestrial ecosystems sequester 60 per cent of global anthropogenic emissions. As of 2019, 25 per cent of those same animal and plant species that provide us with food and medicine are threatened and 85 per cent of wetlands that sequester emissions have been lost or altered due to human activity. To prevent these we need social and environmental change across almost every aspect of our world. To avert the climate crisis we need to reduce the amount of carbon in the atmosphere. It is a critical turning point for life on Earth.[2] Hence we must work on all aspects of the climate equation—stopping sources and supporting carbon sinks, as well as helping society achieve broader transformations. To achieve this, three things are necessary, keeping track of planetary and human health, collaboration and open data and modernising various production systems. That is, three connected areas call for action, which we must pursue globally, simultaneously, and with determination.

Keeping track of planetary health

Nature, economics and public health are intrinsically linked.[3] Scientists have warned that we could lose a quarter of all living species by 2050.[4] The annual loss of ecosystem services that nature provides to humanity over a fifty-year period, due to deforestation, amounts to an estimated $2 trillion to $4.5 trillion each year. That amounts to between two and five per cent of the world's total annual GDP. Moreover, deforestation and fragmentation of landscapes have increased the risks of the outbreak of infectious diseases like COVID-19. We need to therefore plan for a new normal involving connected and healthy forests and agricultural landscapes that could play a pivotal role in preventing future pandemics.

- Forest management can reduce risk of super fires.
- Protecting and restoring forests can reduce soil loss due to intense rain and slow down water runoff.
- Wetlands can absorb and filter flood waters.
- Watersheds can ensure regular supply of water.
- Agroforestry can prevent crop failure.
- Green spaces in cities can lower temperatures and reduce flooding.
- Mangroves, marshes and reefs can buffer costs and absorb floodwaters.

Two-and-a-half years ago, Microsoft launched the AI for Earth programme to put artificial intelligence technology into the hands of the world's leading ecologists and conservation technologists, and organisations around the world. Continuing on its journey, Microsoft has launched an ambitious programme to aggregate environmental data from around the world and put it to work in a new 'Planetary Computer'.[5] This project is over and above Microsoft's ambitious project to be carbon negative by 2030, help suppliers and customers to remove their carbon footprint and to remove all historical carbon generated by Microsoft by 2050. Microsoft has also announced a new $1 billion climate innovation fund to accelerate the global development of carbon reduction, capture, and removal technologies.

The planetary computer will monitor, model and manage Earth's natural, limited resources while tracking ecosystems and species. This will be done by aggregating environmental data contributed by individuals around the world coupled with equipment placed in water, space, land and air environments. For the first time, there will be a comprehensive compendium of international ecosystem data. Not only will this allow for essential environmental information to be readily available to individuals across the world, but the planetary computer will predict future environmental trends through machine learning design. Microsoft customers and partners can use the planetary computer's data and predictions to make eco-friendly business and personal decisions. Microsoft has pledged to use the system to take responsibility for the company's own land footprint and advocate for public policy changes.

An increasing number of funds are investing in clean energy technologies, biomimicry based solutions and more. Deep tech innovation in climate, inequality, food, health matter more than anything else. Accelerators that can speed up innovation in key sectors are being set up.

2020 saw the Cambridge Institute for Sustainability Leadership (CISL) Accelerator run two successful programmes for over fifty UK start-ups and small businesses, focussed on sustainability solutions from low carbon refrigeration to tackling hate speech and fake news on the internet. In 2021, CISL launched the Sino-UK Centre for Sustainability Innovation, enabling opportunities for collaboration in both China and the UK. From fibre modification, to circular design principles and supply chain transparency, the CISL Accelerator works with early stage start-ups and entrepreneurs with tech-driven innovations that have the potential to transform sustainability of the fashion industry. Says Eithne George, Programme Director CISL, 'Accelerators that focus on the topmost things to enable the transition hold the potential to transform sectors rapidly and globally. Hence if used well it they have the potential to help us solve many of the challenges encapsulated in the SDGs. For instance, enabling modern, regenerative agriculture, creating sustainable fashion supply chains and so on can have far reaching impact. We can also potentially make low carbon breakthroughs in manufacturing, materials and impact sectors such as healthcare, agriculture, energy, education and mobility.'

Keeping people healthy

The pandemic has highlighted that in the absence of public health an economy stands on a rocky foundation. The countries that have managed the pandemic well have managed to recover their economic growth trajectory, while others have teetered and fallen. Overflowing hospitals with limited staff and lack of equipment and confusion over what specific insurance plans will cover and what they won't. These scenarios are playing up across the world in developed countries like US and in developing ones like India. They highlight the absence of a robust public health system that can look after everyone. Over time, healthcare has been privatised and the profit motive has held sway in keeping people healthy.

Public health focuses on improving and protecting community health and well-being, with an emphasis on prevention among large groups of people. But, India spends a very small amount on healthcare, just 1 per cent of the GDP. This is one of the lowest in the world. Public health systems in India, that had already been weakened by years of neglect were unable to gear up to the pressures imposed on them when the COVID-19 surge happened in 2020 and then again in 2021.

Vaccinating the world's population against COVID-19 remains a global health priority in 2021. But it is vital that this effort does not overshadow the need to ensure that everyone, everywhere has access to basic health care. Despite ready access to technology, healthcare has largely focused on disease specific interventions. Lack of easily accessible health care has impeded the detection and monitoring of COVID-19 infections. Should another deadly virus emerge in a region with inadequate health care, the world could lose valuable time to contain the outbreak.

Companies like Axtria are realising that this is a big opportunity for change. Axtria helps companies solve several problems by using data, AI and technology. With technology becoming available, data can be tracked across the entire healthcare value chain. The value chain consisting of doctors, hospitals, patients, chemists, diagnosis and testing, and insurance companies is all becoming interconnected. What are the physicians prescribing? What diseases are more prevalent and where? Where are a company's stocks placed? How are the sales people performing? How are they reaching and educating the doctors? These are some of the questions that are now easier to answer in developed countries where data is readily available. In countries like India, where data interchange between healthcare providers is not easy and many processes are still manual, this is still a bridge to be crossed. However, rapid developments in personal care, home care and deep learning are expected to transform healthcare at scale.

Entrepreneurs with telehealth solutions have seen a massive uptake since 2020 with almost everyone who had digital access preferring video consults to in-person visits. The pursuit of value and digital ease has been pushing innovation for a half-decade and this is one trend that is likely to scale even further with the use of deep learning and machine learning start-ups coming to the fore. Some of them are addressing one of the big problems in healthcare of proactive and personalised care. Health at Scale uses a new approach for making care recommendations based on new classes of machine-learning models that work even when only small amounts of data on individual patients, providers, and treatments are available. The company is already working with health plans, insurers, and employers to match patients with doctors. It's also helping to identify people at rising risk of visiting the emergency department or being hospitalised in the future, and to predict the progression of chronic diseases.

As 2021 began, and inoculation drives for COVID 19 started across the globe, governments have realised that they need to track the patients who took the vaccines and also ensure that the vaccines are used up within the allocated time. For public health systems running on outdated tech or no tech this has been a tough ask. For instance, India's public investment in healthcare is one of the lowest in the world. As a result, there is only one government doctor for every 1,445 Indians, much lower than the WHO's prescribed norm of one doctor for 1,000 people. The availability of government beds is abysmally low with only 0.7 beds per 1,000 population.[6] This creaky health system has had to gear up fast by investing in a cloud based vaccine tacking and appointment setting mechanism. Data analytics and interoperability will play a critical role in keeping people healthy. This will be critical for general public health as it ensures accurate record keeping on individuals' relocation or changes provided before the second dose of vaccination. New interoperability rules designed to improve customers' to access their own health data will also likely be introduced.

Collaborating to succeed

Big problems need big solutions and most times, no single company or institution can make the change. AstraZeneca, the British-Swedish pharmaceutical company, has grabbed headlines of late. Its Covid vaccine has been the most administered one across the globe. AstraZeneca has always worked in partnerships of various kinds—academic, commercial, technology, and industry bodies. During the pandemic, the combination of Oxford's strong research capability and AstraZeneca's execution capability was a winning combination.

AstraZeneca's core values focus on following the science, putting patients first and doing the right thing. When it partnered with the University of Oxford in the landmark journey, these values were in focus. This helped stitch together the partnership in record time as its values matched, and they committed to ensuring that they would access as many patients across the world as possible. Gagan Singh Bedi, MD of AstraZeneca India, says, 'We were clear from the start that this was not for profit and was for equitable access.' A number of alliances also worked for this—Coalition for Epidemic Preparedness, GAVI, etc. and were supported by foundations like Gates Foundation. These partnerships ensure that the delivery of the vaccine started across the world, especially in low-income regions like West Africa. The second element of this programme was that no single producer could supply at a scale. Hence partnerships with Serum Institute in India and similar ones in Korea, Brazil, Russia, and others were established to ensure that there are enough vaccines. Finally, it was also AstraZeneca's capability in conducting trials across the world. The interesting feature of the process was that rather than proceeding sequentially, AstraZeneca proceeded parallelly. Thus trials, partnerships with producers and agreements with governments all took place simultaneously. An important element of partnership with producers was technology transfer which was complex and took almost 3-4 months. All this put AstraZeneca in a position to deliver 2.5-3 billion doses a year. The company quickly supplied vaccines to 130 countries and 400 million doses had been administered by early June. This was the most by any vaccine producer.

Similar examples are becoming common across product categories and businesses. In the fashion industry, Adidas and Allbirds, who till now were competitors have announced a first-of-its-kind collaboration to create a sneaker with the 'lowest ever carbon footprint'. In the automotive sector, EV Batteries are expected to create a massive waste management challenge as EV sales pick up. Automotive companies aren't geared to handle the reverse logistics and traditional waste recyclers don't have the expertise and equipment needed to handle the complex recycling that batteries need. The solution lies in collaboration. Which is why Veolia, Groupe Renault, and Solvay are combining their expertise to recycle the metals in electric vehicle batteries in a closed loop. Renault is contributing in this collaboration with its expertise in electric vehicle battery life cycle management, Solvay with its expertise in the chemical extraction of battery metals, and Veolia with its ten years of experience in dismantling and recycling lithium-ion batteries via a hydrometallurgical process. The three partners aim to create a secure and sustainable source of supply for cobalt, nickel and lithium. They are leveraging their respective expertise at each step of the value chain—from collection of end-of-life batteries to dismantling, metal extraction and purification—and by enhancing existing hydrometallurgical recycling processes. With Solvay and Veolia's technologies, strategic materials will be extracted and purified into high-purity material ready to be reused in new batteries, thereby reducing their environmental footprint through this closed loop. Groupe Renault, Veolia and Solvay are committed to setting up a pre-industrial demo plant in France.

The period from 2021 to 2030 will be about producing goods in different ways. As we get into the 5G world, machines will get smarter and quicker. AI and machine learning will be able to anticipate, produce and deliver products based on demand. Reverse supply chains will become an integral part of business as companies integrate into the circular economy. This will be enabled by the new generation of customers who will demand corporate action against waste and brands that care not just for their profits but causes that create a better world. Even if 'how you make things' is standardised, 'how you source' and 'how you ship' have a significant impact on your carbon emissions. Which is why knowledge sharing is so important. While there could be companies who are making radical changes, there could be others who are simply doing things differently. Making small changes to achieve significant impact. Collaboration and knowledge sharing play an important role in raising standards for a net zero world. Reducing carbon is therefore not a one-time effort, it's a journey in which erstwhile competitors can become collaborators. The Fashion Industry Charter for Climate Action[7] has Adidas, Nike and Decathlon France as signatories amongst others and the WBCSD's Tire Industry Project[8] on sustainability issues is currently comprised of eleven leading tire companies. Cross-sector partnerships are also emerging where skills and learnings in one are applied to the other. Shell and Microsoft will collaborate to create and deliver new solutions to help customers, suppliers and other businesses lower emissions.[9]

Incorporating social and environmental benefits makes brands more attractive to their consumers as they rid them of feelings of guilt when they purchase these products, but unless there is concerted action towards the cause it may just be seen as 'greenwashing'. This is impacting beauty, fashion, food, transportation and almost every category. According to the 2019 Retail and Sustainability Survey, more than two-thirds of respondents consider sustainability when making a purchase and are willing to pay more for sustainable products.[10] For consumer brands, this will mean an increased emphasis on understanding local customer needs, new materials and creation of brands with purpose. Companies will therefore need to adopt a systemic perspective to evaluate new sources of value, reverse logistics to take back products, and even collaborate with others so that one companies waste could turn into another company's resource. New value chains will emerge that will drive genuine change, beyond the buzzwords. Teams will need to be prepared for rapid and scalable changes. Companies that are able to create interdepartmental teams that can work together to solve problems will find it easier to navigate these changes. A culture that fosters creative and innovative thinking will help companies create new solutions and ensure that resources are allocated appropriately

Open Innovation and Open data

Companies spend millions on innovations that can give them an edge. These innovations are then protected through trademarks, patents and copyright. When it comes to sustainable packaging and sustainable innovation processes, companies however are open to sharing their learning. This is because, companies are now facing unlikely risks through resource scarcity and unlikely competitors through digital transformation. Open innovation helps hedge risks and controls unexpected threats to some extent.

Levi's has introduced a new technology called WaterLess to make jeans, which as the name suggests use much less water in the production process. Levi's invited twenty competitors to Eureka Innovation Lab and shared their water-saving practices with them. They also open-sourced the WaterLess® innovation for others in an effort to learn and improve.

Creating green and transparent supply chains is the need of the hour as this will result in resilience for the organisation and for the entire ecosystem. Doing this needs scale and high-quality data on impacts. Google has announced a partnership with WWF Sweden[11] to help create an environmental data platform that will enable more responsible sourcing decisions in the fashion industry. This collaboration will bring together projects from each organisation, drawing on the unique strengths of both. As mentioned in Chapter 4, the industry today accounts for 20 per cent of wastewater and 2-8 per cent of greenhouse gas emissions globally—potentially rising by as much as 50 per cent by 2030. Much of this impact occurs at the raw materials stage in the production process, where supply chains can be highly fragmented, and gathering and assessing data at scale is a challenge.

The WWF and Google partnership has been some time in the making. At the 2019 Copenhagen Fashion Summit, Google Cloud announced a pilot in collaboration with Stella McCartney[12] to use Google Cloud technology to provide a comprehensive view into raw materials of clothing manufacturers' supply chains. That work continues with Stella McCartney, whose team have been pivotal in shaping the concept of the platform and will continue as the first fashion brand to test it. WWF Sweden and long-term partner IKEA[13] created a similar tool in 2018, focused on analysing the risk and impact of various textiles raw materials.

Google and WWF Sweden will now collaborate on an updated platform leveraging all of these data types, aiming to further increase the accuracy and relevance of raw materials assessments. This new platform will also move beyond cotton and viscose as first announced, to include numerous additional raw materials based on WWF data and knowledge.

Open data is digital information that is licensed in a way that it is available to anyone. Any data or content that is free to use and distributed falls under the idea of open data. Open data can be used in many ways to drive public good, get people involved and solve big problem across boundaries—both real and virtual. There are many open data projects that have been used in the past and this trend is gathering momentum. In this alliance, Google will also provide access to Google Earth Engine data, which offers satellite imagery and geospatial data which can detect changes, map trends, and quantify differences on the Earth's surface. Google Cloud's artificial intelligence capabilities will allow it to unlock insights fast, filling fundamental data gaps that have prohibited action in this area in the past. In the project each material and sourcing location will be scored on multiple environmental issues such as water scarcity or air pollution, as well as estimating specific impacts such as greenhouse gas emissions and accounting for the 'mitigation benefits' of more sustainable sourcing options.

Hence, to build sustainability, companies need to do three important things. First, reduce the impact on the environment through direct intervention. Two, build transparency so that you know where your raw materials and supplies are coming from and to ensure that they are following the social and environmental standards that have been laid out. And third, share what you know for public good.

This is the time for the corporate world to showcase what they really stand for. Long-term horizons for public good and on-ground action will not only create resilience but companies that will stay strong in an increasingly volatile world. While the current global crisis has touched virtually every industry, retailers and shippers in particular are working overtime to pivot their operations to keep families supplied with essential goods. Green supply chains need to be part of the solution.

The transformation of food systems

The current system of producing food involves industrial farming of land, cattle and marine life. When large tracts of land are taken to grow food, trees are cut and the entire biodiversity of the area impacted. Also the long term unfettered use of fertilisers impacts the quality of soil and water. Moreover, food thus grown is shipped across the world. Each aspect of this food system is highly polluting and harmful. When cattle and oceans are farmed, the harmful impacts intensify. Cattle are a huge source of methane; in fact, if they were a country, they would be the third-largest emitter of greenhouse gases! Large-scale fishing is even more harmful and there are many parts of the world's oceans that have completely been destroyed by over fishing. It takes five times the effort to catch the same amount of fish now as it did in 1950. If the 'business as usual' approach continues, wild fish stocks will decline by 15 per cent. The UN Environment Programme's *Emissions Gap Report 2020* found that GHG emissions, including from land-use changes such as deforestation, hit a new high of 59.1 gigatonnes of CO_2 equivalent in 2019. Scientists are proposing organic and other scientific systems of farming such as precision agriculture that are less harmful. Scientists can also now produce artificially generated products that mimic the taste and texture of meat. But more than the changes in technology, small, traceable and local farming is being advocated.

A large number of apps have frequently emerged to address farmer needs around knowledge and market access. Several years ago, Futurescape[14] undertook a study to understand how technology was helping farmers. The company found that while a plethora of apps existed, their use was at best sporadic or non-existent. Not just in India, this finding was consistent across South East Asia and Africa. While the mobile phone had penetrated the rural communities, it was used mainly by farmers to stay connected. The services which technology companies had launched with much fanfare and copious amounts of funding had barely any traction. Today, five years later, the situation hasn't changed much, as most farmers as who are in dire need of support barely get any help from solutions which seemingly have been tailor-made for them. At a basic level, the farming ecosystem consists of land, seeds, equipment, irrigation, labour, finance, market access, information and some kinds of livelihood protection schemes. Most agri-tech ventures including large multinationals are broadly attempting to organise this sector by either organising and providing access to information, financing, new models and IOT solutions for soil and water management etc. The reality, though is, while the suite of services and solutions is growing, few are getting enough on ground traction. Whichever way you look at it, the situation boils down to a few fundamentals:

- **Discoverability**: Getting people in the agricultural ecosystem to become aware of what is on offer and why they need it is a discoverability challenge that needs to be surpassed in a country as diverse as India.
- **New Models**: Twenty-first-century models have moved from ownership to on demand. Explaining this to people is still a complex conversation even in the urban areas, e.g Ola versus buying a car. A trustworthy person or brand who can build confidence around the offer and ongoing services is needed.
- **Schemes**: Similarly, there are other decisions around livelihood protection schemes, market access schemes and more which need to be decoded in several ways and nuanced so that people can relate to them better.
- **Technology**: With IOT and cloud-based solutions being offered convincing the customer on the efficacy of the product or service is invariably another challenge.
- **Viability**: Many of the agri-tech companies may be startups whose own source of funds may be limited. Should the farmer sign up for the latest, greatest today with someone who may not be around tomorrow?

In other words, the customer journey map has many personas who have specific needs that can be addressed across business models. We also need to keep in mind that this is an emerging ecosystem within an increasingly fragile community. The lessons learnt from the excesses of the recent techno era need to be applied here first. We cannot afford a scorched earth situation for this community in times of climate change. While technology solutions exist, a relevant and trustworthy framework to farming needs and real-life situations is the real need of the hour.

Precision agriculture

Technological interventions in this arena can make a significant impact. Precision agriculture has emerged with tools like drones, robotics and even autonomous tractors. Using technology farmers can gain significant insight into each and every seed that has been planted. This enables them to fertilise the crops with near perfection. IoT sensors that measure and track light, humidity, temperature, soil moisture, etc., will help agriculture overcome its most serious challenges enabling farmers to support increasing population and tackle climate change. Armed with highly detailed 3D maps for soil and field analysis, drones do more than improve decision making about irrigation and crop management. Drones will do more than monitor the crops and assess their health.

Drones can help agriculture in six different ways:[15]

1. **Soil and field analysis**: Drones can map fields accurately and produce 3D maps that capture soil types. This enables the farmer to decide on crop patterns and estimate areas which need intensive care.
2. **Planting**: These systems shoot pods with seeds and plant nutrients into the soil, providing the plant all the nutrients necessary to sustain life. This greatly improves planting accuracy and reduces costs dramatically.
3. **Crop spraying**: Drones use distance-measuring equipment. Thus, drones can assess the correct height and dispense the correct amount of spray on the plants by utilising real data from the ground.
4. **Crop monitoring**: To monitor crops a farmer has to go around the field to check the crops and their health. Weather conditions may impede the inspection. Satellite images are a good option. The images need to be ordered in advance, are available only once a day and can often be unclear. Drones obviate all this. The control moves into the hands of the farmer and they can receive real-time assessment of crops.
5. **Irrigation**: Drones with sensors can identify which parts of a field are dry. They can also check if the fields need improvements. When the crops are growing, drones that can provide data that indicates the intensity of vegetation and heatmaps can indicate the health of the crop. This provides an input for the decision to irrigate the fields both in terms of quantity of water and location of water required.

6. **Health assessment**: It is critical for farmers to assess crop health. They also need to spot bacterial or fungal infections in plants. Drones carrying devices that scan crops using both visible and near-infrared light can help assess the quality of leaves in a plant. This is essential for figuring out how well the plant is doing. As soon as a sickness is discovered, farmers can apply remedies quickly and monitor the results in real time. Continuous assessments and record keeping enables the farmer to make quality insurance claims in case the crop fails.

Synthetic foods

For a long time, humans have been turning biology to their own purposes. They have reshaped crops and livestock through selective breeding and changed the biological ecosystem by moving species around. By the 1950s, we had developed an understanding of the genetic structure and scientists had started moving traits from organisms in which they evolved to organisms where they felt it could be more useful. This ability became the basis of the biotechnology industry. Today, synthetic biology is the design and construction of new biological entities such as enzymes, genetic circuits, and cells or the redesign of existing biological systems. Synthetic biology builds on the advances in molecular, cell, and systems biology and seeks to transform biology in the same way that synthesis transformed chemistry and integrated circuit design transformed computing.

So how does synthetic biology help? There are many applications. Scientists can now produce artificially generated products that mimic the taste and texture of meat. A US-based company relies on engineered microbes for bulk supplies of leghaemoglobin protein (usually found in plant roots) to create plant-based meats. Meat without livestock could in principle be a climate-friendly technology.

There are applications are in the fabric industry too. Bolt Threads[16] is harnessing proteins found in nature to create fibres and fabrics with both practical and revolutionary uses. It creates threads made of proteins from spider silk. It also creates leather from fungal mycelia. This silk would appeal to people who are worried about silkworms being boiled and skinned for their fine clothes. Designers are working to turn these materials into vegan-friendly fashions.

Synthetic biology will help us improve the taste and nutritional properties of our foods. It can create new foods like algae butter and hypoallergenic peanuts. Synthetic biology can help plants grow with less water or land, and design hypersensitive systems at the production level to keep the food we eat safer. This requires finding and eliminating potentially life-threatening bacterium in food before it hits shelves. Test kits have been developed that detect the presence of listeria while the food is still in the processing plants.

Programming biology is extremely complicated and comes with no manual. This does make it risky. Since one does not know what is being turned out the outcomes are both uncertain and, sometimes, dangerous. At the same time, they are pretty helpful too.

The emergence of new materials

The last decade was about making human-to-human connections, where we used Facebook, Twitter and other such social tools to connect with people across the world. The coming decade will be about changing the way we produce and consume things because these processes currently, across sectors, are hugely wasteful. In this context technology that does not harm the environment is critical to maintaining and improving quality of life. The role of materials that don't harm the environment is paramount in this shift. Applied Materials, has grown from a small start-up founded in Silicon Valley in 1967, into one of the world's most admired global companies. Applied is a leader in materials engineering solutions used to produce virtually every new chip and advanced display in the world. Applied Materials has a very active programme called 'Design for Environment'. The goal of this programme is to design products and services to minimise the consumption of natural resources and maximise efficiency. The team asks questions like: What design choices can we be making to optimise usage of electricity? How do we reduce emissions? How do we internally have additional steps so that the output has less impact on the environment? A new crop of materials and companies is emerging that are likely to play an important role in the circular economy.

Learning from nature

Biomimicry is the practice of looking to nature for inspiration to solve design problems in a regenerative way. Impossible materials and Spintex engineering are focusing on this. Impossible Materials uses the bright white scales on the Cyphochilus beetle's exoskeleton as the design inspiration for its more sustainable and better performing white pigment. They are looking to replace the white colourant titanium dioxide with this natural colorant. Spider silk is the strongest material in the world. Spintex Engineering has mimicked the precision of a spider's spinnerets to produce artificial spider silk for use in textiles, apparel, aerospace and automotive industries.

In recent years, there's been a contentious debate in the fashion world between the use of animal (i.e. leather and fur) and synthetic vegan materials. Some say that, while using parts of animals in order to make clothing is neither ethical nor environmentally sound, it is preferable to the plastic alternative. Others vehemently argue the opposite. This debate brings up complex issues and is not easily solvable; however, the rise in vegetable leathers is making the argument obsolete. Hermès has been working to redesign its famous Victoria Bag with a biotechnology company MycoWorks. The bag will now be made of Fine Micellium, a mushroom-based textile, into a leather-like material called Sylvania. Last year, Stella McCartney, Adidas, and Kering have partnered with BoltThreads, to produce another variation of mushroom-based leather-like materials.

Researchers from the Singapore University of Technology and Design (SUTD) have developed a novel approach to manufacture biodegradable substitutes for plastic. The team made use of the two most prevalent organic compounds on the planet: cellulose and chitin. The resulting fungal-like adhesive material(s) (FLAM) are strong, lightweight and completely sustainable, as no organic solvent or plastic is used in their production. They can be moulded or processed using common woodworking techniques, are lightweight and fully biodegradable. FLAMs are cost-effective substitutes of common filaments for 3D printing, and their manufacture is scalable. Their invention won professors Stylianos Dritsas and Javier Gomez Fernandez the innovation prize for the 2018 Purmundus 3D Printing Technology and Design competition—one of the biggest events in additive manufacturing.[17]

There are no simple answers here—we need to think deeply now, not just about the functional benefits of products, but also their impact. Professor Javier Gomez Fernandez says, 'To create a regenerative system we need to define the problem differently. Plastic bottles did not emerge because customers demanded them. They emerged because we had a material i.e. plastic, that was cheap enough, light enough and so easily available that packaging beverages in it became possible. Similarly we need to design better materials which will then on the basis of their suitability find uses.' He further proposes three important principles that are the foundations of his work:

1. **Biological materials are not energy intensive:** From the extreme toughness of bones, to the exceptional strength of silk, biology produces materials without high-energy sources.
2. **Materials for the new economy need to be readily available:** Anything made out of rare ingredients can never really be sustainable as it will need to be shipped around to different places. Hence new materials need ingredients that are readily available.
3. **Closed loops don't exist for materials that don't biodegrade:** Materials necessarily need to get absorbed back into the local environment, hence they should be biodegradable. Recycling products wastes, time, energy and resources.

Converting waste into new materials

JSW Steel, one of India's largest steel manufacturing companies has found a way of converting slag, a form of steel manufacturing waste, into sand for the construction industry. Steel can be described in general terms as iron with most of the carbon removed, to make it tougher and more ductile. Three areas dominate the use of steel: building and infrastructure, mechanical equipment and automotive. Other uses include metal products, other transport, electrical equipment and domestic appliance. India's crude steel and finished steel production increased to 108.5mt and 101.03mt in FY20, respectively making India the world's second largest producer of steel. There are many forms (grades) of steel, each with its own specific chemical composition and properties to meet the needs of the many different applications. Steel manufacturing is a complex, energy and water intensive process. It also generates a lot of waste.

The most basic yet the most essential component required for construction is sand which is used extensively in the preparation of concrete. For each ton of cement used to produce concrete, about seven tons of sand is needed. This makes sand the most-consumed natural resource on the planet besides water. Sand or fine aggregate is mined from riverbeds, banks and floodplains, as well as from lakes and seashores. To meet this ever increasing demand of sand, riverbeds and beaches are being stripped bare. This rampant extraction of sand has many negative effects on the ecosystem. Depletion of sand causes deepening of rivers and enlargement of river mouths and coastal inlets. As a result, the groundwater table in the surrounding areas drops hampering the drinking water availability. It also results in the destruction of the natural balance of aquatic life by causing river bed degradation, bed coarsening and change in the channel morphology. Due to all the harmful effects of river sand mining on ecology and aquatic lifeforms, it has already been largely phased out in many western countries but this practice is still prevalent in India. With restrictions on mining of river sand and stone crushing there has been a growing need in civil engineering fraternity for identification of alternative aggregates.

JSW has taken the lead to address the environmental concern of river sand exploitation by introducing processed granulated blast slag (PGBS) as an eco-friendly alternative. PGBS is produced by treating waste (slag) generated from steel manufacturing processes. This initiative is first of its kind in the country. When the idea of using GBS (granulated blast slag) to replace river sand in concrete was first incepted, the slag was studied for its physical and chemical properties. The team, consisting of the R&D, civil and the environment teams, through several tests confirmed that GBS is inert, non-toxic, free from traditional impurities (i.e. organic impurities, shells, clay) and is similar to an aggregate, chemically. But the challenge lay in the physical properties. Though GBS looks like sand, it does not meet the physical property requirement of the aggregate specifications and when used in civil applications has resulted in lower strengths. JSW Steel identified lesser bulk density (1000 -1100 kg/m^3) in comparison to that of river sand (1300-1600 kg/m^3), higher water absorption and lower specific gravity to be the reasons for its reduced strengths. Through several brainstorming sessions, they were able to develop an innovative processing plan for improving the physical properties.

JSW Steel extensively utilised the granulated slag in all its construction works as complete replacement of fine aggregate and in combination with crushed sandstone. Most of the concrete roads in and around the works, were made using mix of crusher dust and granulated slag or granulated slag alone as replacement of fine aggregate. JSW also utilized slag in making paver blocks and concrete blocks. This helped in spreading the awareness through contractors and visitors. Some of the customers have also started utilising the slag sand. Other steel majors have also started emulating the concept of slag processing for producing slag sand to utilise blast furnace slag generated by them. This not only aligns the steel industry with the UN Sustainable Development Goal 12: Responsible Consumption and Production through substitution of river sand for construction purposes but also promotes circular economy of slag. Many businesses are also showing interest in setting up of separate slag sand units of their own. JSW Steel has started a wave of change in the way industries deal with their waste and hopes that other players in the steel industry as well as other industries will also realize and work on the opportunity in waste.

Clean and Green Cities

In developed nations like Sweden, large quantities of particles and pollutants are removed before incinerating to ensure cleaner air. But the bulk of the world's garbage lands up in landfills. An alternative to burning or burying garbage, is composting. In the US, for instance, yard and food waste makes up 25 per cent of the waste disposed. In addition, there is organic waste that can also be composted, such as bedding made of organic fibres, clothing, wood, sawdust etc. Paper accounts for 30 per cent of municipal solid waste in the US. This shows that well over 50 per cent of the waste being generated in US can be composted. Sadly, this is not being done. India generates over 150,000 tonnes of municipal solid waste (MSW) per day, with Mumbai being the world's fifth most wasteful city. About 83 per cent of the waste is collected, but less than 30 per cent is treated. According to the World Bank, India's daily waste generation will reach 377,000 tonnes by 2025.[18]

While untreated waste is a universal problem, there are countries like South Korea that have one of the world's most sophisticated waste management systems. It has reduced MSW by 40 per cent while its nominal GDP (gross domestic product) has seen a five-fold increase. In the late 1980s, South Korea implemented a volume-based waste fee system—that focused on controlling waste generation and achieving maximum rates of recycling while simultaneously raising additional resources to finance waste management. The country has seen a huge reduction in MSW generation: from 30.6 million MT in 1990 to 19.3 million MT in 2016. South Korea is now the country with the second-highest recycling rate in the world (60 per cent) after Germany.[19] Landfill recovery projects like Nanjido have transformed hazardous waste sites into sustainable ecological attractions. In addition to welcoming 10 million visitors a year to the ecological park, the Nanjido site saves about $600,000 a year by providing landfill gas to be used as boiler fuel. The world's largest landfill, Sudokwon landfill in Incheon, is currently being converted into 'Dream Park', a leisure and environmental education centre. With the world's first landfill-powered hydrogen plant, currently over 60 per cent of new and renewable energy is produced from waste.

Concerns around waste and pollution are transforming how cities and companies are run. C40 is a network of the world's megacities committed to addressing climate change. C40 Cities connects 97 of the world's greatest cities representing 700+ million citizens and one-quarter of the global economy. These cities have taken some path-breaking steps to convert themselves into circular economies by reducing or eliminating waste and making products last longer through reuse and recycling.[20]

Online marketplace for reusing materials

Austin in USA aims to reduce landfill waste by 90 per cent by 2040, and to be net zero carbon by 2050. The city has created the Materials Marketplace platform, a cloud-based marketplace for posting, finding and exchanging unused materials. The users can post an advert listing the type of materials they are looking for, or have to discard—either giving them away for free or selling it at a proposed price. The storage and transportation of the materials is organised by the users. The types of materials typically exchanged include: construction materials, furniture pieces, decor items, office supplies, and electronics.

The world's first circular shopping centre

Eskilstuna in Sweden, wants to attract a broad target group of citizens to enable its vision of creating a circular economy. At the circular shopping centre, visitors donate reusable toys, furniture, clothes, decorative items, and electronic devices in the shopping centre's depot, called 'Returen'. In the depot, staff from Eskilstuna Municipality's resource unit sorts items into what is usable. The items are then distributed to the recycling shops in the centre. The shop staff then perform a second level sort, where they choose what they want to repair, fix up, convert, refine and ultimately sell.

Repair and service centre for electrical goods

Austria's largest independent repair and service centre for electrical goods, R.U.S.Z, is located in Vienna, Austria. The vision of R.U.S.Z is to reverse planned obsolescence and provide 'broken' products an extended life. Also, it aims to promote electrical goods as a pay-as-you-go service rather than ownership. The municipality of Vienna's department for environmental protection supports R.U.S.Z's donation programme which feeds its reuse centre. Private households, which are willing to donate their old washing machine, are supported with two thirds of the transportation costs. Many other municipal and public institutions, including the Austrian Climate and Energy Fund and federal ministries, commission R.U.S.Z as technical practitioners with scientific background and awareness raisers. The organisation has significantly expanded its reach, trainings and visibility over the past twenty years. New concepts have been introduced, such as repair cafés, where people can come in and learn how to fix their items instead of replacing them with new ones.

Trust networks across boundaries

Over half of the global economy is directly linked to natural ecosystems[21] but these very ecosystems are threatened or are already in decline.[22] We are facing a mass extinction of species on the planet as global wildlife is down by 60 per cent and reducing further. Global wetlands that purify and store water have been reduced by 87 per cent and coral reefs have declined by 50 per cent. Insect diversity and abundance has fallen dramatically and this can potentially be catastrophic as more than 75 per cent of the world's food crops are linked to the ecosystem services they provide. Natural ecosystems and wildlife need urgent help. Biodiversity and climate change are large complex problems with direct, indirect and network effects. For instance, climate change can result in higher potential evapotranspiration from soil and plants. When accompanied by stable or increased precipitation it can help in greater carbon sequestration by forests. However, climate change can also reduce or change patterns of precipitation and increase the strength of hurricanes that make landfall, causing adverse impacts on rainforests.[23] Hence, a system that can function at scale, is based on data and rooted in science is needed.

Global collaborations across countries are expected to hold the key to protecting the environment.

In 2009, US political scientist Elinor Ostrom received the Nobel Prize in Economic Sciences for her work on the management of public goods and common-pool resources.[24] What Ostrom established is that, contrary to certain grim predictions, there are numerous examples of effectively managed public goods—Nepalese forests, American lobster fisheries, community irrigation schemes in Spain and many other systems are looked after sustainably by following a combination of eight principles. Ostrom showed that groups of people can self-organise around common interests. But while these principles came into being several years back, not much has happened to them. There are several reasons for this, but an important one is that of paucity of trust. The Amazon forests for instance are in Brazil, the Himalayas cut across India, Pakistan, Nepal and parts of China, and so on. Unless there is political consensus and trust between countries not much can be achieved. Governments also don't trust private companies to look after lakes, forests and mountains, believing that a single entity could exploit them for personal gain. However, in the fight for climate, the increasing cost of inaction and the rise in devastating climate events in spurring people to act. Clearer boundaries are being defined in terms of the carbon budget needed to keep warming in check, further an increasing number of countries are making climate action enforceable by law, UK, Japan, France, Denmark, Hungary and New Zealand. This implies that companies need to seriously consider doing regular risk assessments in terms of regulatory impacts of climate regulation and the way their supply chains will get impacted. Additionally, collaborative partnerships will hold sway in an increasingly fraught series of negotiations as countries, industry groups and large companies try to minimise the financial impact of these regulatory changes.

The G7 meeting in June 2021 and its emphasis on climate change is a sign for all boards to put climate actions front and centre. The seven large economies consisting of US, UK, Canada, France, Germany, Italy, Japan have committed to a multi-year effort to meet net zero commitments and environmental objectives[25]. Steps towards this include

1. **Changing Finance:** G7 recognised the crucial importance of making finance flows consistent with a pathway towards low GHG emissions and climate-resilient development; embedding climate change and biodiversity loss considerations into economic and financial decision-making.
2. **Disclosures:** Support moving towards mandatory climate-related financial disclosures based on TCFD. Baseline global reporting standard for sustainability, which countries can further supplement.
3. **Urgent Decarbonisation:** Shift towards clean energy and doubling the efficiency of four key energy-using products sold globally by 2030: lighting, cooling, refrigeration, and motor systems.
4. **Nature Based Solutions:** Urgent action across ecosystems, including soils, grasslands, savannah, drylands, wetlands, coral reefs, rivers, lakes, coastal dunes, peatland, seagrass beds, mangroves and saltmarshes, whilst ensuring that relevant safeguards are in place.

10

AIMING HIGHER

HSBC ANNOUNCED IN 2020 THAT IT WOULD TARGET NET ZERO carbon emissions across its entire customer base latest by 2050, and provide between $750 billion and $1 trillion in financing to help clients make the transition.[1] But HSBC's shareholders were not satisfied and asked for more. Fifteen institutional investors (including Amundi, Man Group and Sarasin & Partners) with combined assets under management of $2.4 trillion filed a climate change resolution at HSBC, alongside 117 individual shareholders.[2] The resolution asked HSBC to draft and disclose a detailed roadmap to reduce its exposure to fossil fuel, on a timeline consistent with the Paris climate goals. Bowing to investor pressure, HSBC's board tabled a resolution that commits the company to phase out financing of coal-fired power and thermal coal mining by 2030 in the EU and OECD and by 2040 elsewhere.

The reasons for this are clear: simple targets and statements of intent are not enough. Investors are aware that the climate crisis is here now and unless cutting emissions is done quickly, climate risks will rise exponentially. Action for the 2030 timeline is what is urgently needed. Reducing emissions needs business model transformation and deeper insights into second order effects. The people you buy from and the people you supply to also need to be taken into consideration. To restore the climate and have a safe future, we need to maximise mitigation, adaptation and removals. The financial system holds everything together and for it to stand up and be counted it needs to go beyond intent and first order effects. To make the change we need to aim higher and achieve more than earlier imagined.

A superficial approach to ESG implies that business as usual can continue and all we need to do is to add in ESG metrics to address risks from social issues and climate change. This assumption could not be more flawed. Endless consumption and growth are in direct conflict with sustainability. A carbon price or a market mechanism only cannot solve the climate crisis and move the economic system towards a net zero framework. New ways of thinking and acting are required from all stakeholders, including individuals, business executives, social influencers and policy-makers. This is why country after country is transforming their regulatory framework and narrowing the area of operations of companies.

Germany the 4.9 trillion dollar economy will be net zero by 2045, five years earlier than otherwise planned. This is a transition that will eliminate 65 per cent emissions by 2030, 85-90 per cent by 2040 and reach net zero emissions by 2045. Germany is regarded as a global engineering powerhouse with industrial giants in automotive, mechanical engineering, chemicals, electric and electronic equipment. Decarbonising these sectors will have ripple effects across the world too in terms of net zero manufacturing, phasing out coal and investing heavily in renewables.

Russia is joining the sustainability bandwagon. The Association of Banks of Russia has approved recommendations for the implementation of ESG principles by local lenders. At the moment, 7 per cent of Russian banks already apply ESG principles in their business models, while 67 per cent are preparing for the transition to ESG banking, Additionally, Russian Green Finance Guidelines have been issued which focus on promoting private investment into projects aligned to national and international climate targets. The Moscow Stock Exchange has also created a Sustainability Sector for financing projects in the fields of environmental and social sustainability. The new sector will consist of three independent segments: green bonds, social bonds and national projects.

New Zealand has become the first country to introduce a law that will require banks, insurers and investment managers to report the impacts

of climate change on their business. This will cover the all banks with total assets of more than NZ$1 billion ($703 million), insurers with more than NZ$1 billion in total assets under management and all equity and debt issuers listed on the NZ stock exchange. This legislation is in line with the government's policy to create a net zero country. New Zealand public sector will be carbon-neutral by 2025 and will also buy only zero-emissions public transport buses.

Changes afoot in US ESG disclosures

In June 2021, the U.S. House of Representatives passed legislation that would impose new ESG due diligence and disclosure requirements on publicly traded companies. The ESG Disclosure Simplification Act of 2021 would require publicly traded companies to disclose their commitments to ensuring that environmental, social (human rights), and good governance standards (ESG) are reflected in their operations, activities, and supply chains.

The US Securities and Exchange Commission (SEC), which oversees corporate financial disclosures, is also examining transparency rules on climate risk, board diversity and workforce matters.

While several countries are now declaring net zero roadmaps, investor expectations from companies focus on roadmaps for substantive change. Country specific compliance targets are in fact lagging investor demands. In addition, the metrics of evaluation are changing and becoming more and more stringent. Investors are demanding comprehensive carbon mitigation and environmental impact roadmaps. Net zero carbon emissions take precedence over marginal improvements in reducing carbon. In September 2020, the Climate Action Steering Committee, involving more than 500 global investors with over $47 trillion in assets, sent a letter to CEOs and chairs of the board at 161 global companies calling on firms to commit to net-zero business strategies. Signals like these have prompted companies to focus on addressing their GHG footprints— a shift that is visible across several sectors. 57 per cent of APAC investors expect to have 'completely' or 'to a large extent' incorporated ESG issues into their investment analysis and decision-processes by the end of 2021.[3] The area that will have the greatest impact on investments over the next three to five years will be climate risk—31 per cent of investors, disruptive technologies, such as artificial intelligence—19 per cent of investors and sophistication of ESG measurement—14 per cent of investors.

The ESG shift necessitates new thinking

Companies and countries will now need to adjust to ESG requirements. Many of these changes seemed distant a few months back. These are now a reality. This is an opportunity to redesign and recreate a responsive and better experience that can make us healthy, happy and economically sound. But change isn't that easy. The pandemic is a live example of how difficult it is to change behaviour. Despite warnings from the scientific community, most countries were unprepared for the Coronavirus pandemic. Most people just didn't think it would happen, or didn't think it wasn't of immediate priority given the other numerous things of immediate importance. The problem is not of a country, institution or of the absence of a policy, or having enough funds alone. The issue is a deeper one. Despite repeated warnings, we simply didn't prepare ourselves for a different future!

People like to believe in the status quo and bringing about change is really tough. The pandemic lays out in plain sight the gaps in leadership, planning and execution that need to be addressed across all levels in cities, companies and countries. We also need to address the entrenched belief that technology is the solution to everything. Even things like the pandemic and climate change! Technology, innovation and vaccines haven't yet helped us get out of the pandemic. This is because the single greatest weapon in our arsenal to defeat the pandemic is behaviour change. Social distancing, masking, hygiene and cleanliness are the tools that will need to be implemented for several months more if not years, even as mass vaccinations continue. Changing the collective mindset is not an easy task. It takes time, effort and collective will to transform.

The climate crisis is fundamentally about a culture of over consumption, wasteful use of materials, poor design of everyday things that we can't seem to live without and irresponsibility. Believing that start-ups in energy, carbon capture, new materials and maybe even geoengineering will help us solve climate change is wishful thinking. Many of these technologies are in their infancy. Moreover, throwing tech-based solutions at the climate has other consequences too. Technology needs large amounts of energy to function and some technologies like AI need even more. Digital currencies consume more energy than several cities put together. Electric cars, batteries and computers need metals and minerals to manufacture and they come from vulnerable areas that need to be protected. Africa has the largest mineral reserves in the world and it also has the richest plant life, forest cover and biodiversity. For instance, bauxite is mined extensively in the beautiful Republic of Guinea, 98 per cent of which is covered in forests. Cobalt, used in phones and batteries is sourced from the Congo, its neighbour. Hence, depending on technology alone won't take us to net zero emissions if we keep consuming and wasting resources in large quantities or harming biodiversity to mine the minerals we need. For the circular economy to take firm root we need technological innovation, science and policy that enables this move and great design.

However, at this point, in addition to a blueprint of action we need the transformation of the collective and a shift in thinking to create a better world.

Shift thinking is about **mapping the change**
Shift thinking is about **defining the ambition**
Shift thinking is not about bluster, it's about **paying attention to the details**
Shift thinking is about **building trust**
Shift thinking is about **collaboration and partnerships**
Shift thinking is about **taking everyone along**

So, how does one develop shift thinking? This requires moving from logical thinking (using deductive or inductive methods) to lateral thinking (thinking non-linear creative ways). Essential to this is the process of unlearning what is ingrained in us since childhood. Shift thinking also requires a collaborative process—the ability to bring together diverse ideas and integrating them into one's thought process. Much of the decision making is built around believing that much of the future will be like the past. Shift thinking requires breaking down the blocks of the past and visualizing the future in a completely different way. Ken Olson, the founder of Digital Equipment Corporation, had once famously said, 'There is no reason anyone would want a computer in their home.' This was a failure to reimagine the future. These skills do not come ingrained in us. They need to be developed and honed.

Reshape the board

Managing the pandemic needs coordinated global action at one level and behaviour change at another. This is almost exactly what climate change needs as well. These two threats to the human race—the pandemic and climate change are massive in their scale and debilitating in their impact. Not only that. They impact each other. The SDGs are a framework on which to 'build back better' after the pandemic. Most corporate sustainability reports however map SDGs in a non-specific way to their ESG activities; choosing to simply mention the SDGs they support. At one level, it is understandable because the SDGs are vast and are global and country level indicators. However, if you really need to make an impact, choosing a goalpost is imperative. To think differently, you need a new board, with new insight. Companies don't change merely because of external pushes and pulls, they change because the people in them read the signals correctly and then change themselves.

If you look at the news that has come out in the recent past i.e. 2020 and early 2021, you will notice that some of the world's largest companies, Mondlelez International, Dr Reddy's and Diageo, have announced radical strategies to reduce carbon emissions by 2030.

To get ESG right, companies need to get in new people who have the responsibility mindset. The board therefore needs to be redesigned first. While public commitments by companies on environmental and social parameters play an important role in signaling to stakeholders and financial markets that making the transition is essential. ESG issues are now becoming critical in investment decision-making. Investors are incorporating these to reduce risk and seize opportunities by fine-tuning equity exposures, searching for excess returns, remaking bond portfolios and tapping the green bond market (see Technical Note 4 and 6).

The board needs to understand the importance of social parameters that form part of the SDG's and a focus on ethics. There is social inequality, the food and water crisis and a host of other issues that are competing for attention that all add in to the discussion of things that need to be fixed. Child labour, diversity in the workplace, health and safety of employees—all these and more are part of the 'social parameters' that ESG seeks to cover.

Now, and increasingly in the future, respect for human rights across the supply chain is expected from investors worldwide. But above everything else, 'social' just means doing the right thing, all the time. If you have the right intent metrics and processes will follow. It has been proved again and again that transgressions in the social arena are penalised heavily by the markets. Studies have accurately shown that high social standards can reduce a company's systematic risk.

Diversity and inclusion are important parameters that most investors are demanding. Thirty-seven of the companies on 2020's Fortune 500 were led by female CEOs.[4] While the percentage of businesses around the world with at least one woman in senior management has increased significantly, rising from 66 per cent to 75 per cent in 2019-20. However, at the same time the proportion of senior roles held by women has marginally declined. This trend suggests that many businesses may be focusing on merely ticking the 'diversity' box and avoiding an all-male leadership team, over laying out policies that genuinely make organisations more diverse and less biased. It is high time that intent translates to on-ground action, for policy alone (such as equal pay, flexible hours, maternity/paternity leave), is not creating real progress. Female 'overboarding' is being used by many businesses, particularly in the US and across Europe, to enable rapid achievement of diversity targets, but is reducing the wider pool of women available for senior management roles.

What we are looking at, is a comprehensive behavioural change, over a mere checkbox exercise. Business leaders should champion the cause of gender diversity, making it a core company value. This will happen as more leaders realise the commercial benefit of gender diversity. Thus far, improvements have been seen in emerging economies, as these businesses are open to adaptation, with Africa and Eastern Europe leading the way. Latin America also has demonstrated significant improvement. Reports show that businesses in developed countries find it harder to drive change as they operate in environments that have established and ingrained behaviours. What we must keep in mind, however, is that having only one woman on a senior management team is not the goal. Change will happen only when there are several varied voices in a boardroom.

Reskill the board

Investors are asking for ESG to play a role in executive compensation. But, global companies are struggling to comply because ESG standards are not uniform and they don't really have ESG data. For several brands, operations across the world were largely sourcing and manufacturing hubs that have never looked at non-financial parameters beyond country level compliance issues. Hence extending global norms across countries will take time and reworking of processes and systems. As and when ESG data becomes available, directors need to be fluent in these topics when engaging with shareholders. ESG therefore needs to be on the board's training agenda months before the sustainability report becomes public. ESG is also about consistency. Once you make public commitments through your sustainability/integrated reports, you need to track ESG parameters regularly. ESG data is likely to become part of quarterly earnings reports very soon. The board needs to be aware that changing indicators in reports to make them look good is an extremely bad idea, one with serious consequences.

Boards normally have governance expertise on accounting matters. Some of them, after India's CSR legislation that required board oversight, had started focusing on CSR as well. However, ESG is not CSR. It is about corporate strategy and management oversight of core business in the context of environmental, social and governance standards. With ESG standards gaining momentum across institutional investors, it is now expected that ESG should be a part of the board agenda. Boards need to be trained on the following:

1. The difference between ESG, CSR, Sustainability and Brand promise
2. What are the core issues for the company/sector and how this will change in the next ten years.
3. Global risks, country risks and corporate risks.
4. Reputational challenges that can emerge from business as usual.
5. The opportunities for change.
6. Global momentum on ESG and expectations.
7. The challenges of measuring environmental and social risk.

Reskill Finance Teams

Customers and investors are increasingly looking at a company's performance on ESG parameters before undertaking purchasing or investing decisions. Both these shifts will necessitate the CFO and the teams working with them to operate differently. From having the central responsibility for delivering financial results to shareholders, the CFO will have to co-opt the heads of operations, sustainability, product, marketing, technology and the CEO to help figure out the ESG issues that impact financial performance.

The CFO today needs to have an integrated view of the company. Performance across the company's operations, talent, natural capital and, supply chains needs to be measured regularly. Integrated thinking will ensure that not only do companies see gaps in all areas of the organisation on both ESG and functional parameters, but start taking steps to improve performance. Newer standards and regulations are quickly emerging—TCFD (Taskforce on Climate-related Financial Disclosures), Value Reporting Foundation, Business Responsibility and Sustainability Reporting (BRSR) (see Technical Note 10), GRI reporting, etc. Keeping track and building knowledge on these standards and guidelines is a daunting task for the CFO but one that necessarily needs to be done.

CFOs will also need to realise that a focus on share price, and EPS is not enough. The financial statements need to be retooled to capture ESG. Take the case of emissions. Although difficult to measure, the potential harm due to emissions can be captured on the balance sheet as an expense. Similarly, estimates of lack of diversity will appear on the income statement as an expense. These measurements are like those used for valuing externalities. Essentially, there is a need for a framework that generates an 'ESG' EPS. As mentioned in Chapter 3, there are a slew of new financing mechanisms that are now available to help CFOs raise funds for their company's ESG actions. Green bonds, sustainability linked bonds, impact bonds, sustainable development etc. dot the financing skyline.

CFO's now need to ask themselves some important questions:

- How can I build a shared understanding of the fundamental purpose of business beyond profits?

- How do I evaluate projects and proposals beyond maximising value to incorporating ESG concerns?
- How do I keep track of ESG rankings and frameworks? How do I choose the one that works best for my company?
- How do I communicate my approach to stakeholders?
- What internal and external reporting practices do I develop that tie up finance and purpose?
- What new skills and abilities do I develop to function in the ESG centric world?

Widen the role of the Chief Sustainability Officer

As companies join the dots between environmental and social wellbeing and business resilience the role of the Chief Sustainability Officer (CSO) is changing.

Higher standards
Expectations from the sustainability team have increased as companies now demand higher environmental and social standards. The CSO's work now matters even more to the CEO and CFO with increased ESG reporting. Further, there is increasing pressure from the financial world to link financial and business performance with sustainability targets to calculate executive pay.

Strategy and Risk
Sustainability is increasingly expected to be part of core strategy and risk mitigation and the CSO is now expected to be aligned to both strategy and risk teams. In many cases the CSO is now reporting to the board.

Because of the far-reaching impact of sustainability decisions, governance structures for sustainability need to pan across several functional areas and not just the sustainability department. Take a look at the sustainability governance framework adopted by large retail brand. This has been necessitated by the organisation's ambition to build circularity in its operations.

Reporting
Head of Sustainability reports in to the CEO and the Board

Cross functional support
The sustainability department is supported by a cross-functional forum reviewing strategy performance and defining priorities based on business intelligence and innovation processes.

Sustainability managers and teams in brands, retail markets and suppliers drive the implementation across the company.

KPIs
Each central function and brand is measured against a set of sustainability KPIs, in the same way that performance against sales figures and customer satisfaction are measured.

Rethinking the role of business

Companies today have become all-powerful entities even larger than several governments, hence the polluting and damaging impacts are also large. Capital and economic power have led to lifting vast swathes of the population out of poverty and the corporation remains the single most important mechanism for wealth creation and distribution in society today. The predominant thinking since the last few years has been that government needs to step back and allow the private sector a free run in hitherto government controlled sectors such as health, energy, water and waste. This hasn't really worked well so we need to rethink the role of business. Businesses and markets that function with a singular focus on profit maximisation at the cost of lives cannot be allowed a free reign. The link between health and economic wellbeing has never been clearer.

While companies cannot solve many issues there are others, they can certainly benefit. But is that all?

Perhaps the answer lies in intent, collaborations and the articulation of the brand purpose. As seen in the previous chapter businesses from different industries are coming together to develop low-carbon solutions and technologies. They are also engaging with governments and civil society organisations to develop new approaches. But there are many instance of words without action. A great purpose should manifest itself in everything a brand does: from product development, to customer experience, to how it should conduct its marketing. While the profit motive takes primacy for most in the immediate future, the organisation's licence to exist will take primacy in the long game. Working towards the common good has to be the defining metaphor of our times. For this, we don't just need big words but actions that build trust, transparency and authenticity at scale. These trends are likely to have a big impact on the shifts towards the achievement of the SDGs. That's because intent, collaborations and technology help in scaling up progress on the areas of action.

Similarly, the changes in the world of finance will bring seismic shifts in how we value nature. EU's Sustainable Finance Disclosure Regulation aims to push around €1 trillion into green investments over the next decade, address the lack of consistency in the climate-related information that's currently being provided by financial-market participants and provide a competitive edge to those firms offering genuinely sustainable products.

New methodologies such as Natural Capital assessment and Environmental Profit and Loss are entering corporate boardrooms when projects are being assessed. Natural capital investments are therefore gaining importance in the $120 trillion investment management industry. A growing number of private sector investors are factoring environmental concerns into their investment decisions. This is likely to grow even further. The Natural Capital Investors Alliance[5] targeting $10 billion by 2022 was launched in 2021. HSBC Pollination Climate Asset Management, Lombard Odier and Mirova, an affiliate of Natixis Investment Managers, are the three founding partners of the alliance which aims to focus on natural capital as an investment theme and engage the investment management industry to further this trend. The focus has largely been on the greenhouse gas emissions in the past, but now natural assets such as water, soil, air and living organisms are in focus. Using of carbon credits to generate revenue streams for forests, bonds for preventing deforestation, debt-for-nature conversion to protect oceans, protecting coastal assets through insurance are just some of the emerging innovations that value natural capital in ways never been done before.

We need a moral code that defines the relationship between businesses and their stakeholders. To look ahead, sometimes we need to look at the things, philosophies and people we have left behind. One of them is Mohandas Karamchand Gandhi from India. He led India's freedom movement based on core beliefs of non-violence and equity. And it changed the world. He proved that freedom could be one based on non-violence. We need a modern day ethos of defining life on earth and maintaining the balance that has allowed us to progress—the Prime Directive for the 21st century.

The Gandhian Model of Trusteeship is one such approach that, while being uniquely Indian, provides a means of transforming the present unequal order of society into an egalitarian one. It specifies that everything we do must be economically viable as well as ethical—at the same time making sure we build sustainable livelihoods for all. This model was debated in the 1940s and '50s and had no real takers for most of the twentieth century. However, the challenges thrown up by the twenty-first century such as economic collapse, the absence of values and challenges of sustainable growth necessitate another look at trusteeship. Gandhi's economic ideas were part of his general crusade against poverty, exploitation against socio-economic injustice, and deteriorating moral standards.[6] He was not an economist, but at the core of his philosophy was the need for human dignity and not just material prosperity. He aimed at the development, upliftment and enrichment of human life rather than merely a higher standard of living. Gandhi believed that disconnecting production with consumption leads to acts of violence against others. For instance, if production is in the village and consumption is in the cities, the city dwellers would not be interested in the environmental damage that the village went through to produce something. This perspective needs to be studied today, with a deeper conversation on governing public good and creating robust infrastructure to support them.

There will be a significant number of changes that will need rethinking of our economic models. For instance, while the internet has enabled us to work from anywhere, it has also enabled the gig economy (as mentioned in Chapter 1). Employers can now call on experts to do a job, instead of hiring them full-time. This has helped companies reduce costs, get high quality talent and work across geographical boundaries. At the same time, the gig economy has also been exploitative. Employment platforms have been accused of making people work harder and longer for very little pay, no benefits or holidays. In the coming years, while flexible work will rise, so will the need for companies to be more responsible to not just full-time employees, but to the larger ecosystem of flexible workers that serve them. During the pandemic, the gig workers were the first to be laid off. Without any social security and any other opportunity to earn money they sunk into poverty and destitution. Our work is also becoming more and more automated. 'Lights out factories', or unmanned factories that function with robots and don't need lights or air conditioning are emerging. AI and machine learning are also going to impact the number of jobs available. This will cause huge displacement of labour in the short run.

Hence, we need a new way of thinking that prioritises public good. In this context, there are many concepts that till now were not considered as relevant, that need to be carefully evaluated. Universal basic income, a concept that till now had remained on the fringes, has now become mainstream. The concept of a universal basic income is about regular and unconditional cash payments to the underprivileged. In recent months though, with intense economic upheaval spurred worldwide by the coronavirus pandemic, calls for a universal basic income (UBI) have grown even more urgent. US, Canada, Japan, Singapore, India, Spain, UK, amongst several other countries announced cash transfers. The Spanish government aims to roll out a basic income 'as soon as possible' to about a million of the country's poorest households. Scotland's First Minister, Nicola Sturgeon, has said that the virus and its economic consequences had 'made me much, much more strongly of the view that [universal basic income] is an idea that's time has come'.

We believe that leaders in the green transition need to look at 3 core elements to create transformative change.

Build Trust

Public good, can't really be achieved without trust as an important enabler. In order to protect our global commons and turn the tide against climate change and biosphere degradation, humanity must develop new business models to transform the intertwined systems of urban development, food, energy, and the circular economy. Eventually, eventually everything connects—people, ideas, objects. Hence a systems thinking approach, enabled by trust is perhaps the only solution.

Follow the science but work with empathy

Science, data, analysis and standards need to show the way, but we also need to understand that this is not enough. People will be impacted in many different ways because of these changes. We can't progress by leaving people behind, hence understanding their needs, interests and priorities, and working together to create just solutions will be critical.

Have long-term horizons and act as a trustee

The concept of acting as a trustee is therefore, now more relevant than ever. The trusteeship model is a proactive model because it defines the core values of a business which run through how the business needs to conduct itself. It can be surmised that, for Gandhi, sustainable development implied a form of economic growth that would, first, sustain the lives of the poor in rural India and, second, be of the kind that could be sustained by the economy of the country for a long time. His approach to sustainable development rested on the three planks of:

- **Ahimsa (non-violence):** This can be interpreted as causing no harm to planet earth.
- **Swaraj (self-control):** This can be interpreted as better decision-making.
- **Sarvodaya (benefit to all):** This can be interpreted as welfare for tackling areas of human rights, labour exploitation, etc.

Absolute trusteeship is unattainable—but if people act as trustees then we can develop institutions that are economically viable yet benign. There are no easy answers to most of the issues that surround us. But a moral core can help us stay a steady path. Trusteeship has a relevance, but also needs redefinition for the modern age.

Proactive responsibility for a world in transition

What will life be like twenty or thirty years from now? That used to be a question for futurists. Now global climate change makes it something we all think about.

Designing a low-carbon future requires unprecedented levels of collaboration, creativity, and imagination. This is precisely the kind of intricate, thorny challenge designers and design-driven businesses solve best. Take the ambitious independent design project, The Ocean Cleanup, a Dutch non-profit that developed a gigantic floating structure in 2013 with which it aims to clear plastic trash from the oceans. By 2020 the company had collected over 235, 505 kgs of plastic waste. The Ocean Cleanup has been beset by criticism from scientists and environmentalists, who claim its system is flawed, yet its success so far shows how compelling a design endeavour for an important cause can be.

More and more socially and environmentally conscious designers are following suit, including those in parts of the developing world that previously lacked the resources to forge thriving design cultures. A new generation of African designers has emerged at the forefront of Internet of Things technologies in countries where more people have access to cellular networks than to clean running water. Portable diagnostic devices such as the Cardiopad heart monitor, developed by Arthur Zang in Cameroon, and the Peek Retina ophthalmoscope, devised by a group of doctors and designers in Kenya and the UK, are already improving the quality of healthcare for thousands of people.

At one level, all the challenges around climate change are design challenges. Emissions and waste are the result of poorly designed products and the business models that promote this are the result of a financial system that incentivises endless production and consumption. Hence, we need to redesign financial and the economic system, at the same time we need to redesign products and the way they are made and consumed. The growing financial, social and ecological pressures imply that it is time to bring design front and centre in corporate decisions. Design also needs to transcend its traditional function of translating technological advances into new or improved products and services, by emerging as a way of better decision-making—in the form of design thinking (see Figure 10.1). Design thinking is a practice which states that strategic decisions can benefit from being interrogated with the openness, thoughtfulness and rigour of the design process. This will become an important part of the corporate world as we design out waste and pollution, keep products and materials in use and regenerate natural systems to create a net zero world.

One thing though is certain, we need better design of core products, manufacturing process, distribution, usability and end of life. Further

FIGURE 10.1
WE NEED BETTER DESIGN

Focus Areas	Areas for Improvement
Product Design	• Reducing weight and volume • Using biodegradable materials or recycled materials • Using materials that use less resources –water / energy
Manufacturing Process Design	• Designing processes for less waste, less energy, less water
Distribution Design	• Better packaging –lightweight, recyclable • Optimising for high packaging density • Optimising transportation and distribution
Design for use	• Reduce energy / water in use • Easy access to spare parts and repair • Ease of reuse and disassembly
Design for end of life	• Processes that help the product bio degrade or return back to the producer / recycler • Processes for ease of recycling –maximum can be retrieved at minimal cost

products and processes need to be designed with real time early warning systems.

Today's world and increasingly in the future we are looking at real time responses to everything. Sensors on machines give real time information for companies to generate so that they can capture breakdowns. Wearable devices such as smart watches capture health data and can predict a heart attack three hour before they occur. Algorithms can take decisions in seconds and reach tremendous scale with big data. Responsibility in the twenty-first century has to be about creating a better world today and not waiting for harm to happen and then correcting it. Since the world is changing at tremendous speed we can't really have responsibility models that rest on mere compliance or remediation. We need better decisions now!

Current models of responsibility are mostly reactive. They seek to rectify damage to the environment and social systems. In a data-driven world, there is the potential to cause massive damage with far-reaching consequences. In the next few years, existing systems and value chains will need a reboot not just in terms of finding newer markets and growth avenues, they will come under increasing regulatory and public pressure for transparency, trustworthiness and public good. Responsibility is about taking the higher ground, about getting the design right in the first place. Proactive is the default norm. Calling on human ingenuity and collaboration through innovation fusing finance, information, technology and human behaviour.

The connected world magnifies the smallest risk. While the crosscutting nature of connections provide huge benefits they are also incredibly difficult to implement because of the sheer complexity and scale of the task. The system therefore needs to be changed from the inside. From the areas that drive value and not just the areas that contribute to risk. Assessing the planet's health must become a more sustained, integrated practice that allows us to understand exactly what is happening in real time to enable smart decision-making. These initiatives highlight the importance of AI for public good and the way our commons need to be governed. Data about the global commons such as forests, oceans, air, corals is increasingly going to gain prominence and critical mass. Machine Learning and AI will need deep science and a nuanced approach to manage and intervene. A planetary computer is a reality. How should it be used and what should be the laws governing it? What should be the moral code to determine use and impact?

The measures to control the pandemic have clearly shown that complex systems need complex answers and that reaching these can be an iterative process. Further, all AI-based algorithms failed during the pandemic because they were based on historical data. In a world changing at warp speed, the future can't be more of the past, hence new frameworks and models are needed. Experts are repeatedly warning that the frameworks governing AI need to be capable of ensuring accountability over the long term. What may seem unbiased and ethical could develop unconscious biases over time and replicate them to scale. Efficiencies and optimisation are great when you want machines to run in a certain way. But within AI it has different connotations. For instance, to improve commercial outcomes the AI system may sack employees or indulge in unethical practices. In the case of AI for the global commons, we need to be aware that nature runs its own course—ecosystems flow and ebb and so do wildlife and plants.

Perhaps the need of the hour for business is not just about mapping the system but about designing a better system.

Leadership for the fourth industrial revolution has to be about mindfulness. It has to be about people. Climate change and digital transformation are creating new risks, and at the same time, new opportunities are opening up too. A new kind of leadership is needed that builds trust, is driven by values and is open to change. The leader has to be a trustee to all the stakeholders, rising above the stereotypes to decide what she will and will not do. As a trustee to the organisation, there is no exit strategy and the leader takes a long term view of the organization. This is needed, for businesses to transform from within to move towards a digital, low-carbon world.

There are no outsiders anymore. New ways of thinking and acting are required from all stakeholders, including individuals, business executives, social influencers and policy-makers. Deep, meaningful conversations and not just excel sheets hold the key to responsibility. This means thinking not just about what new perspectives might be needed, but finding entirely new ways to create and update our thinking over time in collaboration with other people in the industry, policy makers and customers themselves. The corporate brand needs to move from product attributes, smart logos and great TV advertisements into being more human, responsive and above all trustworthy.

Pro-active responsibility for an accelerating world. Business responsibility therefore needs a modern context. It needs to bring in the many connections and technology interchanges that really define the twenty-first century, as well as build frameworks that reflect the changing realities. If done right, responsibility for the modern world can define the boundaries of the corporation—and its very soul!

The biggest potential for that transformation is in five core actions:

1. **Incentivising transformation through financial markets**
2. **Involving women to increase diversity and drive change**
3. **Transforming key drivers of environmental impact – plastic waste, water security, clean energy and transforming food**

4. **Building new models for cities, healthcare, social change and artificial intelligence**
5. **Defining the new drivers of value and skills**

Implementing these will define the face of the new corporation. What do they mean for you and me and what will be the pathways to the future?

TECHNICAL NOTES

Technical Note 1

CARBON MARKETS

CARBON MARKETS ARE ONE OF THE TOOLS TO TACKLE THE CLIMATE change problem. The climate change problem is simply the accumulation of GHGs in the atmosphere. Given that there is only one atmosphere, it matters little where the emissions are released. The emissions will soon spread around the earth, creating what is known as the greenhouse effect.[1] Going by this logic, if a group of people, countries or companies can agree to limit their emissions to a certain amount (a 'carbon budget'). It does not matter how much each person emits, or where they do so, as long as the whole group does not emit more than what they committed to. Since it doesn't matter where we reduce emissions, the argument behind carbon trading is that the best way to take climate action is to reduce emissions where it is easiest (i.e. least costly).

To achieve emission reductions governments around the world have established carbon markets. Here emissions (or emissions reductions) can be exchanged from one entity to another. In theory, as long as we control the total amount of emissions traded in the market, it does not matter for the climate who buys or sells. Although this works well in theory, in practice establishing a global or even a national carbon market is fraught with significant challenges. Significant risks are present in the system. Loopholes in the system can result in the policy having little or no impact.

According to the Carbon Pricing Dashboard,[2] there are sixty-four carbon pricing initiatives implemented or scheduled for implementation in forty-six national jurisdictions. In 2020, these initiatives would cover twelve $GtCO_2e$,[3] representing 22.3 per cent of global GHG emissions. 61 per cent of the global emissions are covered by carbon pricing initiatives (ETS and carbon tax).

There are various types of carbon pricing mechanisms.

An Emissions Trading System (ETS) is a system where emitters can trade emission units to meet their emission targets. To meet the emission requirements, companies can consider either internal abatement measures or acquire emission units in the carbon markets. Thus, those who have excess carbon units can trade them in the carbon markets with those who are unable to meet their emission requirements. The ETS market creates a demand and supply for emission units through a trading mechanism that establishes a market price for GHG emissions. There are two main types of ETSs—a cap-and-trade and baseline-and-credit.

Cap-and-trade systems: A cap-and-trade programme limits the total amount of CO_2 that can be emitted by certain facilities. In this system or programme, the government issues a limited number of emissions allowances (also known as permits). Each of these permits grants the holder the right to emit one ton of CO_2. These allowances are tradeable. The sale and purchase of the allowances yield a market price for the allowance. This is practically the price of one ton of CO_2.

Baseline-and-credit systems: Here baseline emissions levels are specified for individual companies. Credits are issued to companies that reduce their emissions below the baseline emissions. These credits can be sold to other companies that have exceeded their baseline emission levels.

Banking and borrowing caps: Some cap-and-trade programmes include provisions for the banking and borrowing of allowances over time. Thus permits issued in one year can be submitted to account for emissions in later years (this is like putting money in the bank). Alternatively, permits for future years can be issued and used in the current year (one is borrowing permits today which would have been used in the future).

A **carbon tax** is a price set per ton of carbon per ton of CO_2 emitted. CO_2 emissions that come from the combustion of fossil fuels are proportional to the carbon content of the fossil fuel. Thus the carbon tax is effectively a tax on CO_2. Given that carbon constitutes approximate 3/11th by weight of CO_2, a $1 tax per ton of CO_2 is equal to a $3.7 tax per ton of carbon.

An **offset mechanism** designates the GHG emission reductions from project- or programme-based activities. These emission reductions can then be sold either domestically or internationally. Often a registry is created for the issue of carbon credits. These credits can then be used to meet compliance requirements.

Result Based Climate Finance (RBCF) is a funding approach where payments are made after pre-defined outputs or outcomes related to managing climate change are met and outcomes like reduction in emissions achieved and verified. In many RBCF programmes, verified reductions in GHG are purchased. This creates a market for carbon.

Internal carbon pricing is a mechanism organisations use for its internal decision-making process to value change impacts, and their risks and opportunities.

Carbon taxes and cap-and-trade programmes differ on the type of certainty they provide. Carbon taxes are most certain as companies know how much they will need to pay per ton of carbon they emit. At the same time, it allows companies to get away by paying money. On the other hand, cap-and-trade programmes ensure quantitative reduction in emissions. Unfortunately, the price fluctuates on trading markets making it difficult for business to make decisions. Building in cap and floor features in cap-and-trade programmes reduces price volatility. Carbon taxes can also be designed to adjust dynamically if actual emissions miss the predetermined emissions path.

The graph on the next page shows carbon price in Europe.

Benefits of Carbon Pricing

Carbon pricing policies have several features that make them more efficient, or less costly as compared to other policies to reduce CO_2 emissions (such as technology mandates, direct regulations, subsidies to zero-carbon energy sources, etc.). These features are:

Flexibility

Carbon pricing mechanism allows companies to choose the method or technology to reduce or mitigate emissions. This is unlike technology mandates where the regulator decides on a single method that is then applied

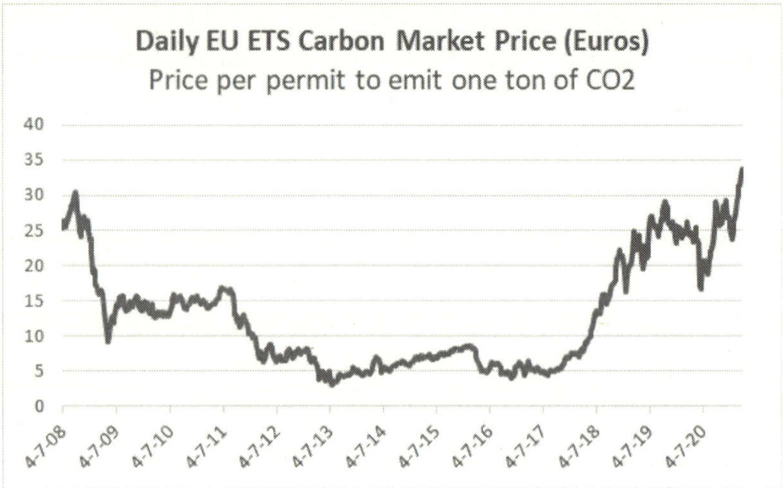

Source: Based on data from Ember (https://ember-climate.org/data/carbon-price-viewer/)

to a wide set of companies. This one-size-fits-all may make it prohibitively expensive for some companies when cheaper methods of emission reduction exist.

Equal Marginal Costs of Abatement[4]

An economy-wide carbon price applies a uniform price on CO_2 emissions regardless of the source. This results in the equalisation of marginal abatement costs across firms and sectors. Regulations, on the other hand, imply different marginal abatement costs across firms and sectors. Thus regulations in sectors with very high marginal abatement costs may require that regulation be removed (as it is cost-ineffective). At the same time, it will lead to more stringent regulations in cases of low marginal abatement costs. Undertaking such balancing acts are difficult for regulators—something that carbon pricing does effectively.

Encouraging Conservation

Conventional regulations put a limit of emissions per unit of output. This leaves little incentive for companies to undertake reductions if they are meeting the regulatory requirements. In contrast, carbon pricing provides incentives to reduce emissions per unit of output, but also charges a price for every additional ton of CO_2 that is not reduced through increased efficiency.

With carbon pricing, costs can increase for high emitters as it charges a price for every additional unit of CO_2 that is not reduced through increased efficiency. This motivates companies to improve their carbon efficiency.

Revenue

A carbon price creates a new revenue stream (for example, money earned by selling carbon credits) that can be used in a number of ways.

Carbon Pricing Design

There are many elements that go into the design of carbon pricing instruments.

Price

Economic theory suggests that the maximum benefits of carbon pricing accrue when carbon price is equal to marginal cost of abatement. This can be achieved by either setting a carbon tax equal to marginal damage[5] or by capping emissions at a level equal to marginal damage.

Stringency

A $50 carbon tax is said to be more stringent than a $5 carbon tax. The more stringent a tax is, it will lead to lower emissions and higher costs. In determining stringency, policymakers face a trade-off between environmental goals and the costs of meeting those goals.

Coverage

The coverage of a carbon pricing policy indicates which sectors and industries or emission types will be covered under carbon price. Take the case of the European Union Emissions Trading System cap-and-trade programme. It covers emissions of CO_2, nitrous oxide (N_2O), and perfluorocarbons (PFCs). Also covered are 11,000 energy intensive plants in electric power and manufacturing sectors that emit these emissions. These are spread over thirty-one European countries.

Point of Regulation

The point of regulation of a carbon price determines exactly who is required to submit permits or pay the tax to the government. For instance, an upstream carbon tax would tax fossil fuel producers for the carbon content of their products. A midstream tax would tax the first purchaser in the supply chain of fossil fuels (say, a refinery) for the purchase of crude oil. A downstream tax applies to the emitter. For example, the coal based power plant will pay for the emissions.

Revenue Use

There can be multiple uses of carbon revenue. For instance, a carbon dividend can be distributed from the carbon price revenue to households. Or there can be tax swaps that use the revenue from a carbon price to reduce taxes. Carbon pricing revenue can also be used to finance green spending programmes. Green spending programmes are aimed at reducing emissions through non-pricing methods. Another option is to reduce the government's budget deficit.

Technical Note 2

CARBON FOOTPRINTING

AN ORGANISATION'S CARBON FOOTPRINT MEASURES THE DIRECT AND indirect GHG emissions arising from all the activities across an organisation.

The quantification of GHG emissions helps companies understand what their key emission sources are, what is the contribution of a company's emission to global emissions, and what opportunities are present to reduce the emissions. The quantification facilitates preparation of a carbon reduction plan. This involves identifying ways to reduce carbon footprint and limit emissions from present and future activities. A carbon footprint reduction plan will help the company asses its progress in the carbon reduction journey. It also helps communicate progress internally and externally.

The Greenhouse Gas Protocol Standard

The Greenhouse Gas Protocol[6] is a widely used standard that sets out how to account for the GHG emissions.

Emissions have been categorised into three groups or scopes:

- **Scope 1**: This covers direct emissions that result from activities within the organisation's control. These include emissions from combustion in owned or controlled boilers, furnaces, vehicles, etc.; emissions from chemical production in owned or controlled process equipment.
- **Scope 2**: This covers indirect emissions from any electricity, heat or steam that the company purchases and uses. Although the company is not directly in control of the emissions, by using the energy the company is indirectly responsible for the release of CO_2.
- **Scope 3**: This covers other indirect emissions from sources outside

the company's direct control. Examples of scope 3 emissions include extraction and production of purchased materials; transportation of purchased fuels; and use of sold products and services.

TABLE 1: EXAMPLES OF EMISSION SCOPES

Scope 1	Scope 2	Scope 3
Fuel combustion Company vehicles Fugitive emissions	Purchased electricity, heat and steam	Purchased goods and services Business travel Employee commuting Waste disposal Use of sold products Transportation and distribution (up- and downstream) Investments Leased assets and franchises

There are several examples of organisations that measure carbon footprint. These include:

- Insurers – Aviva
- Agriculture – Cargill, Monsanto
- Universities – University of Kent
- Retailers – Levi Strauss & Co, Patagonia
- Transportation – Transport for London
- Automotive – BMW, Honda, Ford
- Food manufacturers – ABP Food Group
- Hotels – Hyatt, Hilton
- Restaurants – Starbucks, McDonald's
- Travel – United Airlines, Greyhound
- Manufacturers – Kingspan
- Galleries and museums – The National Gallery
- Supermarkets – J Sainsbury
- Manufacturing – Siemens
- Airports – Gatwick
- Construction – ThyssenKrupp, LafargeHolcim
- Software – Google, Microsoft
- Pharmaceutical companies – GlaxoSmithKline

Calculating an organisation's carbon footprint

Calculating an organisation's carbon footprint involves the following steps:

1. The first step is to decide on the method to be followed. It is important to use a method consistently to ensure that people in the organisation become familiar with it. It is also important to choose a method that produces reliable results that are understandable by all. Prominent approaches are GHG Protocol, the International Organisation for Standards (ISO) and the Life cycle analysis.
2. The next step is to define organisational and operational boundaries. This requires setting clear and explicit boundaries on which parts of the organisation are included in the footprint. This can be complex when many subsidiaries, joint ventures or leased assets are involved. The operational boundary determines which emission sources will be quantified. It should include the full range of emissions from activities under your operational control. All material scope 1 and 2 emissions should be included, but one can choose which scope 3 emissions to include.
3. The accuracy of the footprint relies on collating consumption data for all of the emission sources within the company's established boundary. For gas and electricity, data is collected in kilowatt hours (kWh) from meter readings or electricity bills. For other fuels data can be recorded in a variety of units—litres, kWh or megajoules (MJ). Transport emissions can be measured through fuel usage and mileage.
4. The carbon footprint is measured in tonnes of CO_2 equivalent (tCO_2e). It is computed by applying standard emission factors to the usage data collated in the previous step. For example, the Carbon Trust provides following conversions for fuels:

Fuel	Conversion factor	Units
Grid electricity	0.23314	kWh
Natural gas	0.18387	kWh
	5.38869	therms
	2.02266	cubic meters
LPG	0.21448	kWh
	6.28576	therms

Fuel	Conversion factor	Units
	1.55537	litres
Gas oil	3229.34	tonnes
	0.25672	kWh
	2.75776	litres
Fuel oil	3221.37	tonnes
	0.26775	kWh
Burning oil	3165.32	tonnes
	0.24666	kWh
Diesel	3028.61	tonnes
	0.24057	kWh
	2.54603	litres
Petrol	2942.05	tonnes
	0.22920	kWh
	2.16802	litres
Industrial coal	2380.01	tonnes
	0.32040	kWh
Wood pellets	72.29731	tonnes
	0.01545	kWh

5. Verify the carbon footprint and its reduction through a third party. This provides credibility and confidence to the public reporting of carbon.

One of the issues of carbon footprinting is that it does not take into account consumer end-use. Take the case of shampoo. The emissions associated with a bottle of shampoo depend on how much time one spends in the shower, how hot the water is and what sort of heating mechanism is there. For some goods, customer behaviour can make a dramatic difference to the use-phase emissions. A life cycle analysis carried out for Levi Strauss, found that 57 per cent of the carbon footprint of its 501 jeans was due to the emissions associated with washing them—assuming, that is, that the jeans were washed in warm water and machine-dried. Washing them in cold water and drying them on a line, however, reduces the use-phase emissions by 90 per cent.

Technical Note 3

ESG AND SERVICE PROVIDERS

THE MANAGERS OF ONE-THIRD OF ALL PROFESSIONALLY RUN ASSETS globally—equivalent to over $20 trillion—now use ESG data to inform their investment decisions, and most of them rely on ESG rating agencies to supply it. The development of ESG ratings systems has led to the growth of ESG investing. They provide asset owners and managers an alternative option to conducting such extensive diligence themselves.

Globally, there are over 150 ESG rating agencies. Some of the prominent ones include MSCI, Refinitiv, Sustainalytics, Arabeque, RobecoSAM, CSRHub, Ethos, Covalence, and, Bloomberg ESG. Many of these companies have developed APIs to distribute the ESG data.

Specialised ESG scores are also coming up. For instance, Fitch has started ESG Vulnerability Scores. This helps in companies assessing how vulnerable they are to ESG issues.

Apart from data providers, banks and investment banks are creating proprietary scores to handle shortcomings of data providers' information flow. These organisations are better placed because of their access to companies.

There are several issues around ESG data.

For effective investment analysis, high quality data about companies' ESG practices is required. Without this, sound investment analysis is very difficult.

There is a lack of standardisation and transparency in ESG reporting and scoring. For investors, it is a major challenge to understand rival analysis.

Third-party ESG data providers play an important role by filling data gaps. But there are limitations with this data. Different methodologies used by different providers often lead to wide variance in scores.

Additionally, there is a lack of adequate market infrastructure. This makes it difficult for companies to understand how they are evaluated by differing ESG scores.

Given the wide range and quality of ESG data available, commercial and investment banks have built systems that leverage scores from multiple best-in-class data providers. Their key focus is investment analysis for key customers.

Manufacturing companies, banks and financial institutions and other companies are increasingly looking at taking these insights into corporate strategy and enabling teams to navigate this space. Futurescape India offers experience consulting and learning solutions for executives that make insights actionable for the net zero world. Synstrat Consulting understands ESG performance of companies and provides analysis and training on ESG issues.

Technical Note 4

ESG: FIXED INCOME, FAMILY OFFICES

ESG AS A THEME HAS BEEN AROUND FOR MANY YEARS. IT IS NOW A growing trend in fixed income. Fixed income securities have been used as means of downside protection and as a means of portfolio diversification. The growth in fixed income has come mainly from institutional investors (e.g. pension funds and insurance companies). On the individual investors' side, pensioners prefer fixed income securities for the stability of cash flows (coupon payments) while avoiding much of the volatility associated with equity markets. Thus, they allocate more funds to fixed income securities.

TABLE 1: BOND TYPES AND EXAMPLES

Bond type	Example
Traditional corporate bonds	Incorporating material ESG criteria into corporate credit analysis to better identify credit risk.
Traditional sovereign bonds	Integrating ESG factors, together with traditional analysis that focusses on financial and macroeconomic variables to identify sovereign credit risks. PIMCO has adopted this approach since 2011 in its sovereign ratings model.
ESG money market funds	Applying ESG factors to the investment of money market instruments. BlackRock, for example, launched an environmentally focussed money market fund in April 2019.

Bond type	Example
Green bonds	Specific bonds that are labelled green, with proceeds used for funding new and existing projects with environmental benefits.
Social bonds	Bonds that raise funds for new and existing projects that create positive social outcomes.
Sustainability bonds	Bonds with proceeds that are used to finance or refinance a combination of green and social projects.
Green mortgage-backed securities (MBS)	Green MBS securitise numerous mortgages that go towards financing green properties.

Source: Global Financial Stability Report 2019, International Monetary Fund, https://www.imf.org/~/media/Files/Publications/GFSR/2019/October/English/ch6.ashx

Portfolio managers, asset owners, regulatory agencies, and policymakers are increasingly thinking about ESG issues. At the same time, investors are trying to use their capital in a way that creates positive social impact. Investors need to take into account all factors that can affect the viability of their investments through business cycles that last multiple years and the ever-evolving macro environments.

Integrating ESG issues into fundamental analysis for issuer's credit and leverage profile becomes a critical part of evaluation of corporate bonds. ESG analysis involves understanding non-financial issues. These issues include environmental impacts, employee well-being, product safety, supply chain issues, workforce diversity and such like. In the short run, impact of the issues could affect cash flows of a company. That could result in an impairment of the ability to pay interest (or repay principal) to the bondholders. In the long run, the impact could be detrimental to its corporate culture and affect the operating model. This can erode revenue generating capacity and result in poor profitability.

In the fixed income world, while evaluating securities, governance is given prime importance. It is time that environmental and social factors also receive their due share of focus. For instance, deterioration in environment in a country may lead to social unrest, affect business climate or cause political instability.

While evaluating the ESG factors, we need to assess them in the context of overall credit risk. Understanding a borrower's ability and willingness to service the debt is the bedrock of traditional credit analysis. By incorporating ESG issues in credit risk analysis, a sharper picture of a borrower's ability to service debt can merge.

Materiality and the maturity period of the bond often receive the maximum attention. Materiality measures the likelihood that a particular ESG issue will affect a borrower's revenues, costs, long-term financial condition and, ultimately, ability to repay debt. The maturity period of the bond also determines materiality. Over longer maturity periods, ESG factors can become increasingly impactful. Thus, the maturity period of a bond is a critical lens for any ESG analysis.

As with equities, high quality ESG data is critical for understanding an investment's risks and opportunities. Market data like ESG ratings is an important input into the fixed income research process. However, more holistic and relevant insights require assessing these topics deeply and independently. For instance, there is little data available for private companies and emerging markets which are gradually becoming a focus area for fixed income investors.

While incorporating ESG factors in evaluating investments is a strong way of engaging, there are several other ways in which issuers and investment bankers can create awareness and interest in ESG, especially while dealing with new issues.

Unveiling of the issue: This is an opportunity to provide better public ESG disclosure, discuss underlying ESG issues and enhance sustainability assessments.

Roadshows: While undertaking roadshows, issuers and investment bankers can highlight the ESG characteristics of the bond. This can allow investors to ask questions and lead to a dialogue around ESG issues.

Ad-hoc events: Several selling opportunities arise beyond the roadshows and the issuer/investment banker can utilise this opportunity to promote the ESG credentials of the issue.

Country research trips: These provide an excellent opportunity to understand ESG interest in those countries and incorporate ESG specific details in the presentations to prospective investors.

Investor collaboration: Collaborative platforms, although limited, offer an important channel to improve transparency and showcase ESG best practices.

Like equity, fixed income investing also relies on exclusions. There are two prominent exclusion approaches.

Company exclusion criteria that automatically can exclude companies deriving over 5 per cent of their revenues from tobacco products, commercial gambling, fracking and from the extraction of coalbed methane. Then there are criteria that exclude companies that derive more than 50 per cent of their revenues from the exploration and extraction of conventional oil and gas. Other criteria focus on serious violations of ESG norms and involvement with controversial weapons.

Then there are sovereign exclusion criteria. Some investors exclude countries that are a part of the UN's blacklist of twelve countries that are part of non-cooperative tax jurisdictions. The other set of sovereign exclusion criteria covers corruption, human right violations, and impediments to the freedom of speech. These assessments are provided by Transparency International, information compiled by The Economist Intelligence Unit, Freedom House etc.

ESG Investing and Family offices

A family office is a privately held company that handles investment management and wealth management for a wealthy family. These families generally possess over $100 million in investable assets. They have a goal to effectively grow and transfer wealth across generations.

Family offices have a significant role in promoting ESG culture. Since the wealthy tend to be role models, their investments in ESG are likely to have a cascading effect on other investors. A study by UBS indicates that more than half the families are closely involved in asset allocation and making it a priority for the family office to be a cornerstone for wealth preservation.[7] The study also shows that 39 per cent of the family offices plan to invest their portfolio sustainably in five years' time. However, their focus appears to be on exclusion based strategies. For a family office that wants to limit global warming it is far easier to exclude any company that derives more than half its revenues from fossil fuel than find a company with specific goals of developing sustainable energy. Even where such goals are available they are unsure if they will be met and treat them with scepticism. At the same time, when evaluating impact investments, 43 per cent of family offices prioritise investment performance. They put return on investment among their top three performance indicators. Almost two-thirds of the families regard sustainable investing as important for their legacies. How these intentions are likely to turn into reality is yet to be seen.

One of the concerns that family offices face is that with a surfeit of money available for ESG-compliant investments, greenwashing is likely to proliferate. They worry about how to manage it.

Another issue with family offices is that as they do not have to report to anyone else except the family, much of the investment details remain shrouded in mystery.

Technical Note 5

ESG INVESTING AND EU TAXONOMY

EU HAS INITIATED MANY MEASURES TO FACILITATE COMPLIANCE with the Paris Agreement climate targets and its commitment to adopt the UN SDGs. To this end, it is adopting standardised definitions through EU Taxonomy and standardised processes through its Sustainable Finance Disclosure Regulation (SFDR). These measures are a part of a larger set of ESG initiatives that are designed to push funding to investments that are genuinely sustainable rather than 'greenwashed'.

In March 2018, the European Commission (EC) put forward an action plan on financing sustainable growth. The action plan for the establishment of an EU classification system for sustainable investments, the EU Taxonomy, was initiated in May 2018.

The EC set up the Technical Expert Group (TEG) on sustainable finance for the development of the taxonomy in July 2018. The TEG was tasked with the development of resolutions for technical screening of criteria for economic activities. The screening was aimed at making a substantial contribution to climate change mitigation or adaptation, while avoiding significant harm to the four other environmental objectives. These objectives were: (a) sustainable use and protection of water and marine resources, (b) transition to a circular economy, (c) pollution prevention control, and protection, and (d) restoration of biodiversity and ecosystems.

The Taxonomy Regulation was adopted by the EC on 18 June 2020. It came into force on 12 July 2020. These EU-wide standards are likely to form the basis for economic and regulatory measures that will eventually create labels to enable capital markets to identify investment opportunities. Such identification will contribute to the EU's environmental policy objectives.

What is EU taxonomy?

The EU Taxonomy consists of three key regulations: (i) the Taxonomy Regulation, (ii) the Disclosures Regulation, and (iii) the Low Carbon and Positive Impacts Benchmarks Regulation. These are aimed at furthering sustainable finance and ESG integration.

The term 'taxonomy' is not used anywhere in the Regulations. The term 'taxonomy' appears appropriate since the regulation is a classification system that identifies whether economic activities are sustainable from an environmental perspective (the social objectives are to be considered later).

The regulation aims to reduce fragmentation arising out of market-based initiatives and national priorities. It also addresses the practices of 'greenwashing' so as to allow investors to better compare ESG products. The classification works through the technical screening criteria. The methodology and guidance is described in the EU report on taxonomy designed by TEG.[8]

Although the taxonomy has direct implications for the financial sector, its impact is likely to be felt across many sectors. The focus of the taxonomy, currently, is on key sectors with reference to climate change mitigation and adaptation. This list is likely to grow with the passage of time.

The taxonomy also links to their regulatory initiatives regarding sustainable finance. These include EU Green Bond Standard, low-carbon benchmarks and enhanced corporate disclosures.

Which investments qualify under Taxonomy regulation?

Under the Taxonomy Regulation, sustainable investment is an investment in an economic activity that contributes to an environmental objective. So, how do we measure this? Key resource efficiency indicators ensure that these investments do not significantly harm any of the objectives. They also require the investee companies to follow good governance practices.

To be properly characterised as environmentally sustainable, products should:

- Contribute substantially to one of the defined environmental objectives;

- Follow the 'Do no significant harm' principle: Not harm any of the environmental objectives;
- Comply with a series of minimum social safeguards; and
- Comply with performance thresholds.

The six environmental objectives are:

- Climate change mitigation;
- Climate change adaptation;
- Sustainable use and protection of water and marine resources;
- Transition to a circular economy;
- Pollution prevention and control; and
- Protection and restoration of biodiversity and ecosystems.[9]

Each objective is detailed in the Taxonomy Regulation. It is also linked to any existing EU law on that area. Over time further granularity in the technical screening criteria will be built up. These will be updated regularly to account for changes in the underpinning science and technology.

Target group in the new regulation and disclosure requirement

The Taxonomy Regulation is primarily meant for managers who provide a product that has an explicit sustainability focus ('ESG Products'). Irrespective of whether you are providing an ESG product or not, the framework applies to all. For those who do not offer ESG products, disclosure will be required that confirms whether the product is out of scope and whether it adheres to the taxonomy criteria.

The Taxonomy Regulation incorporates certain concepts from the Disclosures Regulation and amends certain provisions of that Regulation. It builds on the three-tier categorisation of products set out in the Disclosures Regulation:[10]

1. Products that have sustainable investment as an objective (Disclosures Regulation Article 9 products);
2. Products that promote environmental or social characteristics (Disclosures Regulation Article 8 products); and
3. Products that do not fall into either of these first two categories.

For asset managers promoting ESG products there will be additional disclosure requirements. These will be over and above those already set out in the Disclosures Regulation. The regulations on disclosures relating to sustainable investments and sustainability risks were adopted by the European Parliament and Council in April 2019. The regulations require the financial market actors to disclose sustainability risks and impacts thereof of their products. Many of these players invest in several sectors. The sustainability risks and impacts arising out of the wide-ranging investments need to be analysed to provide the disclosure required by the regulation.

The Taxonomy Regulation also talks about the development of technical standards that detail the 'do no significant harm' principle expressed in the Disclosure Regulation.

What does the new regulation mean for various stakeholders?

- The Taxonomy applies directly to Member States, who are prohibited from introducing domestic rules that would compromise the integrity of the Taxonomy regime.
- Non-sustainable investments will be discouraged given the requirement to disclose massively stranded assets and carbon-heavy indicators.
- The financial market actors can be expected to look much more closely at the activities they are financing and investing in. Prior to this new regulation, investors and financiers could easily hide their investments in climate unfriendly areas.
- The actors may develop their analyses of their investment and financing targets and aggregate them in order to define their organisation's risk and impacts.
- Financiers and investors are likely to seek sector-specific best practices as benchmarks for decision making, considering that the Taxonomy thresholds in many cases make use of these.
- Companies need to assess a) if their business supports climate mitigation or adaptation and to what extent, b) are they aware of the sustainability criteria that financiers and investors use c) how does it fare against peers, d) is the needed information easily available for investors and financiers etc.

Challenges

- The biggest challenge to an investor seeking to integrate sustainability risks into their investment practices and outcomes is the availability of good quality, relevant and comparable ESG and green data. To identify the right data, at the right level of granularity, and from the right issuers, is the need of the hour.
- Another challenge is the potential changes to the detailed taxonomy criteria. If the criteria changes, disclosure and analysis need to change too.
- Current green identification solutions are mostly focussed on revenues. More work is required to enhance green identification. Relevant Operating and Capital expenditure needs to be identified and company disclosure of this information needs to be provided.
- It is likely that many competing international taxonomy frameworks will come up. There is a need to avoid this.

What can possibly be done?

- There is an urgent need to engage with companies and issuers to improve disclosure and transparency (see Technical Note 3).
- It has been pointed out that it may be worthwhile to create sector specific screening criteria.
- There is a need to back collaborative initiatives. These could include the Climate Action 100+ initiative or the Net-Zero Asset Owner Alliance. This will push companies and climate solutions providers to share more diverse information sets.

Likely future impact of EU Taxonomy

1. The EU taxonomy will eventually replace the mass of voluntary schemes with a single classification system for the EU. The initial focus will be on environment but will gradually be extended to social and governance considerations.
2. The EU framework is likely to become the de facto global ESG gold standard since it will have the force of law and no other legal frameworks that are being developed are likely to compete with it on legal grounds.
3. Given the legal legitimacy that the taxonomy provides relative to their frameworks, there is likely to be greater interest in investors outside of

EU. These investors are seeking assurance (and even their clients are!) that their investments are genuinely sustainable and not greenwashed.

4. The EU will have a first mover advantage with the first legal and pan-regional framework. This will bring about important network effects. They could serve as a barrier to other players who want to be in the ESG standards game. It may even pose an existential threat to existing voluntary schemes. A new ESG world order is in the making.

Technical Note 6

ESG CONSIDERATIONS FOR EQUITY INVESTMENTS

INVESTMENT IN EQUITIES IS NOW INCREASINGLY INCLUDING ESG considerations. There are many models of achieving focus on ESG issues.

1. Exclusionary/Screened Investing

Screening uses a set of filters to determine which companies, sectors or activities are eligible or ineligible to be included in a specific portfolio. These criteria might be based on an investor's preferences, values and ethics. For example, a screen might be used to exclude the highest emitters of GHGs from a portfolio (negative screening) or to target only the lowest emitters (positive screening). It can be based on the policy of an asset manager or asset owner.

TABLE 1: SCREENING CAN BE DONE IN DIFFERENT WAYS, INCLUDING:

Negative Screening	Norms based screening	Positive Screening
Excluding certain sectors, issuers or securities for poor ESG performance relative to industry peers, or based on specific ESG criteria, e.g. avoiding particular products/ services, regions or business practices	Screening issuers against minimum standards of business practice based on international norms. Useful frameworks include UN treaties, Security Council sanctions, UN Global Compact, UN Human Rights Declaration and OECD guidelines	Investing in sectors, issuers or projects selected for positive ESG performance relative to industry peers

Negative Screening	Norms based screening	Positive Screening
Absolute avoidance of activities such as alcohol, tobacco, gambling, adult entertainment, military weapons, fossil fuels, nuclear energy	A sub-category of negative screening which excludes companies or government debt on account of any failure by the issuer to meet internationally accepted 'norms' such as the UN Global Compact, Kyoto Protocol, UN Declaration of Human Rights, International Labour Organisation standards, UN Convention Against Corruption, OECD Guidelines for Multinational Enterprises	Active inclusion of companies within an investment universe because of the social or environmental benefits of their products, services and/or processes
Sets a materiality threshold (e.g. 10 per cent) based on revenue exposure or business activity/operation Avoidance of worst-in-class investments using quantitative ESG measurements Shariah screening, guided by Islamic principles, is a subcategory of negative screening	Can be called 'controversy screens' or negative screening when companies engage in unethical behaviour	Positive thematic development such as transitioning companies, renewable/ clean tech, social enterprises or initiatives

Source: An Introduction to Responsible Investing: Screening, Principles of Responsible Investing https://www.unpri.org/an-introduction-to-responsible-investment/an-introduction-to-responsible-investment-screening/5834.article

Implementation of screening process involves:

1. Identification of client priorities to ensure that proper investment process and screening is undertaken.
2. Publicise clear screening criteria in contractual agreements such as the Investment Management Agreement or marketing literature.
3. Oversight should be introduced through an advisory committee or by empowering internal compliance to conduct reviews, monitor implementation and results, and criteria changes.
4. Implement screening in the investment process. There are three modes of screening/exclusion:

- **Absolute exclusion:** No investment in exclusionary criteria, e.g. no direct investment in fossil fuels or a company found to be violating human rights
- **Threshold exclusion:** Partial investment, tolerance level set, e.g. up to 10 per cent of revenues derived from indirect exposure to fossil fuels or for services connected to it
- **Relative exclusion:** Best-in-class investments, e.g. where energy transition is occurring or where board diversity is improving, not determined through revenue exposures

5. Review the performance of the investment by looking at tracking errors.
6. Monitor and audit.

Exclusionary investment has achieved significant success, and its ease of use makes it an ideal candidate for ESG investing.

2. Best in class selection

Here investors prefer companies with better or improving ESG performance compared to their sector peers. Some investors look at the level of change in ESG performance while others look at investing in more companies with better ESG performance relative to sector peers. There are two ways of evaluating for best in class:

- **On an absolute basis**: The investors compare the company's ESG ratings with companies across the ESG universe.
- **On a relative basis**: Here the investors compares ESG ratings/scores of companies with other companies in the same industry.

Investors seek to achieve return and risk profile similar to traditional investments while integrating material ESG factors in evaluation. This involves applying a higher weight to companies with favourable ESG scores and lower weights to companies with unfavourable ESG scores. While evaluating for best in class investors often look at

- **ESG quality**: Ability to manage key risks and opportunities arising from ESG factors
- **Distribution of ESG Ratings**: Companies are classified as leaders, average or laggards. The distribution of companies in these categories is then considered for decision-making.

- **ESG Ratings Momentum**: This considers the percentage of holdings that have had a recent ESG ratings upgrade or downgrade.

Implementation of a best in class selection can be done through either of two approaches—active or passive.

In the active approach, managers integrate ESG research into the investment process. This is then used to identify financial materiality. The portfolio managers then choose companies to invest in. This involves selecting companies that exhibit the desired ESG factors that will reduce long-term risk while generating a sustainable alpha. The primary objective is to earn strong risk-adjusted returns with ESG characteristics being somewhat in the background. This approach is popular in Europe but is gaining ground in North America.

Alternatively, investors can passively invest in several available ESG integrated indices (e.g. MSCI ACWI ESG leaders). These indices tend to have static methodologies that adjust the weights of the traditional index constituents based on their underlying ESG ratings. For this strategy performance has varied in different time periods. However, the MSCI ACWI ESG Leaders Index has outperformed the traditional MSCI ACWI on a risk-adjusted basis over the last ten years.

3. Active Ownership

Active owners communicate frequently with companies with ESG issues. They exercise their ownership rights and voice their concerns to bring about a change. They engage with companies to monitor their ESG performance. They may also influence outcomes and ESG practices throught their intervention.

4. ESG Integration

Unfortunately, the traditional equity research process doesn't take note of the ESG risks discussed earlier. Let us take a look at the equity research process and try and understand where ESG elements can be brought in.

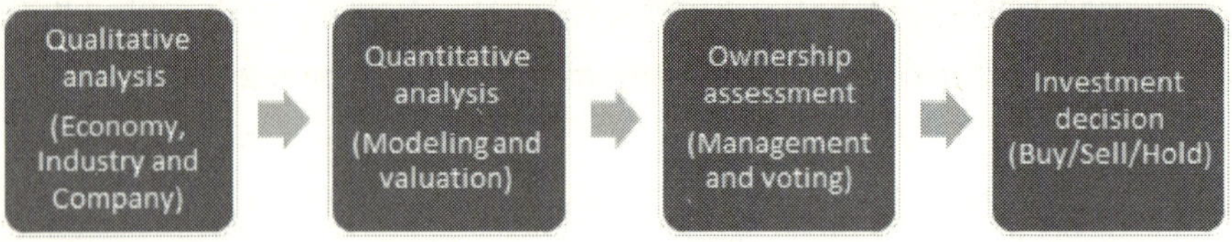

During the qualitative analysis phase, ESG issues impacting the industry and the company can be identified. During the modelling and valuation analysis, ESG risks can be captured in either the discount rate or the cashflows. One should, however, be careful so as not to account for the same risk in both cash flows and the discount rate. While evaluating the management, careful attention should be paid to both management's views on ESG as well as their past track record on dealing with those issues.

There are several techniques of integrating ESG in investment decisions.

Quantitative strategies

Quantitative (quant) strategies utilise data, mathematical models and statistical techniques to outperform their benchmarks.

There are two principal approaches to integrating ESG factors into quantitative models. They involve adjusting the weights of:

- Securities ranked poorly on ESG to zero, based on research that links ESG factors to investment risk and/or risk-adjusted returns;
- Each security in the investment universe, according to the statistical relationship between an ESG dataset and other factors.

Smart beta strategies

Smart beta investing uses a combination of both passive and active investment disciplines. It weights the constituents of a market-capitalisation index by factor(s) other than market capitalisation. These are factors such as value, dividend yield, momentum, growth, quality or volatility. The objective is to outperform the index, lower the downside risk or increase the dividend yield. Some smart beta strategies use these types of data directly, and some use mathematical weighting schemes that can result in similar exposures.

In smart beta strategies, ESG factors and scores can be used as a weight in portfolio construction. This is aimed to create excess risk-adjusted returns, reduce downside risk and/or enhance portfolios' ESG risk profile.

Passive and enhanced Passive strategies

Passive investment strategies seek to match the performance of a market or a section of a market by closely tracking the return of a capitalisation-weighted index. There are a variety of methods that are used by passive investments to replicate an index.

- *Full replication methodology* requires buying all the constituents of an index.
- *Partial replication methodology* (also known as stratified sampling) sees the investment manager invest in a sample set of constituents of an index and adjust their weights so that the fund matches the index on characteristics such as market capitalisation and industry weightings. While this can lower transaction costs, it can increase tracking error as the sample may not closely follow the index.
- Another approach uses derivatives to track an index.

Passive strategies can incorporate ESG factors. One way is to reduce the ESG risk profile or exposure to a particular ESG factor. This can be achieved by tracking an index that adjusts the weights of constituents of a parent index accordingly. Funds that use a partial replication approach can also exclude companies with high ESG risk or low ESG ratings. Often these benchmarks use portfolio optimisation techniques that help minimise tracking error.

Additionally, integration techniques can be applied to enhanced passive strategies. As enhanced passive strategies can make active investment decisions such as adjusting index constituent weights and excluding certain stocks altogether to lower downside risk or outperform the benchmark, managers can integrate ESG factors into these strategies.

Technical Note 7

GREEN BANKS

IN 2020, BUSINESSES SAW MANY CHANGES. THE MOST SIGNIFICANT change in the sustainability narrative has been the entry of banks and large financial institutions which have made substantial commitments in financing the transition to a clean, green economy. Of the world's largest fifty banks, twenty-five banks have made public sustainable finance commitments totalling more than $2.5 trillion.[11]

For instance, Goldman Sachs plans to spend $750 billion over the next decade financing and advising companies focussed on climate transition and inclusive growth. Many banks have signed up to the new UN-backed Principles for Responsible Banking[12] and a host of other initiatives such as Science Based Targets[13] or RE 100[14] which commits to source 100 per cent of energy from renewable sources.

All this has come about due to two key developments. First, the Paris Agreement that created nationally determined contributions that will help limit global warming to well below 2 degrees, preferably to 1.5 degrees Celsius.[15]

Second, UN came out with sustainable development goals that are a 'blueprint to achieve a better and more sustainable future for all.[16]

The 17 goals are required to be achieved by 2030 and are known as Agenda 2030. Given the massive scope of work involved in climate change mitigation arising out of the Paris Agreement and the scale of work required to achieve Agenda 2030, significant funding needs are envisaged. It is estimated that $93 trillion may be needed in infrastructure investment by 2030.[17]

Banks often lack the specialist knowledge to cater to the growing need to fund green projects. This has led to the development of the concept of green banks.[18]

According to OECD, 'A Green Bank as a public, quasi-public or a non-profit entity established specifically to facilitate private investment into domestic low-carbon, climate-resilient infrastructure and other green sectors such as water and waste management.

'According to the Coalition for Green Capital (CGC)—a non-profit Green Bank advisory organisation—a Green Bank is fundamentally 'a focussed institution, created to maximise clean energy adoption'.[19]

A green bank is not to be confused with green banking which is undertaken by commercial banks which involves being conscious of lending decisions, operating from 'green' buildings, reducing power consumption, using paperless technology etc.

The new institutional mechanism of green banks leverages public funds to make private investments in clean technologies. They can become a focal point in helping implement NDCs and achieving SDGs by creating financial products to address market barriers. Many of the projects linked with NDCs and SDGs' achievement often find little support with either large investment banks or venture capital/private equity funds.

So, how are green banks different from other financial institutions? We can distinguish green banks in several ways:

1. They focus on commercially viable technologies.
2. The capital is dedicated to a social or environmental purpose.
3. A focus on leveraging private investment.
4. A relationship with the policymakers and the government.

How does a green bank work? Typically, a green bank will raise resources from public and private sources. Private sources include bilateral and multilateral assistance, and institutional funding. Public sources of funds include funding from government mainly in the form of grants. They may also raise capital of their own. However, these banks typically do not take deposits. These funds are then deployed in green projects that scale up climate solutions and enable multiple co-benefits, including job creation, pollution reduction, energy access, etc. These goals are achieved through the creation of several products and tools. These include co-lending/financing (debt and equity), risk mitigation and credit enhancement (guarantees, first loss, green bonds), innovative financing (tax credits, lien-based financing), debt forgiveness for decarbonisation, etc. They fund projects in areas like renewable energy, energy efficiency, clean transportation, coal plant retirement, waste management, bioenergy, adaptation and resilience, agriculture and land use. The benefits are climate change mitigation, clean air and water, resilient infrastructure, etc. through active interventions with support from funds from green banks.

FIGURE 1: WORKING OF A GREEN BANK

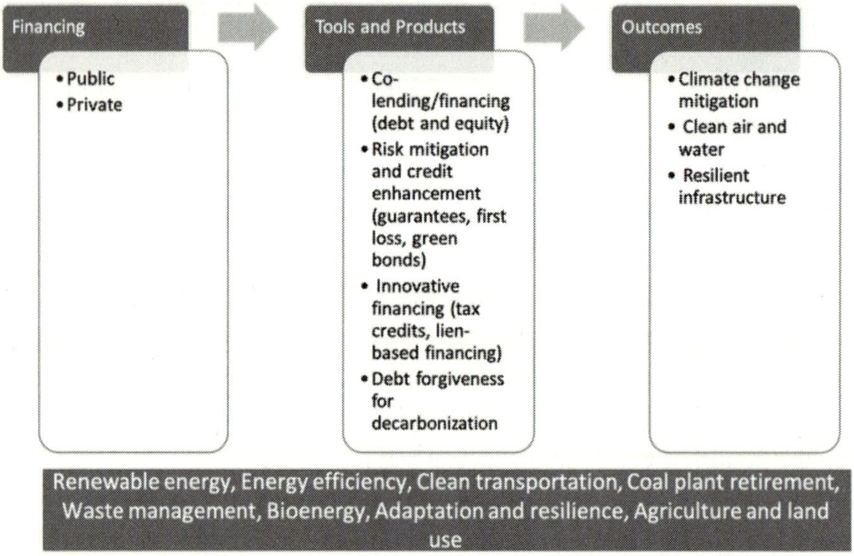

Source: Adapted from: Adriana Becerra Cid et al., State of Green Banks 2020, Green Bank Design Platform, https://www.nrdc.org/sites/default/files/state-green-banks-2020-report.pdf

There are several green banks around the world. In the US, there is the Connecticut Green bank, the UK Green Investment Group in the UK, Technology Fund Switzerland, The Green Finance Organisation in Japan, Masdar in UAE, Green Tech in Malaysia, India's Tata Cleantech Capital Limited (TCCL), etc.

Role of Green Banks

Green banks play a critical role in helping a country meet its nationally determined contributions and SDG targets. This is done through many means.

1. Getting together providers of climate finance through consortium arrangements with development finance institutions and other players. They act as local partners and investors in projects that decarbonise through climate resilient projects.
2. They increase bankability of the projects by creating financial products to mitigate investor risk on initial transactions in low-carbon, climate-resilient sectors
3. Given the control they exert on projects, they can drive project developers and investors to adopt impact metrics. This helps track progress toward national climate and sustainability targets.
4. They help by guiding investors on the technical and economic feasibility of new technologies.
5. They help build a knowledge base and capacity within the financial sector.
6. They can assist policymakers by assisting them in understanding technologies that create enabling environments for low-carbon, climate-resilient projects

Case Study: UK Green Bank

Its definition of 'green impact' relates to the positive contribution to five specific measures. These are to reduce GHG emission, increase natural resource efficiency, protect the natural resources, protect biodiversity, and, promote environmental sustainability. They call them 'Green Purposes'. Every investment must contribute to at least one of the purposes and many contribute to more than one.

UK Green Bank has arranged or committed capital in excess of GBP 20 billion. 198 MtCO2e GHG emissions has been avoided. This is equivalent to removing 2.5 million cars from the road. It has supported 568,243 GWh renewable energy generation, equivalent to the energy consumption of 5.8 million homes

Source: UK Green Investment Group, https://www.greeninvestmentgroup.com/assets/gig/corporate-governance/GIG_ProgressReport_2020.pdf

Case Study: Green Liberty Bond Programme

In July 2020, Connecticut Green Bank in the United States launched an innovative Green Liberty Bond programme modelled on the World War II Series E bonds: 10-year, small-denomination bonds that allowed ordinary citizens to invest in the war effort. The Green Liberty Bond programme issues small denomination ($1,000) green bonds that are used to fund rooftop solar, and that are accessible to individuals. Projected revenues from solar home renewable energy credits that two Connecticut utilities will be purchasing from the Green Bank at a previously agreed upon price over the fifteen-year life of the bond are about $25 million. Through their use of proceeds for green projects that combat climate change, these bonds aim to contribute to several SDGs: poverty eradication, reduced inequalities, good health and wellbeing, affordable clean energy, decent work and economic growth, and sustainable cities and communities.

Source: State of Green Banks 2020, https://rmi.org/insight/state-of-green-banks-2020

Risk mitigation

Not only do green banks provide financial support to lenders, they also help mitigate risks.

Credit risk: One of the key issues in lending is that assets can become stranded. The bank is unable to recover its lending as fossil-fuel based technology comes to a stop and renewable energy gets deployed. The cash flows of the fossil-fuel based technology are disrupted leading to an inability to pay interest and/or principal. Green banks can help mitigate risks through their arsenal of tools.

Legal risk: Compliance with legal environmental rules could have repercussions for banks and investors. Companies and banks may have to share legal risks. Green banks mitigate this risk by shifting to cleaner technologies.

Reputation risk: Green banks help companies reduce reputation risk by helping them shift to cleaner technologies. Not only do they help save reputation loss from dirty technology, they may also help companies enhance their reputation by utilising cleaner technologies. Reputational risk is also mitigated by focussing on social concerns.

Green banks have proven to be a successful model for channelling climate funds. They help drive the private sector into clean technology investments, and developing new green markets. Green banks are helping companies transition to low carbon and climate resilient technologies. This helps bring companies and countries to align with the Paris Agreement by creating capabilities and capacity for transition. Capital pools such as pension funds and sovereign wealth funds are increasingly being utilised to capitalise green banks. They are also partnering to co-invest in projects that promote energy transition. Green banks are becoming a focal point to access available but hard to secure funding. Given these trends, green banks are slowly occupying the banking space where doing good goes in tandem with doing well.

Technical Note 8

THE TERMS THAT EVERYONE IN THE FINANCIAL SECTOR NEEDS TO UNDERSTAND

NATURE AND ECONOMICS GO TOGETHER: Here are the main overarching concepts that fit within the circular economy:

- **Product Stewardship:** The parent company takes full responsibility for reducing the environmental impact of the product they create throughout the entire life cycle of the product, ensuring that there are appropriate end-of-life options and that these are managed by the parent company.
- **Eco Design**: Approaches to designing products so that they last longer and have a limited impact on the environment across their full life cycle. This is also called sustainable design.
- **Industrial Ecology:** Ways of remodelling industrial systems to perform more like ecological ones and maximise value exchange.
- **Industrial Symbiosis:** Part of industrial ecology, a network of diverse organisations collaborate to ensure that resources are used efficiently and value is cycled between them.
- **Waste Equals Food:** An approach where all 'waste' becomes a nutrient to something else in the system.
- **Non-Fossil Energy:** Energy derived from renewable resources.
- **True Cost Accounting:** A type of accounting that takes into consideration the full externalities and costs associated with performing a service, doing business, or creating a product.

- **Cradle to cradle:** A concept of ensuring that the full life of a product is managed in a sustainable way that was made popular in a book of the same name and has a certification system for products.
- **Biomimicry:** An approach to creating products and services that mimic the way nature works by studying and replicating the solutions found in the natural world.
- **Regenerative Design:** A whole systems approach to creating solutions that offer back more than is taken in their creation by exploring the way natural systems solve problems and creating things that are interconnected with natural systems.
- **Post Disposable:** A movement to make waste obsolete by designing solutions that move beyond waste as a socially acceptable concept.
- **Life Cycle Thinking:** A framework that takes into consideration the whole of life environmental impacts of a product or service by looking at the impacts that actions in the economy have on natural systems by looking from the cradle to the grave.
- **Closing the loop:** This is a concept promoted by some businesses as a solution to waste generation and in support of the circular economy. By closing the loop on the end-of-life impacts of a product from the design stage, the business can be redesigned to support end-to-end integrated systems.
- **Technical nutrients:** Materials or stocks that are manipulated by humans and cannot be easily re-integrated into nature (for example, plastics).
- **Biological nutrients:** Materials or stocks that can be easily absorbed or digested by natural systems in a benign way (unbleached paper or food).
- **Zero waste:** This is a strategy and movement to go beyond waste reduction and remove all disposable products from a place, company or lifestyle by embracing a set of strategies that eliminate waste completely. The goal is to avoid sending any waste to a landfill or incinerator.

Technical Note 9

IMPACT MEASUREMENT TOOLS

SEVERAL MEASUREMENT SYSTEMS HAVE DEVELOPED OVER A PERIOD of time. Some of the prominent ones are:

- **Environmental profit and loss (EP&L) statement**: Pioneering development of a means of placing a monetary value on the environmental impacts along the supply chain of a business.
- **KPMG True Value**: A three-step methodology that enables companies to i) assess their 'true' earnings including externalities, ii) understand future earnings at risk and iii) develop business cases that create both corporate and societal value.
- **Natural capital protocol**: A harmonised framework for valuing natural capital in investor decision making.
- **B impact assessment**: Standards, benchmarks and tools enabling companies to assess, compare and improve their social and environmental impacts over time.
- **Redefining value**: A work programme that aims to help World Business Council for Sustainable Development (WBCSD) member firms standardise tools to measure and manage their impact on society and the environment.
- **Shared value**: A management strategy focussed on creating business value by identifying and addressing social problems.
- **Social return on investment (SROI)**: A framework based on generally accepted accounting principles used to help manage and understand an organisation's social, economic and environmental outcomes.

- **Total impact measurement and management (TIMM)**: A new language to assist companies in understanding the overall impact of their activities.
- **True price**: A social enterprise that helps organisations—multinationals, SMEs, NGOs, governments—quantify and evaluate their economic, environmental and social impacts, particularly on a product level.

In June 2021, SASB and International Integrated Reporting Council have merged to form Value Reporting Foundation.

Once the internal tools are set, companies report on their sustainability and social responsibility activities. The primary reporting frameworks being used in India are the Global Reporting Initiative (GRI) based sustainability reports, Business Responsibility Reports and Integrated Reporting (IR).

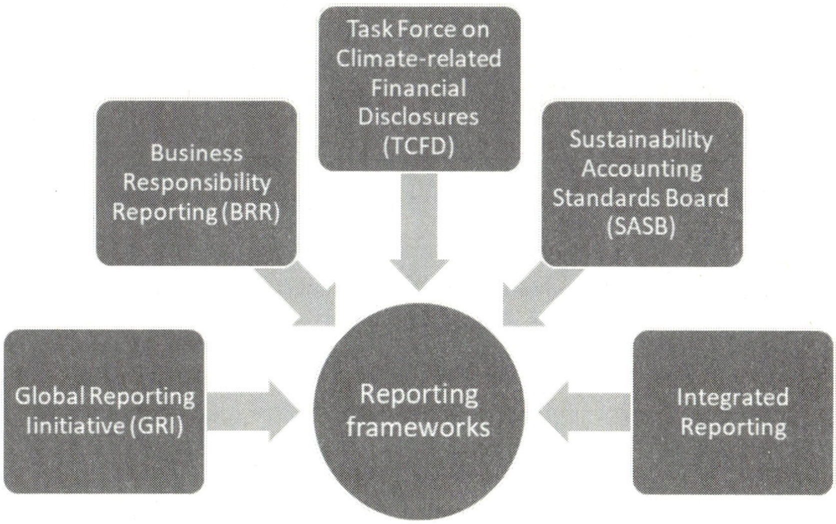

- **GRI based sustainability reports**: The GRI standards were the first standards set out for sustainability reporting. They are seen as global best practices for reporting social, economic and environmental impacts. In India, only a handful of large corporations have adopted GRI-based reporting. Due to the wide nature of requirements and auditing procedures, small firms find it difficult to adopt them.

- **Business Responsibility and Sustainability Reporting (BRSR)**: From the year 2021-22, the Securities and Exchange Board of India (SEBI) has introduced the BRSR that requires top 1000 companies by market capitalisation to provide information that makes more quantitative metrics available, enabling users to evaluate the ESG performance of the company.
- **Task Force on Climate-related Financial Disclosures**: The Financial Stability Board Task Force on Climate-related Financial Disclosures (TCFD) develops voluntary, consistent climate-related financial risk disclosures for use by companies in providing information to investors, lenders, insurers, and other stakeholders.

The Task Force considers the physical, liability and transition risks associated with climate change and what constitutes effective financial disclosures across industries. The work and recommendations of the Task Force will help companies understand what financial markets want from disclosure in order to measure and respond to climate change risks, and encourage firms to align their disclosures with investors' needs.

Although not a reporting framework per se, it is likely to have a significant influence on reporting climate related activities.

- **Sustainability Accounting Standards Board**: Established in 2011, the Sustainability Accounting Standards Board (SASB) is an independent, private-sector standards setting organisation based in San Francisco, California dedicated to enhancing the efficiency of the capital markets by fostering high-quality disclosure of material sustainability information that meets investor needs. The SASB develops and maintains sustainability accounting standards—for seventy-nine industries in eleven sectors—that help public corporations disclose financially material information to investors in a cost-effective and decision-useful format. The SASB's transparent, inclusive, and rigorous standards-setting process is materiality focussed, evidence-based and market informed.
- **Integrated Reporting**: A large number of companies still believe that reporting is a compliance issue and not one that involves a focus on communication to key stakeholders. Integrated reporting seeks to

> overcome this by bringing together material information about an organisation's strategy, governance, performance and prospects. This is done in a way that reflects the commercial, social and environmental context within which it operates. It provides a mechanism to disclose all kinds of capital that underlies any business—financial capital, manufactured capital, intellectual capital, human capital, social and relationship capital and natural capital.

In June 2021, SASB and International Integrated Reporting Council have merged to form Value Reporting Foundation. Non-financial reporting in this case has been at multiple levels, the international standards based GRI report and the India specific reports. SEBI has issued an advisory to companies to provide information required by Integrated Reporting that encourages the top 500 BSE listed companies to use Integrated Reporting as a framework to improve the quality and relevance of the information. Given this development it appears likely that Integrated Reporting will form the foundation of business reports in the near future. However, with the merger of SAB and IIRC it is unclear what shape this reporting requirement will take.

However, one should be mindful of the fact that companies may still end up using differing reporting formats given that the requirements of various stakeholders are different. Consulting firms may want to defend their turfs and not allow new but useful reporting formats to take root. Yet, we believe that if companies were to report more uniformly, comparison across firms will be far more valuable and greater insights will be drawn.

Challenges for the accounting profession

Given the complexity of the task and the proliferation of standards, the accounting profession in India needs to chart out a path that meets the requirements of Indian companies. The profession needs to move from being centred on financial metrics to move towards non-financial metrics. The scope of sustainability reporting is vast and so are business opportunities for the profession. The time is ripe for the profession to meet the challenges of measurement and develop robust practices for sustainability reporting. There is a need for accounting professionals to develop a strategic perspective, adapt to newer technologies and constantly upgrade their knowledge to meet the challenges of sustainability in the age of the fourth industrial revolution.

Technical Note 10

BUSINESS RESPONSIBILITY AND SUSTAINABILITY REPORTING

IN MARCH 2021, SECURITIES AND EXCHANGE BOARD OF INDIA (SEBI) came out with a circular on *Business Responsibility and Sustainability Reporting* (BRSR). The BRSR is a move forward from Business Responsibility Reporting (BRR) and aims to bring sustainability reporting at par with financial reporting and makes ESG disclosures and reporting more prominent.

Since the requirement of BRR disclosures came about in 2012, many changes have taken place. They include the Paris Agreement, UN SDGs, and increased focus on transition to sustainable economies.

The BRSR has three sections:

- **Section A: General Disclosures**

  The objective of this section is to obtain basic information about the company—size, location, products, number of employees, CSR activities, etc.

- **Section B: Management and Process**

  In this section, the company is required to disclose information on policies and processes relating to the National Guidelines for Responsible Business Conduct's (NGRBC) Principles concerning leadership, governance, and stakeholder engagement.

  The purpose of this section is to understand whether the company has the building blocks in place that will enable and ensure responsible business conduct.

- **Section C: Principle-wise performance**
  Responses to this section would indicate how a company is performing with respect to each principle and core element of the NGRBCs. This section requires companies to demonstrate their intent and commitment to responsible business conduct through actions and outcomes. Specific measures are sought on value chain, labour welfare and representation of women and differently abled on the board of directors of the company.

The questions in this section have been divided into two categories:

1. *Essential:* Those that are mandatory for all companies.
2. *Leadership:* Those that are voluntary and which provide an opportunity for companies to present their impacts and outcomes. It is expected that in the next cycle of review, questions from the Leadership category would be moved to the Essential category and so companies should see this as a pathway to transitioning to a more comprehensive disclosures regime.

The circular permits listed entities that already prepare sustainability reports based on internationally accepted reporting frameworks (GRi, TCFD, Value Reporting Framework) to cross-reference the disclosures made in the sustainability reports to the disclosures sought under the BRSR.

Two versions of reporting have been envisaged: (a) Comprehensive format and (b) lite version. The lite version is to enable the first time reporters on sustainability.

The BRSR shall be applicable to the top 1000 listed entities by market capitalisation. The circular states that reporting of BRSR shall be voluntary for FY 2021–22 and mandatory from FY 2022–23. However, it encourages companies to be early adopters of the BRSR and be at the forefront of sustainability reporting.

The BRSR lays considerable emphasis on quantifiable metrics. This enables easy measurement and comparability across companies, sectors and time periods. The BRSR also makes disclosures on climate and social (employees, consumers and communities) related issues more granular.

According to SEBI, access to relevant and comparable information will enable investors to identify and assess sustainability-related risks and opportunities of companies and make better investment decisions.

NOTES

1. Checkpoint 2025

1. Till Kellerhoff, 'A Green Reboot After the Pandemic', *The Club of Rome*, March 24, 2020.
https://clubofrome.org/impact-hubs/climate-emergency/a-green-reboot-after-the-pandemic/.
2. 'World's billionaires have more wealth than 4.6 billion people', *Oxfam*, accessed January 20, 2020, https://www.oxfam.org/en/press-releases/worlds-billionaires-have-more-wealth-46-billion-people.
3. 'Freshwater', *WWF*, https://www.worldwildlife.org/.
4. 'Grossly distorted picture', *The Economist*, March 13, 2008, https://www.economist.com/finance-and-economics/2008/03/13/grossly-distorted-picture.
5. The first industrial revolution took place with the invention of the steam engine and the birth of industrial manufacturing. It lasted between 1700 and 1800. The second industrial revolution was enabled by the discovery of the internal combustion engine and electricity. It lasted between 1800 and 1900. The third industrial revolution came with the growth of computing and later, the internet. It started in the second half of the 20th century. The fourth industrial revolution is happening NOW!
6. 'The Global Wealth Report 2020', *Credit Suisse* https://www.credit-suisse.com/about-us/en/reports-research/global-wealth-report.html.
7. 'Public Good or Private Wealth', January 2019, https://oxfamilibrary.openrepository.com/bitstream/handle/10546/620599/bp-public-good-or-private-wealth-210119-en.pdf?utm_source=indepth.
8. Rupert Neate, 'Ten billionaires reap $400bn boost to wealth during pandemic', *The Guardian*, December 19, 2020,
https://www.theguardian.com/technology/2020/dec/19/ten-billionaires-reap-400bn-boost-to-wealth-during-pandemic.
9. 'The Inequality Virus – Global Report 2021', *Oxfam India*, January 22, 2021, https://www.oxfamindia.org/knowledgehub/workingpaper/inequality-virus-global-report-2021.
10. Total factor productivity (TFP) is a measure of productivity calculated by dividing economy-wide total production by the weighted average of inputs i.e.

labour and capital. It represents growth in real output which is in excess of the growth in inputs such as labour and capital.

11. 'Securing India's Growth over the next decade', February 2018, https://www.citigroup.com/commercialbank/insights/assets/docs/2018/Securing-Indias-Growth-Over-the-Next-Decade//files/assets/common/downloads/publication.pdf?uni=279b9671efcc777ce2bed95e198e8a84.
12. Emma G. Fitzsimmons, 'Why Are Taxi Drivers in New York Killing Themselves?', *The New York Times*, December 2, 2018, https://www.nytimes.com/2018/12/02/nyregion/taxi-drivers-suicide-nyc.html.
13. Suneera Tandon, 'Zomato's Gold delivery plan may be the next food fight', *Mint*, August 31, 2019, https://www.livemint.com/companies/news/zomato-s-gold-delivery-plan-may-be-the-next-food-fight-1567190225703.html.
14. According to an EY report, 20 per cent of organisations globally with more than 1,000 employees have a workforce that is made up of 30 per cent or more contingent workers.
15. Namrata Rana and Utkarsh Majmudar, 'Responsible Business Rankings India's Top Companies for Sustainability and CSR 2020', *Futurescape*, https://www.futurescape.in/responsible-business-rankings/.
16. 'COVID-19 leads to massive labour income losses worldwide', *International Labour Organization*, September 23, 2020, https://www.ilo.org/global/about-the-ilo/newsroom/news/WCMS_755875/lang--en/index.htm.
17. World Economic Outlook, April 2020: The Great Lockdown', *International Monetary Fund*, accessed April, 2020, https://www.imf.org/en/Publications/WEO/Issues/2020/04/14/weo-april-2020.
18. Daniel Gerszon Mahler, Christoph Lakner, R. Andres Castaneda Aguilar and Haoyu Wu, 'Updated estimates of the impact of COVID-19 on global poverty', *World Bank Blogs*, accessed June 8, 2020, https://blogs.worldbank.org/opendata/updated-estimates-impact-covid-19-global-poverty.
19. 'The IMF has a warning about global growth', *World Economic Forum*, accessed October 10, 2018, https://www.weforum.org/agenda/2018/10/global-growth-plateaus-as-economic-risks-materialize.
20. https://opportunity.businessroundtable.org/ourcommitment/.
21. David Gelles and David Yaffe-Bellany, 'Shareholder Value Is No Longer Everything, Top C.E.O.s Say', *The New York Times*, 19 August 2019, https://www.nytimes.com/2019/08/19/business/business-roundtable-ceos-corporations.html.
22. Helen Avery, 'Sustainable finance's biggest problems, by the people who know best', *Euromoney*, accessed December 3, https://www.euromoney.com/article/b1j97rjr74vdoo/sustainable-finances-biggest-problems-by-the-people-who-know-best.
23. 'Principles for Responsible Banking', https://www.unepfi.org/banking/bankingprinciples/.
24. https://sciencebasedtargets.org/financial-institutions/
25. http://there100.org/
26. Natalie Kenway, 'Perfect storm' will accelerate ESG assets to top $53trn by 2025', Natalie Kenway, *ESGClarity*, 25 January 2021,

https://esgclarity.com/perfect-storm-will-accelerate-esg-assets-to-top-53trn-by-2025/.

2. The Net Zero Transition

1. 'Setting countries on the path to Net Zero emissions and a more prosperous future', *World Resources Institute*, https://www.wri.org/climate/long-term-strategies.
2. Yi-Ming Wei and others, 'Self-preservation strategy for approaching global warming targets in the post-Paris Agreement era', *Nature Communications*, April 14, 2020, https://www.nature.com/articles/s41467-020-15453-z.
3. 'Race To Zero Campaign', https://unfccc.int/climate-action/race-to-zero-campaign
4. 'Global Resources Outlook: 2019: Natural Resources for the Future We Want,' https://www.resourcepanel.org/reports/global-resources-outlook.
5. https://ourworldindata.org/emissions-by-sector
6. 'Now's the time to get ahead of the climate crisis', *The Economist*, accessed May 22, 2020, https://www.startribune.com/now-s-the-time-to-get-ahead-of-the-climate-crisis/570707062/.
7. 'Climate Change and Land: An IPCC Special Report on climate change, desertification, land degradation, sustainable land management, food security, and greenhouse gas fluxes in terrestrial ecosystems', https://www.ipcc.ch/site/assets/uploads/2019/08/Edited-SPM_Approved_Microsite_FINAL.pdf.
8. Jonathan Watts, 'We have 12 years to limit climate change catastrophe, warns UN', *The Guardian*, October 8, 2018, https://www.theguardian.com/environment/2018/oct/08/global-warming-must-not-exceed-15c-warns-landmark-un-report.
9. Marshall Burke, Solomon M. Hsiang & Edward Miguel, 'Global non-linear effect of temperature on economic production', *Nature*, accessed October 21, 2015, https://www.nature.com/articles/nature15725.
10. Muthukumara Mani, Sushenjit Bandyopadhyay, Shun Chonabayashi, Anil Markandya and Thomas Mosier, 'South Asia's Hotspots: The Impact of Temperature and Precipitation Changes on Living Standards', *The World Bank*, https://openknowledge.worldbank.org/bitstream/handle/10986/28723/9781464811555.pdf?sequence=5&isAllowed=y.
11. 'Climate Change Could Depress Living Standards in India, says New World Bank Report', *The World Bank*, June 28, 2018, https://www.worldbank.org/en/news/press-release/2018/06/28/climate-change-depress-living-standards-india-says-new-world-bank-report.
12. 'What is climate change and what can we do about it?', Climate Council, October 16, 2019, https://www.climatecouncil.org.au/resources/what-is-climate-change-what-can-we-do/.
13. 'Roadmap for moving to a competitive low carbon economu in 2050: Key facts and figures', https://ec.europa.eu/clima/sites/clima/files/strategies/2050/docs/

roadmap_fact_sheet_en.pdf.
14. Susan Tierney and Lori Bird, 'Setting the Record Straight About Renewable Energy', *World Resources Institute*, May 12, 2020, https://www.wri.org/blog/2020/05/setting-record-straight-about-renewable-energy.
15. 'The Ten Point Plan for a Green Industrial Revolution', *UK Government*, November 18, 2020, https://www.gov.uk/government/publications/the-ten-point-plan-for-a-green-industrial-revolution.
16. 'India aiming to cut its carbon footprint by up to 35%, says Narendra Modi', *Scroll*, November 21, 2020, https://scroll.in/latest/979099/india-aiming-to-cut-its-carbon-footprint-by-up-to-35-says-narendra-modi.
17. https://www.indiabudget.gov.in/economicsurvey/.
18. https://pib.gov.in/PressReleasePage.aspx?PRID=1670351.
19. Schneider Electric Integrated Report 2019, https://www.se.com/ww/en/assets/564/document/145371/integrated-report-2019.pdf.
20. https://missionpossiblepartnership.org/.
21. https://www.xprize.org/prizes/elonmusk.
22. Brad Smith, 'Microsoft will be carbon negative by 2030', Microsoft Blog, 16 January 2020, https://blogs.microsoft.com/blog/2020/01/16/microsoft-will-be-carbon-negative-by-2030/.
23. IEA 'Annual global GDP growth and changes in industrial bioenergy demand, 1990-2019', *IEA*, Paris, May 19, 2020, https://www.iea.org/data-and-statistics/charts/annual-global-gdp-growth-and-changes-in-industrial-bioenergy-demand-1990-2019.
24. 'UK becomes first major economy to pass Net Zero emissions law', *UK Government*, https://www.gov.uk/government/news/uk-becomes-first-major-economy-to-pass-Net Zero-emissions-law.
25. Jillian Ambrose, 'UK launches £315m new tech fund to help industry cut emissions', *The Guardian*, 5 November 2019, https://www.theguardian.com/environment/2019/nov/05/uk-tech-fund-industry-emissions-energy-bills.
26. Hanna Ziady, '2 billion people use these products. By 2030 they'll be biodegradable', *CNN Business*, 7 July 2020, https://edition.cnn.com/2020/06/15/business/unilever-climate-change-commitments/index.html.
27. The Institutional Investors Group on Climate Change, https://www.iigcc.org.
28. 'New Nature Economy Report II: The Future of Nature and Business', *World Economic Forum*, July 14, 2020, https://www.weforum.org/reports/new-nature-economy-report-ii-the-future-of-nature-and-business.
29. https://www.mondelezinternational.com/About-Us.
30. 'Toyota and the world', https://www.toyotauk.com/about-toyota/.
31. Futurescape Responsible Business Rankings.
32. 'Maersk ECO Deliver', https://www.maersk.com/solutions/shipping/ocean-transport/eco-delivery.

33. 'Leading Danish companies join forces on an ambitious sustainable fuel project', *Maersk*, 26 May 2020, https://www.maersk.com/news/articles/2020/05/26/leading-danish-companies-join-forces-on-an-ambitious-sustainable-fuel-project.

3. ESG Transforms Business

1. Nick Cunningham, 'Activist Investors Force Change In The Oil Industry', 3 March 2019, https://oilprice.com/Energy/Energy-General/Activist-Investors-Force-Change-In-The-Oil-Industry.html.
2. Laura Hurst, 'Exxon, Chevron targeted by climate-activist investor group', *OilPrice.com*, 16 December 2019, https://www.worldoil.com/news/2019/12/16/exxon-chevron-targeted-by-climate-activist-investor-group.
3. Daniel Boffey, 'Court orders Royal Dutch Shell to cut carbon emissions by 45% by 2030', *The Guardian*, 26 May 2021, https://www.theguardian.com/business/2021/may/26/court-orders-royal-dutch-shell-to-cut-carbon-emissions-by-45-by-2030.
4. 'Larry Fink's 2021 letter to CEOs', https://www.blackrock.com/corporate/investor-relations/larry-fink-ceo-letter.
5. 'Global Warming of 1.5 °C', https://www.ipcc.ch/sr15/.
6. Namrata Rana. A Trillion Trees and Amazon, Futurescape, https://www.futurescape.in/a-trillion-trees-and-amazon/#:~:text=Human%20activity%20emits%20about%2011,their%20forest%20to%20reduce%20emissions.
7. Ibid.
8. Kara Hurst, 'Three global companies join The Climate Pledge co-founded by Amazon', *Amazon*, 16 June 2020, https://blog.aboutamazon.com/sustainability/three-global-companies-join-the-climate-pledge-co-founded-by-amazon?_amp=true.
9. Amazon Staff, 'Amazon announces five new renewable energy projects', *Amazon*, May 21, 2020, https://blog.aboutamazon.com/sustainability/amazon-announces-five-new-renewable-energy-projects.
10. 'Tire Industry Project', https://www.wbcsd.org/Sector-Projects/Tire-Industry-Project
11. 'Dirty Fashion: How pollution in the global textile supply chain is making viscose toxic,' *Changing markets*, June, 2017, http://changingmarkets.org/wp-content/uploads/2017/06/CHANGING_MARKETS_DIRTY_FASHION_REPORT_SPREAD_WEB.pdf.
12. Viscose fibres are cellulosic fibres like cotton and are derived from wood sourced from sustainably managed forests. They are used in textile and hygiene applications such as garments and wipes.
13. Canopy's Hot Button Ranking and Report is the primary fibre sourcing analysis tool for the fashion sector. This includes the CanopyStyle brands, retailers, and

designers that are committed to eliminating the use of Ancient and Endangered Forests in viscose and other cellulosic fabrics, and to giving preference to textiles made from innovative fibres.

14. Ellen MacArthur Foundation, Completing The Picture How The Circular Economy Tackles Climate Change, Ellen MacArthur Foundation-Material Economics, September 26, 2019, https://www.ellenmacarthurfoundation.org/assets/downloads/Completing_The_Picture_How_The_Circular_Economy-_Tackles_Climate_Change_V3_26_September.pdf?utm_source=newsletter&utm_medium=email&utm_content=2019-10-07&utm_campaign=greenbuzz.
15. Welspun India Limited, Annual Report 2018-19, page 5, https://www.welspunindia.com/uploads/investor_data/W1L%20AR%202018-19%20alongwith%20attendance%20slip%20for%20website%20uplaod.pdf.
16. Ibid., p 34
17. Better Cotton Initiative
18. 'Kannur Kandal Project', https://www.wti.org.in/projects/mangrove-restoration-project/.
19. Kannur has 7.55 sq. kms. of mangroves, i.e. around 45 per cent of Kerala's total mangrove forest cover. Nearly 90 per cent of these forests are under private ownership.

4. Investing in Circularity

1. https://circulareconomy.europa.eu/platform/sites/default/files/financing-the-circular-economy.pdf.
2. Ministry of Urban Development, 'Swacch Bharat Mission, Municipal Solid Waste Management Manual', Government of India, 2016, http://mohua.gov.in/upload/uploadfiles/files/Part2.pdf.
3. Indulekha Arvind, 'Another pandemic: India's fight against single-use plastic falls victim to Covid', Economic Times, 24 October 2020, https://economictimes.indiatimes.com/news/politics-and-nation/another-pandemic-indias-fight-against-single-use-plastic-falls-victim-to-covid/articleshow/78848847.cms.
4. Dorothy Neufeld, 'The Carbon Footprint of the Food Supply Chain', *Visual Capitalist*, February 10, 2020, https://www.visualcapitalist.com/visualising-the-greenhouse-gas-impact-of-each-food/.
5. 'The Circularity Gap Report 2021', https://www.circularity-gap.world/2021.
6. 'These facts show how unsustainable the fashion industry is', Morgan McFall-Johnsen, WEF, 31 Jan 2020 https://www.weforum.org/agenda/2020/01/fashion-industry-carbon-unsustainable-environment-pollution/.
7. Angelica Cora, 'The Fashion Week History and Its Evolution', *The Italian Rêve*, September 11, 2018, https://www.theitalianreve.com/the-fashion-week-history-and-its-evolution/.
8. 'The world's most important fashion weeks', *LookoutPro*, June 13, 2018, https://www.lookoutpro.com/en/las-semanas-de-la-moda-mas-importantes-del-mundo/.

9. Greenpeace International, 'Destination Zero – Seven Years of Detoxing the Clothing Industry', *Greenpeace*, July 12, 2018, https://www.greenpeace.org/international/publication/17612/destination-zero/.
10. 'Fashion's Environmental Impact', https://www.sustainyourstyle.org/old-environmental-impacts.
11. Ibid.
12. Shuk-Wah Chung, 'Fast fashion is "drowning" the world. We need a Fashion Revolution!', *Greenpeace*, April 21, 2016, https://www.greenpeace.org/international/story/7539/fast-fashion-is-drowning-the-world-we-need-a-fashion-revolution/.
13. Ibid.
14. Ibid.
15. 'The Future Of Fashion: From Design To Merchandising, How Tech Is Reshaping The Industry', *CBInsights*, 13 October 2020, https://www.cbinsights.com/research/fashion-tech-future-trends/.
16. Elizabeth Segran, 'Your H&M addiction is wreaking havoc on the environment. Here's how to break it', *Fast Company*, 3 February 2019, https://www.fastcompany.com/90311509/we-have-to-fix-fashion-if-we-want-to-survive-the-next-century.
17. Ibid.
18. Ellen MacArthur Foundation, A New Textiles Economy: Redesigning Fashion's Future', Ellen MacArthur Foundation, November 28, 2017, https://www.ellenmacarthurfoundation.org/assets/downloads/publications/A-New-Textiles-Economy_Full-Report_Updated_1-12-17.pdf.
19. Elizabeth Segran, 'Your H&M addiction is wreaking havoc on the environment. Here's how to break it', *Fast Company*, 3 February 2019, https://www.fastcompany.com/90311509/we-have-to-fix-fashion-if-we-want-to-survive-the-next-century.
20. 'The Size of the Global Fashion Retail Market', https://www.commonobjective.co/article/the-size-of-the-global-fashion-retail-market.
21. 'Online fashion market to double by 2020', *ANI*, March 16, 2018, https://www.business-standard.com/article/news-ani/online-fashion-market-to-double-by-2020-118031600454_1.html.
22. https://www.wbcsd.org/Programs/Redefining-Value/Business-Decision-Making/Assess-and-Manage-Performance/Measuring-and-valuing-impact-business-examples/Kering-Environmental-Profit-and-Loss-EP-L-accounting - The EP&L methodology is open source and has contributed to the Natural Capital Protocol development.
23. 'Kering', https://kering-group.opendatasoft.com/pages/material-intensities-2019/.
24. Alder Wicker, 'The flawed ways brands talk about sustainability', *Vogue Business*, Condé Nast, 16 April 2020, https://www.voguebusiness.com/sustainability/the-flawed-ways-brands-talk-about-sustainability-coronavirus.
25. Kevin Moss, 'Here's What Could Go Wrong with the Circular Economy—and How to Keep it on Track', *World Resource Institute*, August 28, 2019, https://www.wri.org/blog/2019/08/here-s-what-could-go-wrong-circular-economy-and-how-keep-it-track.

26. 'Unilever's purpose-led brands outperform', *Unilever*, 11 June 2019, https://www.unilever.com/news/press-releases/2019/unilevers-purpose-led-brands-outperform.html.
27. 'Student Strikes Around the World – in pictures', *The Guardian*, 24 May 2019, https://www.theguardian.com/environment/gallery/2019/may/24/student-climate-strikes-around-the-world.
28. 'Accelerating India's Circular Economy Shift', http://ficci.in/publication.asp?spid=22977.
29. 'UN Environment Programme', https://www.unepfi.org/
30. 'BlackRock', https://www.blackrock.com/ch/individual/en/products/310165/blackrock-circular-economy-fund
31. James Byrne, 'For BlackRock, Circularity Is Off to a $900 Million Start', *TriplePundit*, October 2, 2020, https://www.triplepundit.com/story/2020/blackrock-circularity/706226.
32. 'End-of-life vehicles', https://ec.europa.eu/environment/topics/waste-and-recycling/end-life-vehicles_en.
33. 'India finally gets a vehicle scrappage policy: 5 key points to note', *Times Now*, 19 March 2021, https://www.timesnownews.com/auto/features/article/india-finally-gets-a-vehicle-scrappage-policy-5-key-points-to-note/734414.
34. https://ec.europa.eu/info/publications/categorisation-system-circular-economy_en
35. Mike Scott, 'Auto sector begins to map more circular road forward', *Reuters*, June 2, 2020, https://www.reutersevents.com/sustainability/auto-sector-begins-map-more-circular-road-forward.
36. 'The changing landscape of the retail food service industry', *Ficci*, December, 2018, http://ficci.in/spdocument/23056/foodzania-release2018.pdf.
37. 'Reducing Waste', https://corporate.walmart.com/global-responsibility/sustainability/sustainability-in-our-operations/reducing-waste.

5. Addressing food, water and energy

1. 'India FoodBanking Network', https://www.indiafoodbanking.org/hunger.
2. Ibid.
3. Ibid.
4. 'Water, Food and Energy', https://www.unwater.org/water-facts/water-food-and-energy/.
5. Chris Arsenault, 'Only 60 Years of Farming Left If Soil Degradation Continues', *Scientific American*, 5 December 2014. https://www.scientificamerican.com/article/only-60-years-of-farming-left-if-soil-degradation-continues/.
6. Lara Bryant, 'Organic Matter Can Improve Your Soil's Water Holding Capacity', *NRDC*, May 27, 2015, https://www.nrdc.org/experts/lara-bryant/organic-matter-can-improve-your-soils-water-holding-capacity.

7. Although banks offer agricultural loans at low cost, these are often subsidised by the government. Although the rates may appear to be low, the cost of default is ultimately borne by someone.
8. 'Population Dashboard', http://datatopics.worldbank.org/health/population.
9. Joe Mariani and Junko Kaji, 'From dirt to data: The second green revolution and the Internet of Things', *Deloitte Review*, 25 January 2016, https://www2.deloitte.com/insights/us/en/deloitte-review/issue-18/second-green-revolution-and-internet-of-things.html#endnote-sup-4.
10. 'ITC', https://www.itcportal.com/sustainability/sustainable-agriculture-programme.aspx.
11. Mahreen Matto, Sumita Singhal, 'Cities journey beyond ODF: India moves to sustainable sanitation for all', 3 August 2020, *Down To Earth,* https://www.downtoearth.org.in/blog/water/cities-journey-beyond-odf-india-moves-to-sustainable-sanitation-for-all-72625.
12. Suresh P. Prabhu, 'India's Water Challenges', *The Atlantic Council*, October, 2012, https://www.files.ethz.ch/isn/154067/PrabhuBrief.pdf.
13. 'Nature Action Agenda', *World Economic Forum*, https://www.weforum.org/projects/nature-action-agenda.
14. 'Priming the Solar Pump', https://shaktifoundation.in/wp-content/uploads/2017/06/Paper_7-FINAL.pdf.
15. Ayal Karmi, 'How Smarter Technology Will Feed the Planet', 26 March 2019, *Scientific American*, https://blogs.scientificamerican.com/observations/how-smarter-technology-will-feed-the-planet/.
16. Nicole Kobie, 'The internet of food: why your steak might have come from a connected cow', *The Guardian*, 5 August 2015, https://www.theguardian.com/technology/2015/aug/05/internet-of-things-connected-cows-agriculture-food-production.
17. Warwick Asford, 'IoT could be key to farming, says Beecham Research', *ComputerWeekly*, TechTarget, February 4, 2015, https://www.computerweekly.com/news/2240239484/IoT-could-be-key-to-farming-says-Beecham-Research.
18. Nicole Kobie, 'The internet of food: why your steak might have come from a connected cow', *The Guardian*, 5 August 2015, https://www.theguardian.com/technology/2015/aug/05/internet-of-things-connected-cows-agriculture-food-production.
19. PM Kusum Scheme, https://vikaspedia.in/energy/policy-support/renewable-energy-1/solar-energy/pm-kusum-scheme.
20. Ploy Ten Kate, 'Half of world's GDP moderately or highly dependent on nature, says new report', *PwC Thailand*, February 28, 2020, https://www.pwc.com/th/en/press-room/press-release/2020/press-release-28-02-20-en.html.

6. Leave no one behind

1. Céline Fornaro and Patrick Hummel, 'Electric transport: Adoption sooner than expected', *UBS*, https://www.ubs.com/global/en/collections/sustainable-investing/latest/2021/trends-electric-transport.html.

2. 'Interest in veganism is surging', *The Economist*, Juanuary 29, 2020. https://www.economist.com/graphic-detail/2020/01/29/interest-in-veganism-is-surging.
3. 'Market size of e-commerce industry across India from 2014 to 2018, with forecasts until 2027 (in billion U.S. dollars)', https://www.statista.com/statistics/792047/india-e-commerce-market-size/.
4. '1.3 billion learners are still affected by school or university closures, as educational institutions start reopening around the world, says UNESCO', *UNESCO*, April 29, 2020, https://en.unesco.org/news/13-billion-learners-are-still-affected-school-university-closures-educational-institutions.
5. 'Glaring digital divide in education in India: Covid-19 gives opportunity for digital inclusion', *India Today*, 11 September 2020, https://www.indiatoday.in/education-today/featurephilia/story/glaring-digital-divide-in-education-in-india-covid-19-digital-inclusion-1720817-2020-09-11.
6. John Fullerton, 'Regenerative Capitalism: How Universal Principles And Patterns Will Shape Our New Economy', *Capital Institute*, April, 2015, http://capitalinstitute.org/wp-content/uploads/2015/04/2015-Regenerative-Capitalism-4-20-15-final.pdf.
7. 'Gender-based violence and environment linkages', IUCN Publication https://portals.iucn.org/library/sites/library/files/documents/2020-002-En.pdf.
8. Sher Verick, 'Women's labour force participation in India: Why is it so low?', *ILO*, https://www.ilo.org/wcmsp5/groups/public/---asia/---ro-bangkok/---sro-new_delhi/documents/genericdocument/wcms_342357.pdf.
9. Ibid.
10. The World Economic Forum (WEF) 2021 Global Gender Gap Report, https://www.weforum.org/reports/global-gender-gap-report-2021.
11. https://www.ilo.org/global/about-the-ilo/newsroom/comment-analysis/WCMS_204762/lang--en/index.htm.
12. Shweta Saini and Pulkit Khatri, 'How India can benefit from the ongoing feminisation of agricultural workforce', 8 March 2021, https://theprint.in/opinion/how-india-can-benefit-from-the-ongoing-feminisation-of-agricultural-workforce/617638/.
13. 'The vital role of women in agriculture and rural development', UN Women, 2011, https://www.unwomen.org/en/docs/2011/6/the-vital-role-of-women-in-agriculture-and-rural-development.
14. 'The World's Leading Resource for Climate Solutions', https://www.drawdown.org/.
15. 'Advancing gender parity could contribute $70 billion to India's GDP by 2025', The *Economic Times*, June 20, 2018, https://economictimes.indiatimes.com/news/economy/indicators/advancing-gender-parity-could-contribute-770-billion-to-indias-gdp-by-2025-mckinsey-report/articleshow/64657487.cms?from=mdr.
16. *Annette Francis and Dheeraj Dubey*, 'Women, Work, and Migration: Why India's Labour Force is Dominated by Men', *News18*, March 12, 2019, https://www.news18.com/news/buzz/women-work-and-migration-why-

india-has-one-of-the-lowest-female-labour-force-participation-rates-in-the-world-2064655.html.

17. Shantanu Das, 'Gender bias in corporate India: The journey from diversity to inclusion', *People Matters*, December 3, 2018, https://www.peoplematters.in/article/diversity/gender-bias-in-corporate-india-the-journey-from-diversity-to-inclusion-20107.
18. Peter H. Diamandis, '5 AI Breakthroughs We'll Likely See in the Next 5 Years', *Singularity Hub*, April 26, 2019, https://singularityhub.com/2019/04/26/5-ai-breakthroughs-well-likely-see-in-the-next-5-years/.
19. 'The 4th Industrial Revolution must be a development revolution" - UNESCO at Davos', *UNESCO*, 2016, https://en.unesco.org/news/4th-industrial-revolution-must-be-development-revolution-unesco-davos.
20. 'Creative Economy Outlook: Trends in international trade in creative industries', https://unctad.org/system/files/official-document/ditcted2018d3_en.pdf
21. 'Crafts and Sustainable Livelihoods in India', https://namratarana.com/2010/03/23/crafts-and-sustainable-livelihoods-in-india/, 23 March 2010
Preethi Chamikutty, 'Crafting a livelihood, a snapshot of the Indian artifacts sector', https://yourstory.com/2013/06/crafting-a-livelihood-a-snapshot-of-the-indian-artifacts-sector, 19 June 2013
22. 'Livelihood Creation Project', https://mittalsouthasiainstitute.harvard.edu/handicraft-livelihood-creation-project/
23. https://www.tatatrusts.org/section/inside/craft-based-livelihoods-programme.
24. Prachi Verma and Anjali Venugopalan, 'India Inc has long way to go in employing disabled people', *The Economic Times*, 11 December 2019, https://economictimes.indiatimes.com/jobs/india-inc-has-long-way-to-go-in-employing-disabled-people/articleshow/72449585.cms.
25. Priyanka Sangani, 'Automation is sweeping across India's manufacturing space', *The Economic Times*, May 11, 2019 https://economictimes.indiatimes.com/tech/internet/automation-is-sweeping-across-indias-manufacturing-space/articleshow/69262579.cms?from=mdr.
26 'A Future That Works: Automation, Employment, and Productivity', *McKinsey&Company*, Januar, 2017, https://www.mckinsey.com/~/media/mckinsey/featured%20insights/Digital%20Disruption/Harnessing%20automation%20for%20a%20future%20that%20works/MGI-A-future-that-works-Executive-summary.ashx.
27. https://www.itu.int/en/ITU-D/Statistics/Pages/stat/default.aspx
28. Division for Inclusive Social Development, United Nations Department of Economic and Social Affairs, 'Leveraging digital technologies for social inclusion', *United Nations*, February 18, 2021, https://www.un.org/development/desa/dspd/2021/02/digital-technologies-for-social-inclusion/.
29. 'Report of the Secretary-GeneralRoadmap for Digital Cooperation', *United Nations*, June 2020, https://www.un.org/en/content/digital-cooperation-roadmap/assets/pdf/Roadmap_for_Digital_Cooperation_EN.pdf.
30. Jane Wakefield, 'Google's ethics board shut down', BBC, April 5, 2019,

https://www.bbc.com/news/technology-47825833.
31. https://www.nytimes.com/2019/04/14/technology/china-surveillance-artificial-intelligence-racial-profiling.html.
32. https://en.wikipedia.org/wiki/General_Data_Protection_Regulation
33. 'LSE Truth, Trust & Technology Commission', http://www.lse.ac.uk/media-and-communications/truth-trust-and-technology-commission.
34. Hristio Boytchev, 'Trust in science at record high', *Research Professional News*, 5 May 2020 https://www.researchprofessionalnews.com/rr-news-europe-germany-2020-5-trust-in-science-at-record-high/.
35. 'Brits demand openness from government in tackling coronavirus', *Open Knowledge Foundation*, May 5, 2020, https://blog.okfn.org/2020/05/05/brits-demand-openness-from-government-in-tackling-coronavirus/.
36. 'Disinformation on Australian bushfires should not be spread by ministers', *The Guardian*, January 14, 2020, https://www.theguardian.com/environment/2020/jan/14/disinformation-on-australian-bushfires-should-not-be-spread-by-ministers.
37. 'Realizing 2030: Dell Technologies Research Explores the Next Era of Human-Machine Partnerships', *Dell Inc.*, https://www.delltechnologies.com/en-in/press/realizing-2030-dell-technologies-research-explores-the-next-era-of-human-machine-partnerships.htm.

7. Green jobs for a Green Economy

1. 'Sustainable Markets 2020 Ten-Point Action Plan', *World Economic Forum*, https://assets.ctfassets.net/69rhyxi5amtf/3wx3uY2JZ1vagDgnZURBHl/842652 1e7c2414eb4b1 808fa669 f99ea/05_ WEF_ Sustainable_Markets_10_pointplan_ 2020.pdf.
2. 'Green Economy', UNEP, https://www.unenvironment.org/regions/asia-and-pacific/regional-initiatives/supporting-resource-efficiency/green-economy.
3. 'New Report: Cities are Trailblazers in the Race to Renewables', *REN21*, March 18, 2021, https://www.ren21.net/report-renewables-in-cities-2021/.
4. Schneider Electric SE is a multinational company providing energy and automation digital solutions for efficiency and sustainability.
5. 'Study warns of poverty surge to over 1 billion due to coronavirus', *The Hindu*, June 12, 2020, https://www.thehindu.com/news/international/study-warns-of-poverty-surge-to-over-1-billion-due-to-coronavirus/article31810064.ece.
6. https://cdn.gca.org/assets/2020-07/Global_Commission_Adapation_COVID_ Resilience_Statement.pdf.
7. 'Green Jobs', *ILO*, https://www.ilo.org/global/topics/green-jobs/lang--en/index.htm.

8. Partners for Inclusive Green Economy is an initiative involving UN Environment, the Deutsche Gesellschaft für Internationale Zusammenarbeit (GIZ), the Global Green Growth Institute (GGGI), the Green Economy Coalition (GEC), the Green Growth Knowledge Partnership (GGKP), the International Labour Organization (ILO), the Organisation for Economic Co-operation and Development (OECD), Poverty-Environment Action for SDGs (PEA), the United Nations Development Programme (UNDP), the United Nations Industrial Development Organization (UNIDO), the United Nations Partnership for Action on Green Economy (UN-PAGE) and UN Research Institute for Social Development (UNRISD).
9. Nearly Zero-Energy Building (NZEB) programmes in EU.
10. Nikita Rana, 'India on track to meet 175 GW renewable energy targets by 2022: ETILC Members', *The Economic Times*, February 16, 2021, https://economictimes.indiatimes.com/industry/energy/power/india-on-track-to-meet-175-gw-renewable-energy-targets-by-2022-etilc-members/articleshow/80976846.cms?from=mdr.
11. 'Future skills and job creation with renewable energy in India', October 2019, https://www.ceew.in/sites/default/files/future.pdf.
12. 'E-vehicles industry to create 10 million jobs in future: report', *Business Today*, May 15, 2019, https://www.businesstoday.in/current/economy-politics/e-vehicles-industry-electric-mobility-mission-create-10-million-jobs-in-future/story/346804.html.
13. Sameh Wahba, 'Future of Cities Will Shape Post-COVID-19 World', *The World Bank*, March 2, 2021 https://www.worldbank.org/en/news/feature/2021/03/02/future-of-cities-will-shape-post-covid-19-world.
14. '5 Lessons for India's Green Recovery', *The World Bank*, 14 September 2020, https://www.worldbank.org/en/news/feature/2020/09/11/5-lessons-for-india-s-green-recovery.
15. 'New Blockchain Project has Potential to Revolutionise Seafood Industry', *WWF*, 8 January 2018, https://www.wwf.org.nz/media_centre/?uNewsID=15541.
16. Brad Smith, 'Microsoft launches initiative to help 25 million people worldwide acquire the digital skills needed in a COVID-19 economy', *Microsoft Blog*, June 30, 2020, https://blogs.microsoft.com/blog/2020/06/30/microsoft-launches-initiative-to-help-25-million-people-worldwide-acquire-the-digital-skills-needed-in-a-covid-19-economy/.
17. 'COVID-19: skills sector impact', *KPMG*, April 2020, https://assets.kpmg/content/dam/kpmg/in/pdf/2020/04/covid19-skills-sector-impact.pdf.

8. Brands We Trust

1. 'Investment Insights 2021', https://www.msci.com/our-clients/asset-owners/investment-insights-report.
2. Imran Amed, Anita Balchandani, Achim Berg, Saskia Hedrich, Jakob Ekeløf Jensen and Felix Rölkens, "The State of Fashion 2021: In search of promise in

perilous times', *McKinsey&Company*, December 1, 2020, https://www.mckinsey.com/industries/retail/our-insights/the-state-of-fashion-2019-a-year-of-awakening.
3. 'CGS Survey Reveals Sustainability Is Driving Demand and Customer Loyalty', *Intrado*, GlobeNewswire, January 10, 2019, https://www.globenewswire.com/news-release/2019/01/10/1686144/0/en/CGS-Survey-Reveals-Sustainability-Is-Driving-Demand-and-Customer-Loyalty.html.
4. 'Study reveals a clear, unmet consumer demand for sustainable products in Singapore: Accenture and WWF', *WWF*, 16 March 2021, https://www.wwf.sg/?uNewsID=366635.
5. '2021 Rome ecoFlight Highlights', *Etihad*, 21 April 2021, https://www.etihad.com/en-gb/news/2021-rome-ecoflight-highlights.
6. https://www.inditex.com/documents/10279/249245/Dossier_JGA_2019_EN.pdf/1664de2f-ca77-3a40-2b78-cace74c06c82.
7. 'The Company', https://www.ghcl.co.in/the-company.
8. Futurescape Sustainability Insights.
9. Polyethylene terephthalate commonly abbreviated as PET is a resin of the polyester family and is used in fibres for clothing and containers for liquids and foods.
10. *Erika Giles,* '25 of the Best Marketing Campaigns of All Time That Spark Inspiration', *Bluleadz*, August 17, 2020, https://www.bluleadz.com/blog/20-of-the-best-marketing-campaigns-of-all-time.
11. 'Consumers are increasingly trusting brands that take a stance', *Smart Insights*, September 30, 2019, https://www.smartinsights.com/online-brand-strategy/consumers-are-increasingly-trusting-brands-that-take-a-stance/.
12. 'Road accidents in India decrease by 4.1% during 2016, fatalities rise by 3.2%', Press release, *Ministry of Road Transport and Highway*, September 6, 2017, http://pib.nic.in/newsite/PrintRelease.aspx?relid=170577.
13. OECD Yearbook 2012, http://oecdobserver.org/news/fullstory.php/aid/3681/An_emerging_middle_class.html?utm_source=newsletter&utm_medium=email&utm_content=2019-10-07&utm_campaign=greenbuzz.
14. Futurescape Research.
15. Ben Cosgrove, '"Throwaway Living": When Tossing Out Everything Was All the Rage', *Time*, May 15, 2014, http://time.com/3879873/throwaway-living-when-tossing-it-all-was-all-the-rage/.
16. Laura Parker, 'We Made Plastic. We Depend on It. Now We're Drowning in It', *National Geographic*, June, 2018, https://www.nationalgeographic.com/magazine/2018/06/plastic-planet-waste-pollution-trash-crisis/.
17. Stephen Buranyi, 'The plastic backlash: what's behind our sudden rage – and will it make a difference?', *The Guardian*, November 13, 2018 https://www.theguardian.com/environment/2018/nov/13/the-plastic-backlash-whats-behind-our-sudden-rage-and-will-it-make-a-difference.
18. Cristina Commendatore, 'Takeaways from Waste Management's 2019 Sustainability Forum', *Waste 360*, February 1, 2019,

https://www.waste360.com/plastics/takeaways-waste-management-s-2019-sustainability-forum.

19. 'Working towards a waste-free future', https://www.nestle.com/csv/global-initiatives/zero-environmental-impact/packaging-plastic-pollution.
20. 'Unilever announces ambitious new commitments for a waste-free world', *Unilever*, October 7, 2019, https://www.unilever.com/news/press-releases/2019/unilever-announces-ambitious-new-commitments-for-a-waste-free-world.html.
21. 'Our planet is drowning in plastic pollution—it's time for change', https://www.unep.org/interactive/beat-plastic-pollution/.
22. Pamela N. Danziger, '6 Trends Shaping The Future Of The $532B Beauty Business', *Forbes*, September 1, 2019, 2019, Pamela N. Danziger, https://www.forbes.com/sites/pamdanziger/2019/09/01/6-trends-shaping-the-future-of-the-532b-beauty-business/#30be0a08588d.
23. Matt Simon, 'Wait, How Much Microplastic Is Swirling in the Atlantic?', *Wired*, October 8, 2020, https://www.wired.com/story/how-much-microplastic-is-swirling-in-the-atlantic/?utm_medium=social&utm_social-type=owned&mbid=social_twitter&utm_brand=wired&utm_source=twitter.
24. 'Zero Waste Week', https://www.zerowasteweek.co.uk/.
25. Brianna Lapolla, 'I'm a Beauty Editor, and I'm Absolutely Appalled by *This* Thing About the Industry', *PureWow*, 28 January 2019, https://www.purewow.com/beauty/what-i-learned-from-being-a-beauty-editor.
26. Amy Westervelt, 'The Beauty Industry has a plastics problem', *Teen Vogue*, December 26, 2018, https://www.teenvogue.com/story/the-beauty-industry-has-a-plastics-problem.
27. 'Naked When it comes to packaging, less is more', *Lush*, https://www.lushusa.com/stories/article_our-values-naked.html.
28. Christina DesMarais, 'How Hasbro, Lego and Mattel stack up as green toy makers', *GreenBiz*, October 31, 2013, https://www.greenbiz.com/blog/2013/10/31/how-hasbro-lego-and-mattel-stack-green-toy-makers.
29. Lindsay Brown, 'Plastic toys: Is it time we cut back?', *BBC*, April 11, 2019, https://www.bbc.com/news/science-environment-47868871.
30. 'Circularity, Sustainability Take Hold in Toy Industry', *Sustainable Brands*, February 2, 2018, https://sustainablebrands.com/read/waste-not/circularity-sustainability-take-hold-in-toy-industry.
31. https://rejoue.asso.fr/.
32. 'Celebrate Earth Day with Radical Recycling for Minecraft: Education Edition', *Microsoft Blog*, 13 April 2021, https://educationblog.microsoft.com/en-us/2021/04/celebrate-earth-day-with-radical-recycling-for-minecraft-education-edition.
33. 'Castrol launches its new sustainability strategy - PATH360', Press release, *BP*, 30 March 2021,

https://www.bp.com/en/global/corporate/news-and-insights/press-releases/castrol-launches-its-new-sustainability-strategy-path360.html.

34. 'Building meaningful is good for business: 77% of consumers buy brands who share their values', *Havas Media Group*, February 21, 2019, https://havasmedia.com/building-meaningful-is-good-for-business-77-of-consumers-buy-brands-who-share-their-values/.
35. Namrata Rana and Utkarsh Majmudar, 'Responsible Business Rankings India's Top Companies for Sustainability and CSR 2020', *Futurescape.* https://www.futurescape.in/responsible-business-rankings/.
36. '90+ Companies Now Certified Climate Neutral', *Sustainable Brands*, April 21, 2020, https://sustainablebrands.com/read/walking-the-talk/90-companies-now-certified-climate-neutral.

9. Transformation at scale

1. 'Planetary Health', https://unfccc.int/climate-action/momentum-for-change/planetary-health
2. 'Drawdown Framework', https://drawdown.org/drawdown-framework
3. Pavan Sukhdev, 'The economics of ecosystems and biodiversity', , Study Leader, 2008, http://www.teebweb.org/media/2008/05/TEEB-Interim-Report_English.pdf
4. James O'Hare, 'Half of the Species on Earth Could Go Extinct by 2050: Scientists', 27 February 2017, https://www.globalcitizen.org/en/content/half-earths-species-extinct-2050/
5. 'Planetary Computer', https://innovation.microsoft.com/en-us/planetary-computer
6. Prasanna Mohanty, 'Coronavirus Lockdown III: Is India's public healthcare system prepared to fight the COVID-19 menace?', *Business Today,*3 April 2020 https://www.businesstoday.in/current/economy-politics/coronavirus-lockdown-covid-19-pandemic-public-healthcare-system-doctors-nurses-patients/story/400039.html
7. 'About the Fashion Industry Charter for Climate Action', https://unfccc.int/climate-action/sectoral-engagement/global-climate-action-in-fashion/about-the-fashion-industry-charter-for-climate-action
8. 'Tire Industry Project', https://www.wbcsd.org/Sector-Projects/Tire-Industry-Project
9. 'Shell and Microsoft form alliance to help address carbon emissions', 22 September 2020, https://www.shell.com/energy-and-innovation/digitalisation/news-room/shell-and-microsoft-form-alliance-to-help-address-carbon-emissions.html
10. 'CGS Survey Reveals Sustainability Is Driving Demand and Customer Loyalty', *Intrado GlobeNewswire,* 10 January 2019 https://www.globenewswire.com/news-release/2019/01/10/1686144/0/en/CGS-Survey-Reveals-Sustainability-Is-Driving-Demand-and-Customer-Loyalty.html - The survey took in responses from over 1000 US individuals (aged18-65+)

on how sustainable products and business practices are driving their buying preferences.

11. 'WWF and Google Partner on Fashion Sustainability Platform', 10 June 2020, https://cloud.google.com/press-releases/2020/0610/wwfandgoogle
12. 'WWF and Google Partner on Fashion Sustainability Platform', 15 May 2019, https://cloud.google.com/blog/topics/inside-google-cloud/googles-new-pilot-aiming-to-measure-the-environmental-impact-of-the-fashion-industry
13. 'WWF and IKEA', https://www.wwf.se/ikea/
14. Futurescape, www.futurescape.in
15. Michal Mazur, PwC, 'Six Ways Drones Are Revolutionizing Agriculture', *Technology Review*, 20 July 2016, https://www.technologyreview.com/s/601935/six-ways-drones-are-revolutionizing-agriculture/
16. 'Bolt Threads', https://boltthreads.com/
17. Effie P., 'Novel bio-inspired materials to substitute plastics', 11 January 2019, https://www.greenoptimistic.com/novel-bio-inspired-materials-to-substitute-plastics-20190111/
18. Soyen Park, Ramandeep Singh, 'India's waste management problem, *Mint, 1 March 2018*, https://www.livemint.com/Opinion/V2CgeiUq89kl1k2fDwJXML/Swachh-Bharats-waste-management-problem.html
19. Ibid.
20. 'C40Cities', https://www.c40.org/about
21. Marie Quinney, '5 reasons why biodiversity matters – to human health, the economy and your wellbeing', *World Economic Forum*, 22 May 2020, https://www.weforum.org/agenda/2020/05/5-reasons-why-biodiversity-matters-human-health-economies-business-wellbeing-coronavirus-covid19-animals-nature-ecosystems/
22 'The global assessment report on Biodiversity and Ecosystem Services:Summary for Policymakers, 2019, https://ipbes.net/sites/default/files/202002/ipbes_global_assessment_report_summary_for_policymakers_en.pdf
23. 'Climate Change Impact', https://www.sciencedirect.com/topics/earth-and-planetary-sciences/climate-change-impact
24. Jay Walljasper, 'Elinor Ostrom's 8 Principles for Managing A Commons', 2 October 2011, *Commons Magazine,* http://www.onthecommons.org/magazine/elinor-ostroms-8-principles-managing-commmons
25. https://www.g7uk.org/g7-climate-and-environment-ministers-communique/

10. Aiming Higher

1. 'HSBC sets out net zero ambition', *HSBC,* 9 October 2020, https://www.hsbc.com/news-and-media/hsbc-news/hsbc-sets-out-net-zero-ambition
2. Natasha Turner, 'Shareholder pressure on HSBC to reduce fossil fuel exposure

intensifies', *ESGClarity*, January 11, 2021, https://esgclarity.com/investors-urge-hsbc-to-reduce-fossil-fuel-exposure/.

3. 'Investment Insights 2021', *MSCI*, https://www.msci.com/our-clients/asset-owners/investment-insights-report
4. Emma Hinchliffe, 'The number of female CEOs in the Fortune 500 hits an all-time record', *Fortune*, 18 May 2020, https://fortune.com/2020/05/18/women-ceos-fortune-500-2020/
5. Susanna Rust, 'New natural capital investment alliance aims to mobilise $10bn', 11 January 2021, IPE magazine, https://www.ipe.com/news/new-natural-capital-investment-alliance-aims-to-mobilise-10bn/10049966.article
6. Y. Kesavulu, 'Gandhian Trusteeship as an 'Instrument of Human Dignity', Gandhi Marg, Vol. 25, No. 4, Jan-March, 2004, https://www.mkgandhi.org/articles/trusteeship.htm

Technical Notes

1. The greenhouse effect is the process by which radiation from a planet's atmosphere warms the planet's surface to a temperature above what it would be without this atmosphere.
2. Carbon Pricing Dashboard, The World Bank, https://carbonpricingdashboard.worldbank.org/.
3. Gigaton Carbon dioxide equivalent.
4. Abatement cost is the cost of reducing negative externalities like pollution. The marginal cost of abatement measures the cost of reducing one more unit of pollution.
5. Damage caused by adding one additional ton of carbon dioxide into the atmosphere. This marginal damage is often called the social cost of carbon (SCC).
6. 'Standards', *Greenhouse Gas Protocols*, https://ghgprotocol.org/standards.
7. Global Family Office Report 2020, *UBS*, https://www.ubs.com/global/en/global-family-office/reports/global-family-office-report-2020.html.
8. 'TEG report on EU taxonomy', *European Commission*, https://ec.europa.eu/info/files/190618-sustainable-finance-teg-report-taxonomy_en.
9. Tara O'Reilly, Kevin Murphy, Sarah Cunniff, Cormac Commins, Ian Dillon, Dara Harrington, Siobhan McBean and Audrey Giles, 'European Union: ESG For Fund Managers: The EU Framework Regulation / The Taxonomy Regulation', *Mondaq*, September 11, 2020, https://www.mondaq.com/ireland/fund-management-reits/983958/esg-for-fund-managers-the-eu-framework-regulation-the-taxonomy-regulation.
10. 'SFDR brings new ESG disclosure rules for asset managers', *Bovill.com*, August 21, 2020, https://www.bovill.com/new-esg-disclosures-for-asset-managers/.
11. Helen Avery, 'Sustainable finance's biggest problems, by the people who know best', *Euromoney*, December 3, 2019

https://www.euromoney.com/article/b1j97rjr74vd00/sustainable-finances-biggest-problems-by-the-people-who-know-best.

12. 'Principles for Responsible Banking', *UNEP*, https://www.unepfi.org/banking/bankingprinciples/.
13. 'Financial Institutions', *Science Based Targets*, https://sciencebasedtargets.org/financial-institutions/.
14. http://there100.org/.
15. 'The Paris Agreement', *UNCC*, https://unfccc.int/process-and-meetings/the-paris-agreement/the-paris-agreement.
16. 'Green investment banks', OECD, https://en.wikipedia.org/wiki/File:A_RES_71_313_E.pdf.
17. https://www.oecd.org/environment/green-investment-banks.htm.
18. 'Green Investment Banks Scaling up private investment in low-carbon, climate resilient infrastructure', Green Finance and Investment, *OECD*, Paris, 2016, https://read.oecd-ilibrary.org/finance-and-investment/green-investment-banks_9789264245129-en#page1.
19. 'What is a Green Bank', *Coalition of Green Capital*, https://coalitionforgreencapital.com/what-is-a-green-bank/.

ACKNOWLEDGEMENTS

Many people have shaped our thinking on responsible business.

We are grateful to a host of professionals and friends for their perspectives and guidance:

Abanti Sankaranarayanan, Abhinav Agrawal, Amit Malhotra, Anil Varghese, Anna Varghese, Anurag Rana, Apoorva Shah, Abhimanyu Sahu, Ashok Kapoor, Prof. Archana Shukla, Arman Ali, Ashok Bhasin, Aviral Singh, Prof. Bharat Bhasker, Bibhuti Ranjan Pradhan, Chhavi Chadha, Dilip Gaur, Debabrata Ghosh, Dr. Parul Sharma, Prof. Debashis Chatterjee, Deepak Ajwani, Dhruv Bogra, Francis Joe, Gaurav Agarwal, Gautam Gode, Gayatri Appaya, Irina Ivashkovskaya, Prof. Janat Shah, Jassi Chadha, Lalit Kumar, Kapil Jain, Manu Bhatnagar, Manu Kapur, Meenal Bhatia, Palak Gupta, Manoj Kumar, Mrithyunjay Amblimath, Mukul Agrawal, Namita Vikas, Naveen Soni, Navtej Johar, Neha Misra, Nozer Shroff, Ophira Bhatia, Panrinjay, Prabodha Acharya, Prasanto K. Roy, Poonam Bharadwaj, Poonam Sharma, Rajesh Madhavan, Rajat Deep Rana, Rinika Grover, Ritu Jhingon, Sandeep Mahajan, Santosh Desai, Prof. Shailendra Singh, Sharada Prasad, Shalini Jain, Shefaly Yogendra, Shyamala Gopinath, SP Mohapatra, Soumitra Pandey, Sunil Mehra, Sudhir Bahl, Syamant Sandhir, Tejas Arur, Vikram Kirloskar, Vineet Gautam, Vipin Aggarwal, Vishal Bhardwaj, Prof. Ganesh Prabhu, Neelima Khetan, Prof.PD Jose, Prof. Rajesh Chakrabarti, Prof. Sudhir Jaiswall, Vinod Mahanta, and Vrushali Gaud.

A special word of thanks for the lead researcher Neelam Agrawal for her support and insights.

A big thanks to Karthik Venkatesh, our editor from Westland, who helped us shape the book.

Namrata would like to thank her parents Jaishree Rana and Major Rana, sister, brother and husband for their constant support and motivation. Syona, Avantika and Antara this book is for you. A heartfelt thanks to Sunrita Sandhir for her blessings. A special shout out to the extended family of Mreenal Deshraj, Chandni, Anupam, Shakti, and Aditya Vardhan, and Amrita Maan. Warm and wonderful memories of Harsh Vardhan, Yash Vardhan and K.K. Sandhir. A special note of thanks to the amazingly fabulous IIMA '93 girls.

Utkarsh would like to thank his father, Mr Nitin Majmudar for his inspiration, his mother, the late Mrs Saroj Majmudar for her blessings and his best friend and wife, Kanan, for being positive, patient and motivating He acknowledges and thanks his sister Sonali, and brother-in-law Bharat for their continuous encouragement and ideas. Gratitude and thanks to the extended family, Mr and Mrs Mehta, Amit, Ishna, Ishan, Ishita and Rajat. Also thanking Abhay & Sirpa, Smruti, Sonal & Pranav, Saumil & Darsha, Ketki & Ajay, Chandni & Anil, Rupal & Anup, Nancy and Ramesh Gandhi for their optimism. A special note to acknowledge my grandniece, little Zaha's contribution in providing so much joy and entertainment. Finally, my mates from IIML and IIMA for always being there.

Namrata Rana
Gurugram, India

Utkarsh Majmudar
Bangalore, India

17 July 2021